HIGHER PSYCH
DEVELOPM

C000262416

By the same author
YOUR PSYCHIC POWERS AND
  HOW TO DEVELOP THEM

HIGHER PSYCHICAL DEVELOPMENT
(Yoga Philosophy)

by
HEREWARD CARRINGTON, Ph.D.

NEWCASTLE PUBLISHING CO., INC.
NORTH HOLLYWOOD, CALIFORNIA
1983

A NEWCASTLE BOOK
First printing October 1983
Printed in United States of America

PREFACE

The following work consists essentially of a series of twelve lectures, delivered before the Psychological Research Society, of New York, in 1918. These lectures were given *impromptu*, without manuscript, and with no thought at the time of their ultimate publication. Because of this fact, they contain certain minor repetitions, and lack, perhaps, a certain literary quality which they might have contained, had they been written out in advance. I have, however, retained practically their original form,—making only a few verbal changes,—from shorthand notes made at the time.

At the conclusion of every Lecture, a number of questions were asked and answered, and a few of these I have retained—thinking them, perhaps, of especial interest to the general reader. It is hardly necessary to say that the vast majority of these questions and answers have been omitted!

The present book is, in a sense, a sequel to my earlier work, *Your Psychic Powers: and How to Develop Them,* and the serious student is advised to read that volume first,—if he has not obtained a thorough knowledge of the fundamental groundwork of psychic science. *Higher Psychical Development,* as its name implies, is a "postgraduate course" for more or less advanced students, and contains information and "secrets" which have never before been published,—so far as I am aware,—in any work in English. The book contains many of the hidden, carefully guarded, inner "secrets" of the Hindu Yogis—obtained as the result of several years' actual experience and experimenting on the part of the author, as well as embodying his extensive—indeed exhaustive—examination of all published material. One of the chief aims of the book, moreover, is to link-up, or show the connections between, these Yoga practices and our Western science, philosophy and psychic investigations. Much of this material has hitherto existed only in Sanscrit, or has been passed on, by word of mouth, from teacher to pupil. The actual *method* for the development of these powers is now explained, for the first time, and in considerable detail—with practical exercises suitable for the student.

The Lectures constituting this book were of course delivered before the publication of Arthur Avalon's great work, *The Serpent Power*—a massive treatise of nearly 500 pages, dealing with the subject of *Kundalini* and the *Chakras* in great detail. I did not have the advantage of consulting this work, therefore, in preparing these Lectures; but I have added several quotations and foot-notes, drawn from it, as my own book was passing through the press. These I hereby acknowledge, —as well as much other valuable information drawn from this source. Avalon's book is of so highly technical a character, however, and so filled with Sanskrit terms, that it will probably be almost unintelligible to the average reader. After reading the present book, however, Avalon's work might be studied with both pleasure and profit; and I take this opportunity to call the reader's attention to that masterful treatise. (Arthur Avalon is also the editor of the *Tantrik Texts*

(*Tantras*)—which constitute, of course, the great store-house of Hindu Occult wisdom.)

I have no doubt that I shall be criticized for publishing these Lectures on several grounds. In the first place, my nomenclature may be challenged—as, for instance, when I translate *Pratyahara* as "meditation." I have, however, used this word in a special sense throughout, and usually employed "introspection" as synonymous with my use of the term. It is in this sense that I use it; and for this use I believe I have ample authority.

In the second place, I shall be reproached for giving the public such "inner" and "dangerous" secrets! I have answered this objection on several occasions, and need only say here that I have little sympathy with those "psychic cowards" who are afraid to experiment, who fear investigation, who lack the courage of their convictions, and who are constantly warning others of the "dangers" connected with psychic investigation and experimentation in any form. Nothing is learned without experimentation,—in this field, as in any other; and if a few unbalanced persons have harmed themselves while trying these experiments, it is safe to say that thousands have derived benefit from them; while the majority have, probably, dropped the subject, after slight investigation, without noticeable influence, one way or the other! In many cases, however, great help has been derived from these exercises.

I wish to say in conclusion—and particularly emphasize the fact—that the "dogmatic" statements and assertions contained in this series of Lectures do not at all times necessarily involve my own personal point-of-view or beliefs. I have merely endeavoured to present, as

PREFACE

clearly and forcibly as possible, the conceptions, teachings and conclusions of the Hindus and Yogis; and it would have been pedantic to have qualified every statement by such words as "It is said," or "it is believed," or "the Hindus claim," or words to that effect. Partly to omit all this,—which would have detracted from the force of the statements—(and also interjected my own personal qualifications and views where they were not wanted and had no place), I have usually omitted them from the text, and merely described the phenomena as they are said to exist—and in many cases as I also believe them to exist. I wish it to be distinctly understood, however, that, in thus stating the facts in this manner, I do not invariably endorse their accuracy; I have merely endeavoured to present the *teaching,* and each reader must determine for himself what degree of objective truth such statements contain.

I wish to acknowledge, here, my very great indebtedness to Mr. Frederick T. Harris, for his invaluable assistance in the preparation of this work.

H. C.

CONTENTS

There are seven Keys to the Great Gate,
Being eight in one and one in eight.
First, let the body of thee be still,
Bound by the carements of will,
Corpse-rigid; thus thou mayst abort
The fidget-babes that tease the thought.
Next, let the breath-rhythm be low,
Easy, regular and slow;
So that thy being be in tune
With the Great Sea's Pacific Swoon.
Third, let thy life be pure and calm,
Swayed softly as a windless palm.
Fourth, let the will-to-live be bound
To the one love of the Profound.
Fifth, let the thought, divinely free
From sense, observe its entity.
Watch every thought that springs; enhance
Hour after hour thy vigilance!
Intense and keen, turned inward, miss
No atom of analysis!
Sixth, on one thought securely pinned
Still every whisper of the wind!
So like a flame straight and unstirred
Burn up thy being in one word!
Next, still that ecstasy, prolong
Thy meditation steep and strong,
Slaying even God, should He distract
Thy attention from the chosen act!
Last, all these things in one o'erpowered,
Time that the midnight blossom flowered!
The Oneness is. Yet even in this,
My son, thou shalt not do amiss
If thou restrain the expression, shoot
Thy glance at rapture's darkling root,
Discarding name, form, sight, and stress
Even of this high consciousness;
Pierce to the heart! I leave thee here;
Thou art the Master. I revere
Thy radiance that rolls afar,
O Brother of the Silver Star!

CHAPTER I

An Outline of Yoga Philosophy [1]

"It openeth wide,
Plain for all feet to tread, easy and near,
The Noble Eightfold Path; it goeth straight
To peace and refuge."

Yoga Philosophy is one of the six main systems of philosophy which exist in India. It is best known in countries of the Eastern civilization, because it contains in it an element of mystery and miracle. But mystery and miracle appeal to all humanity.

There are, of course, more than six systems of Hindu philosophy. There are agnostic and materialistic systems,—corresponding with those of the West. There is the doctrine of Buddhism and Sufiism, which somewhat resembles Vedanta, and other doctrines; but the six systems above referred to are those which claim the greatest number of followers throughout India and the Orient. These six systems are the following:

First: the SANKHYA system, which was founded about 700 B. C. by Kapila. This system contended that

[1] "Yoga" is the Yoga Philosophy. "Yogi" is a person practising Yoga.

1

there are, in the universe, two active principles, and that our universe is the resultant of their interaction. Just as flint and steel will produce sparks when brought into sharp contact, so these "sparks" are the phenomena of nature which are studied by us. The two active principles are, respectively, *prakriti,* which is the primordial energy, and *purusha,* which is the spiritual principle. *Prakriti* has three *gunas* or qualities; namely, harmony, activity and inertia. It will thus be seen that this system is, in a sense, a form of dualism,— though it can be traced back ultimately to a system of monism, as Sri Ananda Acharya has shown in his book, *Brahmadarsanam, or Intuition of the Absolute.*

The *second* system is the VEDANTA, which is strictly monistic in character, and contends that there is ultimately only one reality in the universe, all the multiplicity of phenomena which we see being merely MAYA or illusion.

It must be understood here that *monism* is a doctrine in philosophy which contends that there is ultimately only *one* reality at the basis of all things, while *dualism* contends that there are *two* such realities, and *multiplism* or *pluralism* contends that there are many such. Most of the Oriental philosophies are monistic in character, and this is the central keynote of the doctrine of Vedanta.

The *third* great system is PATANJALI'S YOGA PHILOSOPHY, which depends upon work rather than upon mere adoration and religious rites for its results, and is the doctrine we are about to study. It was founded or systematized by Patanjali, and although he did not found the doctrine, as such, he nevertheless systematized it, and the Yoga philosophy has borne his name ever since. His "Aphorisms," which are the basis of the teaching, are published in Swami Vivekananda's *Raja Yoga,* and lately in the Harvard Oriental Series, Volume XVII, edited by Dr. Woods.

The *fourth* system is called VAISHESHIKA, and was founded by KANADA several hundred years B. C. It depends on the existence of six so-called "categories" or fundamentals of existence,—namely, substance, quantities, action, generality, separateness and coherence. There is also a curious portion of the doctrine which deals with non-existence; but this paradoxical side of the teaching need not here detain us.

The *fifth* system is that founded by GOTAMA (not to be confounded with Gautama Buddha), and is called NYAYA. It depends upon the attainment of truth by analysis and knowledge (a) through the senses, (b) by inference, (c) by analogy, and (d) by the testimony of others. Here in the West, we seek truth very much by these same means, and it will be seen that this system is more in line with our Western science and teachings than the majority of Eastern philosophies.

The *sixth* system is that of JAIMINI, and is known as PURVA MIMANSA, and aims at the complete freedom of the soul by means of orthodox rites and courses of action. It is in a sense an orthodox system of Hindu philosophy, in line with our own orthodox teachings.[1]

---

[1] Those who may be interested in following more in detail the religious doctrines and teachings of India will find them summarized in Yogi Ramacharaka's book *The Philosophies and Religions of India.* There are, in the East, various sacred books which might be studied by the student with advantage, such as

There are various forms of Yoga. This philosophy is extremely systematic in its development, and begins with the doctrine of the body, and proceeds through the active powers of the mind up to the higher principles of spirit. Thus, HATHA YOGA deals with the body and its training through specific methods of training, etc., and later by means of the systems of ASANA, PRANAYAMA and MANTRA YOGA.[1]

RAJA YOGA deals with the training of the mind and the psychic powers, and this includes PRATYAHARA, DHARANA, DHYANA and SAMADHI.

KARMA YOGA deals with the freedom of the soul by means of *work,*—largely work for others.

BHAKTI YOGA is a system of Yoga aiming at perfection through devotion. It is a doctrine of *love.*

Finally, in JNANA YOGA we have a system which endeavours to obtain union with God, or the universal consciousness by means of *wisdom.*[2]

All of these, of course, to some extent interrelate. In HATHA YOGA we deal with such subjects as diet, sleep, rest, hydrotherapy and general hygienic measures, in addition to certain physiological discipline, which trains the body and develops the ascetic from that side. The effect of this is to render the body completely sub-

the various *Vedas;* the *Brahmanas,* which are commentaries on the Vedas; the *Upanishads,* which deal largely with metaphysics; the *Bhagavad Gita;* etc.

[1] For a further and more detailed study of these facts, see Swami Abhedananda's book: *How to be a Yogi,* etc.

[2] See the series of volumes on the various forms of Yoga, written by Swamis Vivekananda, Abhedananda, and Ramacharaka. Layayoga deals with the supersensible seats or centres, and the forces and functions of the inner world of the body.

servient to the spirit, so that it may have complete control of it.[1]

The object of Yoga philosophy is to merge into the Supreme Spirit. The Hindus, however, mean a different thing by the word GOD than we do. It does not mean an anthropomorphic deity; it is a kind of all-pervading universal spirit, of which we form an integral part. Their aim is to become *one* with that, to form part of it, to merge into it, and at the same time to absorb it. Extracting powers from it, they thus build themselves up mentally and spiritually to the point where they also become omniscient and omnipotent.

The aim of the Hindus is to eliminate the sense of personality, because they believe this to be an illusion (*maya*). Everything is part of the one Spirit; everything *is* God,—everything animate and inanimate,—and for this reason the Eastern and Western doctrines are fundamentally opposed in this respect.

The derivation and the meaning of the word "YOGA" is uncertain. Sanskrit scholars say it comes from the word "Yug," to bind, to yoke; and this source seems to me the most reasonable and probable, as the philosophy of that name aims at—in a way—yoking, or binding Self to the Supreme Being. I am using the term loosely, as will be seen later.

It is no longer possible to trace the history of this philosophy to its founders. It stretches out its fingers from the dim background of shadowy ages, whose history has never been written,—till now the life-story of Yoga has become vague to the memory of Man. Yet

[1] See Swami Abhedananda's *How to Be a Yogi*, and kindred books, for further details upon these topics.

we may date its origin to some two or three thousand years before the birth of Christ without fear of wandering far from the truth. Patanjali is the reputed founder of this school of philosophy, but we find traces of it in writings before the date of that venerable sage, though we may with certainty assert that he was the first to systematize the Yoga Philosophy.

WHAT IS YOGA PHILOSOPHY?

It is a philosophy which plans, designs, arranges, and graduates ascetic practices, and the manner of living and thinking by which its disciples may learn that concentration which unites them with God, the Supreme Spirit. The object of Yoga Philosophy is to merge into the Supreme Spirit. The word "merge" can scarcely be used correctly, for all Indian philosophies teach and affirm that all *is* God. Everything animate and inanimate—as we popularly use the word—*is* God. Form and individuality are caused by our senses and ignorance. *We are,* therefore, God. And as such we cannot merge into Him. So it is really not merging into God, but becoming conscious of our real Selves, and thus resuming, or assuming, Divinity.

> "................. He is one with Life.
> ....He is blest...............
> OM MANI PADMI OM! The Dewdrop slips
> Into the shining Sea....................

And we can "slip" into that sea of Light and Infinity by the lubricant of Knowledge.

KNOWLEDGE AND DIVINITY

KNOWLEDGE, as the word is popularly used, means either the comprehension of the true nature of things around us, or the possession of any kind of information.[1] Knowledge, as a technical term of Yoga Philosophy, means the understanding of Self, *i.e.*, the Supreme Being. Knowledge of the former kind is gained by learning and experience, while that of the latter kind can be attained only by mental activity, and the avoidance of all experience, *i.e.*, external passivity. Nor is the mental activity brought into play by thinking of things read or heard, but by turning the mind inwards and recognizing Self, which leads to the unconscious contemplating of, and complete concentration on, the ONE-ALL. For when the Self is known, the mantle of Ignorance is dropped, we see God, and become God. God is OMNISCIENT. In the same way Omnipotence is mastered by the Yogi. By recognizing Self, he becomes GOD, and GOD is OMNIPOTENT.

It will be necessary to possess some knowledge of the Indian idea of Cosmic Evolution, and of the doctrine of KARMA to understand what is meant by SELF and the ideals of this wonderful system of philosophy. Whatever we may think of the right and wrong of their ideas, and the mode of attaining their ideals, we cannot refrain from admiring the boldness and ingenuity of their

---

[1] Knowledge, according to our Western ideals and standards, has a very pragmatic and practical meaning and aim, viz.: to "guide action." That it is the *use* of Knowledge; what it is for, according to us. As will be seen, the Hindus have a very different conception of its meaning and use.

thought and the labour expended in thinking-out a theory of such marvellous minuteness, and the pains taken in formulating such difficult thought as they contain. This reaching out for the highest, together with the difficult practices, the indomitable courage and the untiring patience and perseverance that must necessarily attend that ambition, is to me one of the most beautiful as well as the saddest of spectacles which is to be witnessed in the tragedy of Human Life.

HINDU COSMOGENY

Nearly every action of Man is done with reference to some future result, and any religion is an example of this truth. It is the bait of future good or happiness that makes religion so powerful in this world among men. Nothing that does not deal with a future state has any power, as a doctrine, in human hearts. And the greatest potency of Yoga Philosophy lies in its reference to the future state of its disciples. It is nothing short of "Master of the Universe,"—Omnipotence, Omniscience, Infinity! This, then, is the future state of the Yogi. Now we want to know how the founders of this school came to promise so brilliant and wonderful an after-life. We shall be able to understand this when we comprehend the Hindu idea of the creation of the World and of Man.

Here, in short, is the history of the Creation, according to some Hindu philosophers. It seems to me that the point they set out from is "History repeats itself. All things move in a circle." Rolling onward eternally, the universe proceeds through aeons, or *Kalpas,* as the Hindu calls them. Each *Kalpa* is made up of a thousand *Maha-Yugs,* and each *Maha-Yug* contains 4,320,000 years. When the Universe has passed through all these years, once more the Universal Matter returns into the Primal Being and lies inert, or perhaps no more *as* Matter, for an indefinite period. Then by the activity of the Primal Being, again Matter is thrown out of Equilibrium—or freshly "created"; and once more the Universe becomes nascent.[1]

THE PHILOSOPHY OF BUDDHA

Buddha taught that "All is sorrow." This life is, after all, nothing but a continuous series of ills and pains; the death penalty hangs over every one of us. We die, but only to be reborn again into this vale of tears. Thus the tragedy (or comedy) goes on for ever![2]

Absorption in the One-All means freedom from further rebirths; therefore, from further sins and troubles, for life is a series of troubles and sorrows which, though they are all *Maya* or illusion, are troublesome to the existence of the human soul, inasmuch as they bind it to individuality, and the experiences and consciousness

---

[1] It is interesting to note the agreement of modern science with this view. Thus, Marion Erwin, C. E., in his book, *The Universe and the Atom* (1916), p. 289, says:—"We must therefore conceive that in the universe matter is being created by radiations from other matter all the time; and there is going on all the time the gathering up of this new-born matter by gravitation into clusters and suns; that in time these suns go to a Kinetic death, and finally the matter of which they are composed is converted again into ether substance. Thus we have an endless cycle of births, lives, deaths and resurrections in the material universe."

[2] See Kitch, *The Origin of Subjectivity in Hindu Thought*, pp. 65–68, for discussion of this point (1917, University of Chicago Press).

of variety, and thus keep it from the fulness of itself. Now then, how is this evil to be overcome? What causes pain? Birth! What causes birth? Karma! What causes Karma? Ignorance! Therefore, kill ignorance! But now, if we stop Karma, we shall stop birth, and with it pain. If we stop birth we resume our Original Nature, which is omniscient and omnipotent and infinite; then we are no more ignorant, *i.e.*, Ignorance is killed. Therefore, the chief thing is to prevent Karma,—and this is the aim of the Yogis.

We must bear in mind that Karma is the product of the "eleven senses," so that if we conquer all the senses we shall stop Karma. This the Yogi proceeds to do by training his mental faculties to be conscious of nothing else but *Jiva* (consciousness). Thus even mental activity is not permitted. The training is consummated in eight stages.

According to the doctrine of the "Eight-fold way," the Yogi state of life is entered upon in the last stage of this existence, when man has fulfilled his three obligations, his hair has become grey, and his face wrinkled. It is then that the Hindu betakes himself to the forests primeval to wean himself from this world in order to enter the Higher Life.[1]

1 One objection should be noted here, viz., that all this is impracticable in our active, busy Western civilization. That is very true; but this is no argument against studying Yoga. Everyone who plays the piano does not hope to become a concert pianist; everyone who takes up any physical exercise does not expect to become a professional athlete. But we can all progress *to some extent*, in our chosen line—according to the amount of work we choose to devote to it; and we must remember that Yoga means work! In what follows, therefore, I am not outlining what

The whole life of the Brahman is a preparation for the ascetic life. The first part he spends with his books, and under the almost servile subjugation of his master or *Guru*. The second is spent as a priest and a man of the world, with his wife and family, earning bread for them, performing the rites and ceremonies of his office, and living a strictly honest and continent life. No luxuries are allowed to him. The third part is spent apart from the world. He leaves his family and possessions and retires to the forest to solve metaphysical problems, and is allowed to take his wife with him, if he wishes to do so. It is only later, when abstruse metaphysical problems have ceased to trouble him, and he feels himself ready for the lonely life with his thoughts and God, that he sends his wife home and is thenceforward a man free from all earthly ties.

The passing from one stage to another is very gradual. At first any one was allowed to lead this life of the "Eight-fold way"; but when the power of the Brahmans or priests increased, they declared that those of the lower castes were not required to become ascetics. After a time even this negative permission was withdrawn. When Buddha came, he abolished such restrictions, and further said that it was not necessary for a man to wait till old age overtook him in order to enter into the path of the higher life.

There are two kinds of Yoga practised, the *practical* and the *superior*. It is necessary to do the practical to rise to the superior.

The Sacred Books of India prescribe eight stages
my present readers should attempt, but merely describing the method of life pursued by the Hindu Yogis.

to attain perfection. The whole course may well be likened to an educational curriculum. Thus the "Four-fold Path" is the school course, when the man is prepared to do his part well here and taught to apply his learning to everyday life. The first four stages of the "Eight-fold Path" are the college course, when the student dips more deeply into the mysteries of being; and the last four grades are the "postgraduate course," when he has risen above the ordinary theories and experiments, and knows more than he can teach. Degrees are of no more value to him, and the deepest theories propounded in books and by men are but incipient wisdom,—finger directions to the truth of which he has caught a glimpse. Bearing this in mind, we shall see how good and rational is the "Eightfold Path," and we shall be able to understand it better. Let us take each stage and grade and extract all the meaning we can out of it.

The *first* grade is called *Yama*. The Fourfold Path has taught man to live as a man of the world,—working, doing, enjoying all the good things of earth and experiencing the passions, emotions and vicissitudes that are a part of the worldly life. Now he must rise higher. He must learn to avoid the deceits and illusory pleasures of life. Life among men is full of petty lies. He must speak nothing but the strictest truth,—the absolute Truth. Not only must he cease to ask for anything, but even cannot receive gifts, so that the desire to possess may die, and he may be under obligation to no one. Theft, even in the most far-fetched application, may not be committed. For instance, no food may be taken, no fruit broken from a garden without permission, even to satisfy the last stages of starvation. Nothing that belongs to another must be touched. Chastity in its broadest sense must be practised. Above all, SELF-CONTROL is the lesson of this school-room. This lesson is gathered by the acquirement of INDIFFERENCE. INDIFFERENCE is much discussed and not infrequently ridiculed in the Occident, and among occidental races. I venture to say it is because the West has not understood the full import of this word, as used by the Oriental, because of its ignorance of the ideals of the East.

The real and inner meaning of indifference in this case is "intensity and rapidity of thought and calm,"—a calm perhaps tinged with fatalism. Everything that comes to the mind is instantly felt and entirely grasped; and when that is done it is put aside and the mind is ready to receive new impressions in the same swift and complete manner. Thus all unnecessary agitation is avoided, for when the real nature of a thing or deed is understood, the mind becomes calm. It also kills desire, for the mind wants nothing illusory. All is illusory except One, i.e., God. Thus it does not want what it understands as the illusions of the senses. It only wishes to know, to experience; not to possess. This indifference is meant to develop equally in every direction—strongly. Therefore, it must not be undervalued or considered unnatural.

The exterior must be the physical demonstration of the inward thought, and waste detracts from the mental force and purity of the Inner-Self, also,—for the loss of force must be accompanied by a lessening of purity, because the ability to resist the undesirable is weakened. Such a useless expenditure reduces the acuteness and vi-

tality of concentration, which further reduces the force
and power of the Will. Life is made up of many interests, and if an undue amount of energy be expended
on one object, the others suffer and no good results are
gained. Such indifference must be cultivated, to gain
control,—or how can we work, especially such strenuous
work as the Yogi has to perform?

Everything requires just so much force and no more,
—the rest is superfluous. Further, what is gained in
one direction is counteracted in another, for in Nature
all things have a just equipoise,—that is compensation.
So if too much be spent on the material side, the abstract will lose. Nor is this indifference to be acquired
by killing, *i.e.,* avoiding passion, but by the subjugation
of it, and by satiety, aided by comprehension. We do
not cease to feel, but cease to show and care, *i.e.,* we
control and master by understanding. Christ himself
instances this indifference in all the recorded events and
crises of his life. Moses once lost command over himself,
and he was not allowed to enter the Land of Canaan.[1]
To sum up, indifference teaches:

1) To think inwardly, by oneself, without outward
expression. This means bodily youth,—for our body is
destroyed, and our countenance lined, wrinkled and rendered ugly by the expression of the thought on the body.
Therefore the faces of people who have beautiful
thoughts *are* beautiful.

2) The thought is intensified by the reservation or the
proper direction of energy.

3) To understand the real nature of things readily,
and to dismiss the thought when understood.

[1] According to the Hindus "anger is the worst of sins."

The benefits of the system are:

1) One is able to think of many more things; therefore the interest becomes wider, *i.e.*, the mind develops
in many more directions, and so more equally. It is a
well-known fact that Yogis can work continually for a
long time, and are extremely versatile in their knowledge and interests.

2) Man is enabled to master thought instead of
thought mastering him, *i.e.*, the will is strengthened.

3) Man is given power over man, for silent thought
and feeling is domineering. Silence is greater than
verbiage.

These are only a few of the advantages gained. From
the above exposition one can see that *Yama,* the first
grade, is meant to develop man's mental equipment to
something higher, by developing him fully. So we shall
find, on closer inspection, that each grade deals with a
new development, and lifts the student rung by rung
higher on the ladder to perfection.

Says Edward Carpenter (*Pagan and Christian
Creeds*):

"Rest is the loosing of the chains which bind us to
the whirligig of the world; it is the Stilling of Thought.
. . . Obtain power over your thoughts and you are free.
You can then use the outer things or dismiss them at
your pleasure. . . .

"In the Katha Upanishad you will find these words:
'As rainwater that has fallen on the mountain ridge
runs down on all sides, thus does he who sees a difference between qualities run after them on all sides.'
This is the figure of the man who does *not* rest. But
the Upanishad goes on: 'As pure water poured into

pure water remains the same. Thus, O Gautama, is the self of a thinker who knows.' "

But what if our minds be not "pure"—what if the water be muddy? If you pour muddy water into the reservoir, what do you see? The muddy water will taint all the rest. What, then, must we do to render our minds clear and pure—to prevent the water (pursuing our analogy) from being muddy?

The solution is simple, and was clearly stated by the Chinese philosopher Lao-tze, hundreds of years B. C. He wrote, in the Tao-Teh-King—"Who is there who can make muddy water clear?" And Lao-tze has a ready answer. He says: "If you *leave it alone* it will become clear of itself." So, "the muddy water of the mind,—muddied by all the foolish little thoughts which like a sediment infest it—but if you leave it alone it will become clear of itself." Here we find a beautiful example of the value of non-resistance, passivity, so constantly urged in the Hindu writings. . . . By non-resistance we achieve everything! As Lao-tze again says: "By non-action there is nothing that cannot be done." And the Bhagavad Gita also says: "He who discovers inaction in action and action in inaction is wise among mortals." It is by meditating upon these apparent paradoxes that Truth will be discovered.

The second grade is called NIYAMA. Now the neophyte has been taught to regulate his behaviour to his fellow men. His ethical education is complete. He must now withdraw himself more completely from the outer world, and turn his mind within himself,—directing his thoughts Godward. This is done by conscientiously performing his religious observances, by sacri-

fice and worship,—like Catholic priests, who have daily
to say Mass and read their Breviary. All impure
thoughts are resolutely put aside; the mind must be as
pure as the body. Contentment in all things must be
cultivated, as discontentment robs the mind of peace,
and good, kind thoughts. Simplicity in all things is
one of the lessons of this class-room. Vedic verses are
continually muttered and thought over, so that their
inner meaning may enlighten the soul. One more lesson is learnt in this grade, namely, trust in God. The
thought of the morrow is banished from the mind.
"Sufficient unto the day is the evil thereof." Absolute
and unwavering trust in the Lord! The mystic syllable
AUM (OM) is used in this stage. "Detachment" is
learned.

"Detachment" or "renunciation," according to the
Hindu teachings, means more than merely giving up
what one wants; it means giving up *the desire to want it.*
As Avalon says: "Those who seek the joys of any
'Heaven' can never attain the end of high Yoga." For,
as William James has pointed out: "In the more positive and refined view of heaven many of its goods, the
fellowship of the Saints and of our dead ones, and the
presence of God, are but social goods of the most exalted
kind. It is only the search of the redeemed inward
nature, the spotlessness from sin, whether here or here-
after, that can count as spiritual self-seeking pure and
undefiled." (*Principles of Psychology,* I, p. 309.)
How far all this is removed from the "Christian" Bib-
lical materialism,—with its streets of "pure gold" like
transparent glass, its foundations of "precious stones,"
etc.,—it is easy to see.

The *third* stage is ASANA or Posture. A period has now been reached when the pupil is required to undertake work of a very strenuous character,—so much so that it appears almost a superhuman labour. The sages of old discovered that so long as the mind is in the body it requires the help of the brain to do its thinking, therefore the body must not be neglected.

No great work can be done without Strength and Health.

They had also noticed, as doctors and men of science are now beginning to recognize, that certain thoughts develop themselves best in certain postures of the body,— just as diet very often regulates the current of thought. Therefore, after careful observation and experiment, they discovered those positions which aided their lines of thought most. There are eighty-four (84) such positions which the Yogi has to practise. Those postures will not all be described here. Many English books do not provide a detailed description of these postures, because they say they are vulgar and disgusting. ''To the pure all things are pure.'' Besides, what part of the human body can be disgusting or impure? Nothing that God has made is unclean. It is false modesty, caused by an imperfect social and ethical standard. The Indian philosophers are not hindered in their search after Truth and Life by such petty considerations, which have no value. Those who have practised them have found bodily health and strength and mental vigour. It is as unjust as it is unfair to condemn anything without due trial. Those who seek for the Truth cannot afford to be narrow or prejudiced. Suffice it to say that these bodily postures are necessary both for the body and the mind.

The *fourth* grade still attends to the body. Deep breathing and the regulation of breath are taught. (This is known as PRANAYAMA.) The process of breathing is in three parts,—inhalation, retention and exhalation. The time taken to perform each action is proportionate. The Yogis have discovered the proportion, and its apprentices are taught to breathe accordingly. Gradually the aim is retention, *i.e.*, suspension of breath. Any one who will try the experiment will find that the brain works with dizzy celerity when the breath is held in the body. This, then, is the object. Another object it has,—namely, by suspending the breath, life—it is said—may be prolonged indefinitely. How well Yogis have succeeded in this wonderful art may be gathered from various accounts which narrate the interment of Yogis in sealed, air-tight coffins for periods varying from seven to forty days. The experiment was tried on a Yogi, with his consent, by some well-known British officers, who testified to the incident on their word of honour, and also signed a paper giving an account of the whole experiment in all its details.

Nowadays it seems hardly necessary to tell of the effects of deep breathing. It is known to everybody that deep breathing makes the blood pure, the eyes so bright that they dazzle, the complexion clear and clean, the skin smooth, and that it fills the body with the exhilaration of health; but few know that it makes the body glow—actually *glow*. For many decades the occidental scientists laughed at the idea that the human body glowed and gave forth light; but lately, within the last few years, a series of experiments on chemicals and other substances sensitive to light, undertaken by French and also American scientists, have proved clearly that the human body *does* emit a form of light. Youth radiates more light than the aged, and the so-called "beauty of youth" is said to be largely due to this glow. Deep breathing produces more glow than most ordinary youths have,—and brings new life, youth and beauty to age. It is a most noticeable and remarkable fact that Yogis, however old they may be,—and some of them are said to live three and four times the span of 70 years, an ordinary man's life,—always look young, some positively handsome; all have brilliant eyes, and all are strong and healthy.

Together with the above-mentioned exercises, there are, in the third and fourth stages, others whose purpose it is to strengthen and cleanse the body, such as cleaning the nasal organs by drawing water through the nostrils, passing water right through the body, regulating the heart-beats, sharpening the five senses, and other exercises for the control of every limb and muscle of the body. I refrain from detailing the practices,—however interesting may be their results,—in deference to the false ideas of propriety now current in our present-day social life. Suffice it to say that, after a man has submitted himself to the above discipline, he is perfect master of every little action of his body.

Now stands before one a man who is as complete as the world can expect him to be. He is correct in his relations with men; his piety is of a high order, but still

conventional.   He is master of his body and to a certain
extent of his senses, *i.e.*, of his *five inward* senses; but
as yet he is not immune from the action of the *outward*
senses on him,—though he began their control with the
practice of Indifference in the very first stage, and carried the process in modified forms through the succeeding stages.   But now, in the fifth stage, he must devote
himself wholly and solely to the subjugation of the
effects of the senses of sight, hearing, touch, smell and
taste.

This *fifth* state is called *Pratyahara*.   In this grade
the practice is to withdraw the attention from all objects and to accommodate the thought to the nature of
the mind.   He is rising on the mental plane, and can
control his own thoughts: "I do not want you; I want
another!   You have come unbidden,—go at my command!"   But yet he is not in a position to say, "*All*
thoughts go away; I wish to rest my mind."   Now, to
attain this complete mastery is the aim of the neophyte
in the *sixth* stage.   The fifth grade is more a preparatory to the sixth than a grade distinct by itself.

The exercises grow difficult in the *sixth* grade, called
DHARANA.   Its object is two-fold, *viz.*, (1) to gain mental composure, (2) to steady the mind.   The first is
gained by holding the mind perfectly blank, allowing
no thought to enter into the consciousness, and permit-
ting the senses to perform none of their functions.
This is a most difficult object to attain, for the mind
must not be even conscious of its prohibition to itself.
It must be maintained perfectly blank.   When this difficult task is learned, the mind is taught to fix its atten-

tion without swerving on some object or point. Very
often the tip of the nose is selected. This is called
steadying the mind.

DHYANA is the *seventh* grade. Material objects are
discarded, and thought is fixed on knowledge, the Supreme Being, or some other abstract idea, to the exclu-
sion of all other thought. Unification is attained.

In the *eighth* stage, called SAMADHI, the last grade is
reached. It is one of profound contemplation; the
thought is trained on the Supreme Being *only* and there
held. The soul becomes enlightened, the man divine,
and all powers of heaven and earth are said to belong to
the Yogi. His condition thereafter is ecstatic. Cold
and heat do not touch him, prosperity and adversity
have no influence; joy and sorrow are not for him; he
is above all earthly states,—he is one with the Supreme
Being. It is after this state has been attained that the
Yogi is able to perform "miracles."

This, in brief, is the object of the Yogi,—to attain
a state of universal consciousness and become one with
the Absolute; but in the course of this development, and
as it were as an offshoot or resultant from it, certain
psychic powers are automatically developed by certain
practices which the Yogis adopt. The prime object of
the Yogi is not to attain these psychic powers,—and
hence they differ from our psychics and "mediums"
here in the West, who desire phenomena above all else.
The Hindus believe, however, that these psychic faculties will come of themselves when a certain state of
inner development has been reached; and their object
is to attain this development not by passive sitting for
phenomena, but rather by intense inner development and

activity, coupled with certain exercises or practices devoted to the purpose of arousing certain secret energies
within the system, and when this end has been accomplished these psychic powers come of their own accord.

As the student proceeds, he will see that the Hindus
have a whole system of physiology, of which we in the
West know nothing, and which the average physician
would wholly deny. Thus, they speak of certain *nadis*
or infinitely small vessels which traverse the body, and
of these there are more than seven hundred million!
They also tell us of certain inner, psychic centres which
they call *chakras,* but which would not be discoverable
by the dissection of the Human body; and of a hidden,
latent and sacred energy, known as *Kundalini,* which is
said to reside at the base of the spine, and which, when
aroused, vivifies these various *chakras,*—thereby rousing
them into activity, and stimulating the psychic powers
of the Yogi.

All this, however, we will explain in detail in the
chapters which follow. For the present, this brief outline of Yoga will suffice to give the reader an idea of
the philosophical system in which the Hindus believe
and of their methods of attainment, by means of certain
scientific mental and physical practices which are, we
might say, modes of development of the inner psychic
powers, and the attainment of Cosmic Consciousness.

In the next chapter we shall begin a concrete study
of the methods of development, by which these powers
are to be stimulated into activity.

CHAPTER II

Asana—(*Bodily Posture*)

Yoga, then, is a system of graduated ascetic practices, which the Hindus have developed to a very finished degree,—as the result of many years of experimentation. Yoga is very closely allied to the Vendanta, which is a religious philosophy. Yoga is the practical side of it, as it were,—in the same way as in occult science,— which is a sort of philosophy and scheme of things, ceremonial magic is the practical part of that,—*i.e.*, the working part. Occultism has a perfectly definite scheme of the universe, and magic is devoted to the psychical or practical work,—very much in the same way that Yoga is the practical work which travels along the lines of psychic development in this direction.

Bear in mind very clearly that this whole conception of the Hindus is that our individual consciousness, the ego, the self, is not an isolated "thing," which is tied up in our own brain, as we think in the West, but is a fragmentary part of the Universal Consciousness. It is all part of one Being,—in the same way that a drop of water is a portion of the bucket of water; you can lift it out and pour it back again. It is separate and it is universal. That is one of the great points; while we *appear* separate, here in this life, we are all part of the Great Scheme, and we desire to get in touch with that Universal Consciousness. The Hindus think they can draw upon it. Just as there has been an extraordi-

nary power,—electricity,—all through this world, in the
atmosphere, for hundreds and hundreds of years,—but
humanity had not reached the point where it could em-
ploy it,—so the Hindus say, "We have this extraordinary amount of energy which is going to waste; let us
harness it and utilize it!" And in addition to this,
there is a certain metaphysical or religious training
which accompanies it. It has been written:

"Existence is full of sorrow. . . . No religion has
failed hitherto by not promising enough. Let us begin
by doubting every statement. Let us find a way of
subjecting every statement to the test of experiment"—
(which Yoga does). "Is there any truth in all the
claims of the various religions? There is, . . . one
form of miracle which certainly happens,—the influence of the genius. There is no known analogy in nature. There are supermen of different kinds, but they
are none of them of the same character as the great
spiritual teachers of the world. What is there in common between Christ and Buddha and Mahomet?
Buddha was born a prince and died a beggar. Mahomet was born a beggar and died a prince. Christ
remained obscure until a good many years after his
death. Elaborate lives of each one of these have been
written by devotees. There is one thing common in all
three,—an omission in their life histories. We hear
nothing of Christ between the ages of twelve and thirty.
Mahomet disappeared into a cave. Buddha left his par-
ents and went for a long while into the desert. Each
of them was perfectly silent up to the time of his re-
appearance, but came back and immediately began to
preach some new law. This is so curious that it leads

us to inquire whether the histories of the men were not very much the same.''

The point is this: what happened to them during their absence? They all three went away, disappeared for a certain length of time, a number of years, and alone, and came back with an extraordinary, new conviction. What did they do? We think that they went through certain initiations.

There is in Thibet a stone tablet bearing an inscription which records the presence there of some one who corresponded very remarkably with our conception of Christ; so that, apparently, he went to this monastery in Thibet and studied there.[1] And Buddha and Mohammed did much the same thing; they apparently went through certain practices and experiences,—not only talking and reading about religion, but they *experimented* with it themselves, and this gave them their belief.

Now, the Hindus have a perfectly definite scheme of the world,—a philosophy; and it is not *Dualism,*—or the belief in *two* ultimate things,—but *Monism,* or the belief in *one.* It is that all ultimately leads to *one thing,*—which is Spiritual Consciousness, and they strive to attain *that.*

In the last chapter, I outlined the eight stages of development,—the EIGHTFOLD PATH,—beginning with YAMA and NIYAMA, which are various methods of renunciation, practices in daily life, during spiritual training.

Annie Besant, in her little book, *An Introduction to Yoga,* gives a useful summary of some of the ''Obstacles

---

[1] *The Unknown Life of Jesus Christ,* by Notovitch.

to Yoga,''—that is, obstacles to be overcome—as follows:

"The obstacles to Yoga are very inclusive. First, disease: If you are diseased, you cannot practise Yoga; it demands sound health, for the physical strain entailed by it is great. Then, languor of mind: you must be alert, energetic in your thought. Then, doubt: you must have decision of will, must be able to make up your mind. Then, carelessness: this is one of the greatest difficulties with beginners; they read a thing carelessly, they are inaccurate. Sloth: a lazy man cannot be a Yogi; one who is inert, who lacks the power and the will to exert himself, how shall he make the desperate exertions wanted along this line? The next, worldly-mindedness, is obviously an obstacle. Mistaken ideas is another great obstacle, thinking wrongly about things. (One of the great qualifications for Yoga is 'right notion.' 'Right notion' means that the thought shall correspond with the outside truth,—that a man shall be fundamentally true, so that his thought corresponds to fact; unless there is truth in a man, Yoga is for him impossible.) Missing the point: illogical, stupid, making the important unimportant, and *vice versa*. Lastly, instability: which makes Yoga impossible, and even a small amount of which makes Yoga futile; the unstable man cannot be a Yogi.''

Flagg, in his work, *Yoga, or Transformation*, says:

"The means or ways of attaining Yoga which we will term 'Yoga practice' all resolve themselves into concentration of mind. And to this concentration Hinduism, which is both philosophy and religion, makes all its vast collection of Gods of every degree, all its temples with their countless symbols, in which those gods are worshipped, all its theology and ritual of devotion,—but the subservient means. For Yoga is above and beyond all these; they merely conduct the devotee up to it, and at its portals vanish as guides and ushers should.   To the whole thing, the work and what is worked for, the term Yoga is commonly applied,—just as in old Chinese literature, the word *Tao* means 'way to travel on,' but when used in relation to the practice in question, means 'the way in which it is performed,'—the method, art, and mystery of it. . . .''

Swami Vivekananda, writing of the practical utility of this subject in his *Raja Yoga,* says:

"The science of Raja Yoga, in the first place, proposes to give men a means of observing the internal states; and the instrument is the mind itself. The power of attention of mind, when properly guided, and directed towards the internal world, will analyse the mind, and illumine facts for us. The powers of the mind are like rays of light being dissipated; when they are concentrated, they illumine everything. This is the only source of knowledge that we have. Every one is using it, both in the external and the internal world; but, for the psychologist, this minute observation, which the scientific man can throw upon the external world, will have to be thrown upon the internal world, and this requires a great deal of practice.

"From our childhood upwards, we have been taught

only to pay attention to things external, never to pay attention to things internal, and most of us have nearly lost the faculty of observing the internal mechanism. To turn the mind, as it were, inside, stop it from going outside, and then to concentrate all its powers and throw them upon the mind itself,—in order that it may know its own nature, analyse itself,—is very hard work. Yet that is the only way to anything which may be considered a scientific approach to the subject.

"What is the *use* of such knowledge? In the first place, knowledge itself is the highest reward of knowledge; and in the second place there is also utility in it. It will take away all our misery. When, by analysing his own mind, man comes face to face, as it were, with something which is never destroyed, something which is, by its own nature, eternally pure and perfect,—he will no more be miserable, no more unhappy. All misery comes from fear, from unsatisfied desire. Man will find that he never dies, and then he will have no more fear of death. When he knows that he is perfect, he will have no more vain desires; and, both these causes being absent, there will be no more misery—there will be perfect 'bliss,' even while in this body."

These Yoga practices also have a very practical resultant benefit, from a worldly point-of-view. Miss E. A. Fletcher, in her book on *The Law of the Rhythmic Breath*, says:

"When we consciously subordinate the physical to the spiritual, all the atoms of our bodies feel an impulse toward order from the rhythmic flow of the *Tattvas* (ethers) ; and even the most rebellious yields to the magnetic attraction, and vibrates in harmony with the prevailing rhythm, when the currents are fully established, and maintained in perfect equilibrium. This is the secret of all the miraculous recoveries of bed-ridden invalids; for in moments of supreme elation, through faith or enthusiasm, the *Tattvic* currents are raised to so high power as to sweep all obstructions from their path, and to impart synchronous action to the hitherto wandering elements, which almost instantly thrill the body with a sensation of strength. . . .

"The higher we raise our vibrations, through the purifying action of rhythmic breathing and beneficent thinking, the more we shall be in touch and co-operate with the finer forces round us—their waves even breaking over us—and waiting for our recognition to lift us to higher states of efficiency,—of comprehension, of intuition, of power to think and to do. Spiritual perceptions and spiritual strength make possible a degree of activity—both mental and physical—a power of accomplishment in a given task, utterly beyond the capacity of mere physical energy. Work which on the physical plane is effort, becomes a joy and an inspiration when we call to our aid our ever-ready, ever-waiting, spiritual forces."

Thus you will see that Yoga has a very practical bearing upon our daily lives; and will help us, from any point-of-view whatever. Indeed, the whole system of Yoga is so beautifully graded, so logical, so consistent, and so thoroughly supported by personal experiences throughout, that one might almost be a thorough materialist, and yet experience all the phenomena, and the highest states of ecstatic consciousness! All Yoga begins with the body—with physiology—and works gradually upward, through the mental, the psychic, to the spiritual; and the transition is so gradual, and so consistent, that one hardly knows he has attained that state until he finds himself there. It is this foundation of the Yoga system upon the body,—upon physical and sensual experience,—that makes it so intelligible to Westerners, when once they have duly appreciated its inner meanings, and its *raison d'etre*. So, as I have said, we must, in all Yoga practices, begin at the beginning, with the *body;* and the Yogis begin, as we have seen, with certain postures of positions, which are calculated to subdue the body, and thus leave the consciousness free for meditation and concentration,—when these exercises are, later one, undertaken.

So, therefore, we come to the actual bodily positions or postures,—known as ASANA—which are the groundwork, so to speak, of the whole system of training.

Before doing so, however, I want to touch upon one or two philosophical questions. The Hindus have always been very keen on this point: that the mental or spiritual life *is dependent on the body;* and they say that you can affect the current of thought by the kind of food you eat; and we know that food is an enormous and important factor. For instance, you can take bees, and by feeding them one kind of food, they will give birth to male bees, and by feeding them another kind of food you will get female bees; and the same with tadpoles. Food is an extremely important factor in all these biological questions.

In the West, we are inclined to be omnivorous. There are various grades of different kinds of animals which naturalists have classified or placed into groups,—such as carnivora, herbivora, omnivora, the rodents, and the frugivora,—or those that eat fruits,—of which the monkey is an example. This is so true of those divisions of animals which only eat certain kinds of foods, that a naturalist can take any animal and tell exactly what kind of food he eats; or, if you tell him what sort of food an animal eats, he will name the animal for you. And the reason they can do that, is because every part of the anatomy is different, all through the body. The whole physiology, the character of the secretions of the body, and everything else, is entirely different.

For instance, a carnivorous animal has a relatively short, thick intestinal tract; a herbivorous animal a very long and slim one; and carnivora, of course, have certain teeth, secretions, saliva, etc., which are suited to the kind of food they eat. Here are one or two examples which show the difference: all animals which eat meat *lap* their drink,—like a cat or dog; but vegetarian animals drink *by suction.* And carnivorous animals *do not perspire,* although they have perspiratory glands. But horses and other vegetarian animals, as we know, *do* perspire.

The point is this: when you take man, and you say, "Now, according to this category of differing animals, what should man eat?"—in every conceivable part in the body, throughout, structure and all, he comes into the frugivorous class,—the class which eats fruits and nuts,—and this I believe to be the ideal diet of man. (See my book *The Natural Food of Man.*)

Now, you may say, "What is the result of this diet?" Well, personally, I had a very great deal of energy, ability to work, a very clear brain, worked a long time without stopping, required very little sleep, and in fact felt in every way better than I do now; I do not feel very much different on the mixed diet except that if I want to sit down for a long period of intense work, on the present mixed diet, I cannot do it, but on the other diet, I could. That is due to the fact that the body, on the fruit diet, is so clean that very few poisons are accumulated; and on the mixed diet, there are many poisons, which are the cause of fatigue. Proteid foods,—such as meat,—are the great causes of fatigue or "tiredness," and that has been proved by taking different squads of men, and feeding them on one diet, then putting the same squad on another diet, and they were found to outpoint themselves a hundred per cent., or more, on the vegetarian diet.

It is easy to see why this should be so; all of us create certain poisons within ourselves. A clever Frenchman has called the human body a "poison factory"; and those poisons are in the tissues, in the blood, and all through it.

If you stop the circulation of the blood by strangling a man, he does not die because the air is cut off; it is because the blood has circulated through the body two or three times without meeting oxygen, and has got so poisoned that it is practically *black*. We create, therefore, poisons all the time. The reason we do not die, is because we throw them off all the time. Now, if you were to kill any animal, all the poisons which were in the tissues of that animal, at that moment, would be retained in the tissues; you could not force them out, so that, in addition to the "good" part of meat, its nutriment, you get in addition all those poisons. It amounts to this; that we have all the poisons created within ourselves, plus the poisons in the meat, and these are the great causes of fatigue. It is a fact on record that in a very long race, not long ago, it was found that the seven men who came in first were all vegetarians.

There is this further, occult doctrine regarding food, which should perhaps be mentioned here. It is that a vegetarian diet tends to make the molecules of protoplasm in the body smaller and more sensitive to shorter wave-lengths. It is quite conceivable that it should actually do so. We know that a bar of iron becomes magnetized when all the molecules of its structure are, as it were, "pointed" in the same direction. If you strike a magnet of this type a sharp blow with a hammer, or heat it red-hot and allow it to become cool again, it will be found to have lost its magnetism. What has happened? Probably, the molecules of the iron, which before had been uniform, in their polarity, are now "pointing" in all directions, and hence the energy which formerly played on or through the bar of iron, in one continuous unbroken stream is now broken up, and playing in a thousand different directions. Hence, the iron will be no longer a magnet. It is possible that something of the same sort takes place in the body; and that its molecules, when finely attuned by rhythm, and acting in unison, may allow a flow through the body of energies which would otherwise be limited or altogether restrained in their action. This is merely by way of suggestion, which you can take for what it may be worth.

Mr. Prescott F. Hall, in a most interesting article in the *Journal* of the American Society for Psychical Research (Vol. X, pp. 680–81) says:

"A vegetable diet tends to loosen the vibric matter of the astral body; and vegetables, fruits and prunes make the blood able to attract spiritual power. Carrots also are beneficial. Nuts, especially peanuts, are bad,—especially near the time of sitting for development, as they tend to make one's atmosphere of one colour. Raw eggs are favourable. Liquids are favourable for development. . . . Fasting often helps the liberation of the astral body."

I do not enter into all this in order to persuade you to change your form of diet; but those who go seriously into initiation will find that a very abstemious diet facilitates their progress so much that they will adopt that system of living. In addition to this, a great deal of water-drinking is very good. The body is about eighty per cent. water! It is just a few solids in solution, as it were! To maintain that state or ratio, you should drink plenty of water,—four to six glasses a day at least. The various eliminating organs should be kept as open as possible; likewise the skin.

The subject of *fasting* I ought perhaps to touch upon. I have observed patients who have undergone fasts to cure themselves of various diseases, fasting from thirty to fifty-five days,—taking nothing but water,—and they did not die, but they *all got well!* They cured themselves of the diseases they had, by giving nature a chance to ''catch up.''

The remarkable fact is that if you feed a person who has a disease, you feed the disease and not the patient! He does not get any benefit from the food. If you put food into a sick person's body you starve and poison him at the same time. They are now curing diabetes at the Rockefeller Institute, by the fasting process. Nearly all the great scholars have undergone long periods of fasting. I have seen people fast over forty days with benefit. Christ probably did fast forty days, as stated. *The Philosophy of Fasting*, by Mr. Edward E. Purinton, discusses the philosophical and spiritual sides of fasting, and I have treated the physiological side of the question at great length in my book, *Vitality, Fasting and Nutrition*.

Two other questions: Regarding the nature of *life* and regarding *sleep*. The ordinary theories held by the physiologists are simply these: Here we have a body, a human machine like an engine,—an ordinary fire-engine; you put in so much coal and you burn it up, and you get so much energy; and in the care of the body you put in so much fuel (food), and you get so much energy; and they say we can calculate exactly how much it is, and figure it out on the basis of so many ''calories.'' I believe that this is all absolutely untrue; that the body is not at all like an engine, but rather an *electric motor,* which is recharged with energy, during the hours of rest and sleep. If the body were like a steam engine, then when we were very tired, all we should have to do would be to eat some food, then exercise and burn it up! But that is not so; we must have sleep and rest.

And that factor of *sleep* distinguishes our (human) machine from every other machine in the world, and shows it to be a separate thing. *Sleep* is the great restorer of energy; it distinguishes man from any other engine. Bear that in mind, because sleep is of a very mystical nature, as evidenced by dreams, etc., as we shall see.

Doctors tell you we need so much sleep,—say eight hours, usually. If you sleep eight hours a day you spend a third of your lives in sleep! It seems rather a waste. And the Hindus said: "Cannot we get rid of some of this waste? Cannot we reach a state in which we no longer miss sleep?" And they found that, by following out these exercises,—this diet and this system of living,—they *could* cut down their hours of sleep very much.

In practice, we find that the curve of sleep runs thus: we start with what we call the "threshold of consciousness"; it goes down when you fall asleep, and then gradually rises again; so that immediately you fall asleep you are at the deepest point, and from that point it is a gradual curve upward until you awaken. The query is: Is it possible to deepen that curve so that you get *deeper* into sleep and require *less of it?* The Hindus think they have found this method of artificially deepening sleep, and not spinning it out so long; and we in the West have done that by *hypnotism.* Put a hypnotized patient to sleep, and in an hour he derives as much benefit as in three or four hours of ordinary sleep.

A curious thing about the thinking processes is that bodily posture has a great deal to do with them. You will find that when you begin to meditate. If you close your eyes, the stream of consciousness is broken into by all kinds of stimuli or sensations,—chief among which are *physical* sensations,—coming from the body. So, the Hindus said, the first thing to do is to put the body into such a state that it will not keep interrupting consciousness. In other words, if you put your body in *any* ordinary position, you are, after a time, uncomfortable. The Hindus said, "There must be *some* positions that won't keep interrupting consciousness,—so that we can think without these breaks in consciousness, during meditation." And there are such physical postures which you can assume. They may be painful at first, difficult to assume,—but if you once "get" them, you will find yourself in a peculiar position, which the body can assume and maintain, and you will find that you are then free from these "breaks." So the Hindus studied and worked on it for hundreds of years, and finally they settled on 84 different postures,—many of which, unfortunately, it will be impossible for me to illustrate. The definite object in ASANA is to place the body in such a state that it will be free from interruptions.

You must first of all learn *relaxation*. The first thing to do is to relax the "solar plexus,"—to feel it "open," —because that is the beginning, essentially, of right breathing.

One of the best practical exercises is the following: A low pillow is necessary,—or, better still, none at all. With eyes closed, *think* of the back of the neck. Just let the pillow hold the weight of your skull. Think separately of the right arm, the left arm, right leg, left leg, and the structure of the body. Go over it again eight or ten times,—dwelling about eight or ten seconds on each member. Breathe deeply, relax, and control yourself so that you can absolutely relax every muscle of the body; and you will find you will go to sleep. The second point is that you will be as refreshed in ten minutes of this simple method of relaxation as you would be by hours of sleep.

Before going into the Asana positions, one thing you must learn, viz., *balance,*—the balancing of the body.

1) Lift up the right foot with the left hand, standing on the left foot; balance the body, keeping the *back straight* and the *knee down;* try to get the foot as far up as possible, until you begin to feel a pain in the knees. The idea is to keep the balance with the back *straight.* Do that once slowly; then, without using the hands, do it rapidly, alternating. Kick as high as you possibly can. Use a chair to balance yourself, if you absolutely have to.

2) Another exercise: The Hindus can do what we Europeans cannot do very well. If you squat down, you will find that you squat on your *toes,* which is easy,— but if you look at the Hindu, you find that he is sitting on his *heels,* balancing,—extremely difficult because our bodies are not properly balanced.

The above are balancing Exercises. We now come to the regulation

ASANA (POSTURES)

3) The first position is to insert the insteps into the bend of the knee-joints of the opposite legs. Bring the

right instep up through the hole made by the left leg.

4) The next position is, sitting flat on the floor with the knees straight out, toes out, keeping the spine straight, holding the toes, keeping the knees rigid.

5) The second part of this position is the same, while bending the head down, touching the knees with the forehead.

6) Holding the same position (and holding the toes), pull one foot up to the ear, like an arrow in a bow,— holding the other toe in the other hand.

7) Sitting on the hands balancing, lift the feet up in the air (feet outside hands).

8) Right foot under body; the other foot out straight; hands flat on thighs, spine erect and chin back.

9) Vary the last by bringing up the other foot instead. In this position you do your breathing exercises.

10) Lying flat on the floor (like a corpse).

11) This position is called ''THE GOD,'' and it is nothing but sitting in a chair, with feet and knees together, spine and head straight, hands on the knees.

12) The IBIS. Bring up the right foot as in the balancing experiments, only this time hold the right foot with the right hand, and with the left hand on the lips with a straight forefinger. Knees together. Then stand on the other foot.

13) The DRAGON. Kneeling on the toes and knees, hands flat on thighs; spine straight, head erect.

14) The THUNDERBOLT. Sit on the left leg, with the right foot straight out, hands on the knees, spine straight; the first finger and the thumb of each hand together, on the two knees. It is believed that a mag-

netic current is established in the body by those fingers, held in this manner.[1]

Asana positions are difficult, but if you can do them at all, you finally get to the point where you can hold them for hours without getting tired,—in fact you sink into them with the same sense of relief as you would into a warm bath. In these positions the mind is free from physical interruptions.

Patanjali merely points out the best positions, and leaves each one to settle for himself which one is the most suitable. Asana is primarily intended to facilitate and clear the thought; hence "a suitable steady Asana produces mental equilibrium."

We must get the body subjected first; otherwise, as you shut your eyes, you will be conscious of your body. As to the relaxing exercises, when lying flat on the back place a book on your abdomen, over the "solar plexus." While breathing, cause the book to rise and fall. Learn to *relax;* get some sort of balance to the body; and then try any position which you find is comfortable, and can be retained for some time without constantly annoying you. Practise this every day for at least ten minutes, so that you can get into a condition in which you are not conscious of the body, when you are sitting in this position, with the eyes closed. Then gradually work into a suitable *Asana* position, and hold *that* every day until it becomes easy and comfortable for you. Once you have acquired this, you have taken the first definite forward step towards psychic unfoldment, according to the Yoga teachings.

[1] The famous Yoni-mudra is made by touching the thumb with the first finger. This is the posture in which Buddah is often depicted.

CHAPTER III

PRANAYAMA (*Breathing Exercises*)

WE now take up the question of energy or *prana* distribution,—mainly through certain breathing exercises.

A great deal of the material contained in the last chapter may have appeared quite irrelevant, at the time; but it was not so, because you have got to learn balancing and relaxation, and these positions of the body, before you can progress to the mental exercises later on.

The chief thing to do, first of all, is to place the body in a restful and relaxed state, so that it will not keep intruding itself into the conscious mind; and that you must learn to do by means of these ASANA positions. Seat yourself in a comfortable chair, with the spine *straight*. That is really quite essential, because of certain exercises to be given later on, in connection with the spine—that is psychic practices. The spine must be fairly straight, and the muscles must not be too relaxed. They must be relaxed in a way, but yet there must be a certain tension there, as though you are ready to spring. You must feel you are *not* going to get up, you are *not* straining to get up, but preparing to get ready to get up! *That* you must practise,—that attitude you must try to have and hold,—while keeping the head fairly loose, the spine straight, and the hands open. Placing the thumb and first finger together has certain mystical meanings; it represents the circulation of the "magnetic" currents; the marriage of the sun and

42

moon; male and female; and various other things,—
more especially if they are resting on the knees. You
must be "at home" while holding these positions for
some considerable time.

Do not lean the body too far forward or backward;
and do not, above all, get any "kink" in the spine
either way! It must be relatively straight, up-and-
down. The reason for this is that when you come later
on to the psychic, internal practices, in connection with
breathing, you will find that there are certain internal
currents which travel up and down the spine; and these
would be interfered with immediately by any curvature
or bend.

The first thing to do then, is to practise these positions, and also relaxation,—particularly relaxation in
and around the neck and the "solar plexus." It is
very essential to *feel* the relaxation there, so that you
can consciously feel that it "opens," like a flower,—
just below the spot where the ribs divide. If that be
tense, it will stop your development until you can relax
it. The thing to do is to concentrate and get enough
"control," so that you can feel it, and then you can
relax. The plexus itself is like a great octopus; it is
the biggest nerve-centre in the body, aside from the
brain, and is the ruler of the "sympathetic system,"
the stomach and other vegetative functions; so, for that
reason, the stomach should not be full when these Yoga
exercises are undertaken, because it would press against
the plexus and against the heart. That is one of the
reasons why it is very important that the stomach should
be empty, and the food very light.

We now come to *breathing,*—which is, in one sense,

the most important keystone of the whole Yoga system.
There are two ways of considering it, the exoteric and
the esoteric,—the outer and the inner. Our exoteric
or Western doctrine is, of course, propounded in books
on physiology. The blood flows through the lungs; it is
at the beginning dark; it then comes into contact with
the oxygen in the lungs, and is rendered by that contact scarlet, arterial blood, and in that way is changed.
If it circulates two or three times through the lungs
and they are imperfectly filled with oxygen, it does not
meet enough oxygen, and it is only partially transformed into scarlet blood, and goes on its way semi-
loaded with impurities; but if there be plenty of oxygen
in the lungs, it is, of course, changed completely.[1]

From any point of view, deep breathing is very effica-
cious. But another thing! We find that breathing has
a tremendous effect on the mind, the character, the flow
of thought and the whole stream of consciousness. If
you feel depressed, just take a few of these exercises,
with loose clothing, and the feeling will pass away,—
showing that it is largely due to the circulation.

Here is an interesting physiological fact, very little
known,—in fact I have rarely spoken to a doctor who
knew it,—though it seems to bear out very strikingly
the Eastern philosophies. If you put your hand on
the wrist, you can feel the pulsation,—or in the upper
arm, or in the ankle or wherever there is a pulse. It
simply shows the rate of the heart-beat. The pulse
varies from seventy to eighty to the minute, or more,

[1] For a full and interesting discussion of the physiological side
of breathing, see Dr. J. S. Haldane's *Organism and Environment:
as Illustrated by the Physiology of Breathing* (1918).

according to the degree of excitement, exercise, and so
forth. That pulse-rate is the same all over the body,—
into the neck, the head, even the coverings of the brain.
But the circulation *in the brain itself* is synchronous
with—or correspondent to—*not* the heart pulsation but
to the *breathing rate*,—that is, twelve or fourteen to the
minute! This is a very striking fact and it seems to
show us that there is,—in the circulation of the brain
itself,—a pulsation which is synchronous with, or correspondent to, the breathing-rate.

This has been demonstrated by a series of very fine
anatomical experiments made by an English surgeon,
and certainly seems to bear out the Hindu contention
that there is a definite connection between consciousness
and the breathing rhythm.

If you take painting lessons from a Japanese artist,
he will begin with breathing exercises,—to obtain, first
of all, the "Rhythm of Nature."

In addition to our Western knowledge of breathing,
therefore—which physiologists possess,—there is an inner or esoteric doctrine,—which says that, in addition
to taking in oxygen from the air into the lungs, you at
the same time take in a vital *something,*—a "principle"
or "essence," which is known as *Prana;* and this *Prana*
is the supporter of vitality,—that it is the creator of
vitality; and it exists in a sort of fluidic form in the
atmosphere,—so that, as we breathe in the air, we also
take in this *Prana.* By certain mystical exercises, we
can raise the degree of circulation of this *Prana* in the
organs of the body. The *Prana* circulates through the
nerves and through the blood-vessels; so that we can
force the circulation of *Prana,*—once we get it inside

ourselves,—throughout the body, *i.e.*, through the nerve-centres.[1]

The Hindus have a whole mythical system of physiology, which we will come to a little later on in more detail. They claim that there are certain energy-carriers or *Nadis*, as they call them. There are 72,000 of these, and each of them has innumerable ramifications. If you take a scalpel or a knife, and dissect the human body, you do not find these centres. But the Hindus say, "Ah! they are not composed of *physical* matter, but of *astral* matter; therefore, not having any astral senses, you cannot see them." These energy-carriers are the storage-centres and chief means of circulating the *Prana.*

Now, the first thing to learn, in breathing exercises is: *Nose vs. Mouth Breathing.* Every doctor will tell you to breathe through the nose, but very few people know how to do that properly. You ought to breathe as though you were smelling a flower, and taking the scent right down, into the lungs. But you must do it in this way: instead of the air striking between the eyes, so to say, you must try to relax the nose and the passages all round, so that the air goes right down into the throat. You must feel the cold in the throat, instead of in the nose or between the eyes. Different sounds are made in the different kinds of breathing.

A good way to obtain a large volume of air without opening the mouth is this: hold the *teeth open* (just enough to get a finger in between them), and *close* the *lips.* They call this position the "rabbit throat," be-

[1] "Prana in the body of the individual is a part of the Universal Breath (Prana) or the 'Great Breath'" (*op. cit.*, p. 212).

cause it makes one look like a rabbit! When you have done this, you must draw down the lower or under part of the throat and mouth. Normally that is very soft; when you press down it makes it tense and hard. Do this as you hold the teeth apart and the lips closed. This opens all the passages and gives you an enormous passage for air.[1]

Now you have passed the air into the throat. In doing this,—when you analyse your sensations—you will find that you tend to keep the back straight and the chest high. Now, by muscular effort, without breathing at all, you must lift the chest up *at the top*. That is the position which you must hold during all the breathing, and all the expansion must come practically from the sides and bottom of the chest. You must relax thoroughly. There must be no strain at all, but perfect relaxation. This breathing must become so natural that you do not know you *are* breathing!

There are three kinds of breathing,—upper, middle and lower; diaphragmic, etc. You should be able to fill any one of those three parts *separately*.

The full breath of the Yogi is from the abdomen up. Bend slightly forward, in practice, and breathe out thoroughly first. Now inhale until you have a full breath; retain it. The chest must be kept elevated more or less all the time. Now, when you get to this

---

[1] There are theoretically *two* breaths which flow through the right and left nostrils. *Ida* is the nerve current on the left side of the spinal cord; the left nostril. *Pingala* is the nerve current on the right side of the spinal cord; the right nostril. They are also known as the Sun and Moon Breaths: but all this we shall come to in Chapter 7, when we shall treat it at length.

point, you must begin certain exercises; and the first
and the most simple of these is to *hold* the breath for
a definite period and then exhale. That establishes the
rhythm. If you breathe-in five seconds, hold it five,
and breathe-out five.

Kumbhaka is the retention of breath between the inspiration and expiration.

The great desire of the body is to eliminate poisons.
There is a poison residuum which always gets left in
the body; and if that is allowed to remain, the body
will try to rid itself of that before taking in any more
air. This rhythmic breathing is very important. You
should practise it morning and evening, for some time,
beginning with six or seven seconds, and raising it up
to ten,—which is a fair medium; twelve or fifteen is
pretty good. Get the cycle even; close the eyes and
empty the mind; think of nothing *but* this cycle; and
after three or four times the body seems to get into a
rhythm by itself, when the breathing seems to go on
mechanically. That is what you want it to do.

Later on, when we talk about mantras or chants,—
rhythmic syllabic words which are pronounced,—you
will find that they should be performed in the same
manner. In fact, these mantras are very intimately
connected with the breathing exercises, and you can
often attain rhythmic breathing exercises by saying the
mantras.[1]

A friend of mine who was working at Yoga, and was
very far advanced, told me that for *thirty-six hours* he

---

[1] Says Avalon: "Breathing is itself a Mantra, known as the
Mantra which is not recited, for it is said without volition."
(*The Serpent Power*, p. 97.)

said a mantrum without stopping, and he finally fell asleep and woke up again and was still saying it! The body had got into such an absolute rhythm that it went on by itself,—even though sleeping. And this is what you want to attain,—this complete rhythm, unconsciously. William James once said that all our civilization is based upon making as many acts as possible unconscious. The baby who learns to walk has first of all to make a tremendous conscious effort; but as he learns it becomes totally unconscious so that grown people can walk along the street, reading, breathing and able to see and hear, —all these things going on mechanically at the same time. And you should do whatever you can mechanically; for instance, buttoning your coat. In other words, it is just like delegating work to other people; the more you can delegate to them the less you do yourself. That is important for two reasons. In the first place, we have found that only those parts of the body and the nervous system get fatigued upon which consciousness works, but that all the vegetative functions of the body,—the heart, and so forth,—go on mechanically during sleep. The parts which tire are the parts which consciousness uses. So that the thing to do is to get as many parts to function unconsciously as possible.

The second point to observe is that it leaves your mind free for other things,—the labours of life, or anything you want to do,—particularly exercises of this kind, meditation, and so forth.

There are two things you may cultivate, as aids to breathing. One is breathing through a straw. The other is, closing a single nostril, breathing in through one and out through the other, which cleanses all the passages and at the same time improves the lungs and adds to the strength, by pulling and pushing the muscles of the abdomen.

We now come to various specific or particular *kinds* of breathing. First of all there is what the Yogis call the CLEANSING BREATH. This is very important, and one that is used after many other breathing exercises are mastered. Inhale a full breath, fill the lungs with air; then, when you are holding the breath, put the lips into the form of a sort of whistle, and breathe out very quickly; then hold; then out again in little gasps, as it were. It is very stimulating. Laughing, and all exercises which stimulate the diaphragm, are very beneficial. The "cleansing breath" is used after many of the Yoga exercises. You cannot think if the muscles are in tension anywhere in the body. Persons will sometimes say that they cannot remember things. Now, that is because they are tense! When they relax they will find they *can* remember clearly. You will find an intimate connection between memory and all the functions of physical and nervous and muscular relaxation.

Here is a very good exercise,—it is not altogether a Yoga exercise but is a good one to practise: with the shoulders slightly stooped, arms forward, begin breathing in and at the same time, extend the arms limply upward in front of you. Now, when you get to this point (arms horizontal), then the hands should be clenched and brought back to the shoulders,—tighter and tighter,—holding the breath all the time. Then hold this position, still tense, arms out; then relax and exhale at the same time. Throw the arms out with a jerk *before* you let-out the breath,—which you do as

they fall to the sides.   That is called the NERVE VITALIZ-
ING BREATH, and is very useful.

Now, the VOCAL BREATH.   Take in the breath, retain,
and then force out the whole breath through the open
mouth *suddenly*.   It must be done from the diaphragm.

Prana gathering exercises should be done on a flat,
hard bed or something of that kind.   You must lie down
for them, so as to relax and send the whole breath to the
solar plexus; and then, when you have taken in your
complete breath and held it for a moment—(now begins the psychic breathing)—imagine that you are, at
the same time, breathing in *Prana,* psychic energy.
Imagine or conceive that there is an enormous field of
energy or force all around you, which you only have
to "tap"; that this is vitalizing, and that you are drawing it into you at the same time that you are breathing.
As you inhale this, and retain the breath, you then begin to *will* that the *Prana* shall circulate through the
entire system in the same way that the blood circulates.

Now, in this PRANA GATHERING AND DISTRIBUTION, hold
the breath and at the same time feel, be conscious,—if
you can,—of every part of the body, and follow that
Prana-current as it circulates.   After it has made a
complete circuit of the body, you can exhale.   Usually
you should begin at the heart,—then go down, and up
the left arm, over the head, down and up the right arm;
and so forth.   Outline the body.   *Will* it down the
centre of the leg,—not on the side,—on the inside of
the foot, as it were, and so on.   You follow the arterial
nervous system, in other words; from the heart up to
the shoulder, down and up the left arm, and so forth.
When you get back to the mouth, exhale.

This teaches you, for one thing, to *be conscious* of every part of the body, and to *feel* with every part of the body; and that has a very interesting analogy to certain psychic phenomena. Lombroso has cited a case in which a medium illustrated or displayed what we call "transposition of the senses,"—which is quite frequently known. That is to say, she "saw" with the lobe of the ear, apparently; but mediums sometimes "see" with the "solar plexus." We bandage the eyes, in these tests, and then hold an open book in front of the body,—and the subject reads. It is as though the sense of sight had been transferred to the ear or to the "solar plexus," or to some other part of the body.

This "transposition of faculties" is something which results, in some unknown way, from the ability to be conscious of, or to feel with, every part of the body. Every part of the body should be conscious, and controlled. The Hindus can move the heart and control all the actions of the internal organs by complete conscious mastery.

This rhythmic breathing is also the basis of many other psychic phenomena. Telepathy between the Hindus is practised while they are breathing rhythmically; and we ought to practise or experiment in this manner. Two people who are breathing in perfect synchronism should try experiments in telepathy. So far as I know, this has never been tried systematically; but we *ought* to try it. For instance, it was known in India, long before the telegraph was in operation, that the natives at the bazaars always knew events a long time before the Europeans. It seemed to be "in the air." The natives knew all about it; and perhaps six or twelve hours later, the news that such-and-such an event had taken place would arrive,—which was already common knowledge among the natives. *How* they got it no one knows, but we suppose it was by some species of clairvoyant or telepathic power which they possessed.

During Prana-gathering and Prana-distribution,— you should be able to charge-up the "aura" of the body. It has been said that "obsession" is due to the fact that our aura is very permeable and very loose and flabby; and we should seek to strengthen it. These "vital rays," which come from the body, instead of being rigid are, in such states, relaxed; and the object of these experiments is to strengthen these rays, and make them stand-out all over the body; and when you do that, you are said to be impervious to disease and to obsession, and so on.

There are two experiments that will show you the existence and reality of this aura,—of this vital fluid. One is to take a glass of water, and hold your fingers over it, and *will* intently that the energy shall pass from your fingers into the glass of water. Quite a few people can so "charge" the water that it has a perceptible taste, like carbonic. In fact, you can take ten glasses on the table, and "charge" one, and a sensitive person will pick out the glass that has been so "charged." When the subject who does the selecting is in a hypnotic trance, the right glass is nearly always picked out.

Another experiment (this may be tried in the dark or in a dim light): Hang up a piece of black cloth, and then hold the fingers together (finger-ends touching). Hold them against the black cloth in such a way that the light does not shine directly on the hands; *i.e.*, they remain in the shadow. Now, when the body-shadow is thrown on the hands, hold them together for about thirty to fifty seconds, and then gradually move the hands apart. You will see streams of "vapour" coming from the fingers. Every one can see this, practically. And as you move the hands apart, and up and down, you can see these filaments or threads become more and more tenuous and thin, and finally break off. You can really see these threads moving with the hands, —against the dark background. This shows us that there is a magnetic current or fluid established, and in circulation in the body,—and that when the hands are separated, this fluidic, cobwebby, spidery material is seen. It is, I think, probable that this is the first, faint beginning of materialization,—this fluidic substance which is thrown-off by the body; and this energy is closely related to the *Prana* of the Hindus.

To return, however, to *Pranayama*. Up to this point we have had purely physiological breathing, you might say. But the Hindus have developed two offshoots from this—the "Psychic" and the "Spiritual" breathing. Psychic breathing is practised in connection with mental exercises; and they have a saying, "Blessed is he who can breathe through his bones." That means that you can apparently absorb this Prana not only through the lungs but through every pore of the body, like a sponge, and particularly through the long bones of the legs.

We must also learn to *force* this *Prana* through all our cells and even through our very bones. And what you should do, to develop this power, is to lie perfectly flat,—relax, and breathe rhythmically. Maintain a perfect rhythm,—we will say 10 in, 10 hold, 10 out,—10, 10, 10, over and over again; and when you have done this, *will* that this Prana shall be absorbed through the legs,—the bones of the legs and the body,—and you will feel a perceptible current established through the body in this way. I think that many people can get the first faint tinges of this,—a sort of "prickly" sensation,— very soon. It is hardly necessary to say that these exercises should be undertaken *cautiously* and *gradually.*

Yogi Ramacharaka, in his *Science of Breath,* thus describes the "Grand Psychic Breath":

"1. Lie in a relaxed position, at perfect ease.

"2. Breathe rhythmically,—until the rhythm is perfectly established.

"3. Then, inhaling and exhaling, form the mental image of the breath being drawn up through the bones of the legs, and then forced out through them; then through the bones of the arms; then through the top of the skull; then through the stomach; then through the reproductive region; then as if it were travelling upwards and downwards along the spinal column; and then as if the breath were being inhaled and exhaled through every pore of the skin, the whole body being filled with prana and life.

"4. Then (breathing rhythmically) send the current of prana to the Seven Vital Centres, in turn, as follows,—using the mental picture, as in the previous exercises:

"(a) To the forehead.

"(b) To the back of the head.

"(c) To the base of the brain.

"(d) To the solar plexus.

"(e) To the sacral region (lower part of the spine).

"(f) To the centre of the stomach (navel).

"(g) To the reproductive region.

"Finish by sweeping the current of prana, to and fro, from head to feet several times.

"5. Finish with cleansing breath."

I should not advise the student to attempt these exercises, however, until later,—when we have entered more fully into the question of these Seven Vital Centres, and seen how to arouse them properly, and in the right order.   For the present, the simpler exercises alone had best be attempted.

In this connection, it is interesting to note that Flagg, in his work on *Yoga, or Transformation,* says:

"In performing these (the breaths) there will be felt a peculiar tensive fulness of the whole body, reaching to the nails of the fingers and toes, and even the roots of the teeth.   Says Chung Tzu, in his only allusion to the breathings: *'Pure men draw breath from their heels . . .'*"

The question naturally arises: why do not ten "breaths a minute let in as much or more of the vital force (*prana*) as one long drawn breath, retained for a whole minute?   The ordinary breathing, short and frequent, certainly suffices to supply the blood with oxygen.   Why not also to supply the organism with whatever else it wants,—that comes in with that oxygen?   But there is a difference between ten quick taps and one slow pressure,—between ten short vibrations and one long one,—difference enough to make of one thing quite another thing, both as to action and effect. Whoever tries them will know that the Yoga breaths *do* in fact produce effects which ordinary ones do not, and be apt to presume that this is because the long ones give more time than the short ones do for the inflowing force to act,—as imparting, and the organism, as receiver, to appropriate,—the beneficial effects of the breathings, and there is no *a priori* reason why they should not be what they seem. . . ."

As you practise these breathing exercises, in connection with concentration, you will probably pass through four stages: (1) the body breaks out into a perspiration; (2) everything appears to go black before you. That passes off, and then you experience the sensation of (3) hopping about like a frog. If you are sitting cross-legged,—this is a curious feeling. Physically, people do not move, although apparently in some cases they *do;* and the theory is that you only hop about like this because the body is not properly balanced. If, they say, it were properly balanced, then, instead of hopping about, you would go straight up into the air,—which is (4) LEVITATION. That is what the Hindus aim to attain,—this equilibrium of force; and this is the chief thing which this breathing does, viz., to establish equilibrium.

You must establish this rhythm between yourself and the rhythm of nature; and when you have done that, you adjust yourself to your environment in this way, and then these curious things happen!

Now, there are two analogies for this. One is by

showing how creatures are adapted to their environment. I do not know if many persons have ever seen a deep-sea fish,—very curious and usually horrible looking beasts. If you pull up these deep-sea fish towards the surface, they *explode* before they reach the top, because the internal pressure is so great that, being adapted to their enormous pressure, the fish cannot withstand the lack of it; and when you pull it up, this enormous inner pressure rends the fish apart and it explodes. That shows you how the internal conditions are adapted to the external, by nature.

Another analogy is this: when we saw Palladino levitating the table,—she would sit at one of the short ends, put her hands on the table, and wait for five or ten minutes,—even an hour sometimes,—before anything would happen; then her fingers would apparently "charge-up" the table, and it would become vitalized, as though there were *life* in it. You could then put your hands on the back of the table, and it felt like a live thing,—like the back of a dog! Apparently it was "charged" with this vital energy, this *Prana,* through her finger-tips,—gathered from the circle and flowing through the table. The latter seemed to possess a capacity for absorbing it. When this *rapport* had been established,—this "charging" had taken place,—then she would *will* that the table should go up into the air, and it *would* go up,—about a foot usually,—but I have seen it go so high that we all had to stand with our hands above our heads and walk about the floor; when it fell to the ground,—about three or four feet.

Hundreds of times the table was levitated without any one touching it,—except for our hands upon the top. We would look and see that the medium was not touching it with her hands and feet. She would often say, "Push it to the floor," and we would try, but could not budge it;—that is to say, it was as though supported on elastics,—a kind of elastic resistance. And, on the contrary, sometimes it would be on the ground, and she would say, "Lift it up," and you would try, but could not budge it. She could make it heavy or light!

The point I want to bring out, in all this, is that this vital emanation, coming from the medium, and passing into an inanimate object, seems to "charge it up"; and when this "charging" takes place, then, by an effort of will, the inanimate object can be moved. In the same way, through psychic breathing, when you get this vital current going, you can use it for various purposes within yourself, and even project it beyond yourself,—to cure people, or perform various marvels with it, in many ways. I am sure it is a real thing, this current of *Prana*, which is established by this rhythmic breathing; and the establishment of this rhythmic state is very important.

Says Miriam M. French, in an article in *Azoth* (April, 1919):

"In Hathayoga, the science of the Five Breaths and control of the five *Tattvas* (ethers) literally relate to the vital lung breath, whereas in Rajayoga, it refers to the will breath. By correlating the two, and making them respond to each other, our Ego can strike the keynote in our entire body, and can play upon these *Tattvas* so that the combination of harmonious notes will create the most beautiful melody, and thereafter only those chords that are beneficial and musical need ever be struck: no crashing discords need ever be heard, and by constantly raising our breath and aspirations upward, in a grand crescendo, we can strike one perfectly rounded note in the beautiful symphony of the higher spheres.'' [1]

One or two final remarks and I must close. In connection with these currents within the body, we will come later on to the so-called *Kundalini*, which is the great secret spring of life, or sacred ''serpent''; it is very closely connected with these breathing exercises, and with the passages or tubes in the body,—particularly with the two nostrils and the mythical ''hole'' in the spine, up which this current passes; and it is because of this that the spine must be held *erect* in all these breathing exercises.

Besides the PSYCHIC BREATHING, which we have just studied, the Hindus practise what they call SPIRITUAL BREATHING. The object of this is, again, largely to meditate upon some ideal,—that is, some spiritual conception, usually an abstract conception,—such as the Infinite, or Cosmic Consciousness, or Abstract Good, or something of that sort. It may be some more concrete thing, but usually it is some abstract idea, in connection with spiritual breathing. While the breathing is going on, these ideas are retained in the mind. We shall

---

[1] Levi speaks of several distinct breaths—the breath of *animal life,* that is the breath of the physical body; the breath of *aspiration,* which is the second of the "vital breaths"; the breath of the *heart;* the *magnetic* breath—feeding the magnetic body, and the breath of the *spirit,* feeding the spiritual body.

consider this more fully in the chapters devoted to the awakening of the *Kundalini*.

This is all I have to say at present about breathing. The rest is merely a question of practice. Keep constantly in mind the idea of relaxation during the period of breathing,—relaxation of the body, and the *Asana* positions, with the spine straight; and deep breathing, in this sort of rhythm. Get a metronome or a watch or clock; set it going, so that you have an *exact* measurement. There must be perfect rhythm established. . . .

I cannot conclude this chapter better, perhaps, than by quoting the following fine lines from Don Marquis,— intended to symbolize and portray the power of rhythmic Breath:

BREATH

We are the shaken slaves of Breath:
For logic leaves the race unstirred;
But cadence, and the vibrant word,
Are lords of life, are lords of death.

Not facts nor reasons absolute
May touch the crowd's composite soul,
But rhythm, and the drum's long roll,
The orator, the arrowy flute.

The gods mixed music with our clay . . .
Rune-giving Odin, Krishna, Pan,
Move in the running blood of man,
His tidal moods they mete and sway.

We soar to heaven on a tone,
Or shod with magic syllables
Glide on like shades through shadowy hells . . .
Breath more endures than steel or stone!

CHAPTER IV

Mantrayoga (*Chants*) and Pratyahara (*Meditation*)

We must now take up for consideration three different topics. The first is an extension, really, of pranayama or breathing,—in fact, it is very intimately connected with it. I refer to so-called mantra yoga or Yoga through mantras,—a series of words uttered rhythmically. These are certain formulae, which have been worked-out by the Hindus, mostly in the Sanskrit, but later in the Pali dialect; and the effect of these words on the body is to produce a certain result,—which has been proved by actual experiment. The power of these words seems to create a sort of rhythm in the body,— which is quite remarkable.

Before we proceed to the actual mantras, I may perhaps make a few general remarks as to the effect or power of *words*. The actual production of words, of course,—physically, exoterically,—consists simply in the production of certain air-vibrations, which are carried by the air to the ear of a listening individual, causing the ear-drum to vibrate. This is connected, by an indirect mechanism, with the nerves of hearing, and conveyed to the auditory centres in the brain,—where, by some mysterious process, which no one understands, it is then translated into *sound*. Strictly speaking, there is no ''sound'' in the universe;—only vibrations which are themselves soundless! If the elevated railroad structure were to be smashed to bits, and an elevated train were to fall off and break to pieces, it would be an enormous crash *to us;* but if there were no living being in the universe, there would be no "sound,"—because there would be no ear to translate those vibrations into sound. All sound exists in the human brain. Between that crash and the ear that hears it, there would be nothing but air vibrations—(not ether vibrations, which are the conductors of *light*)—but noiseless, silent vibrations, travelling in the air.

Suppose you see a man on the stage playing a violin. Between that violin string and your ear-drum there is no sound,—just vibrations in the air, themselves soundless; and it is only when they enter the brain that they are translated into sound. In the same way, there is no such thing as "sight." We will speak of this more particularly when we come to the question of concentration upon objects, and so forth. Between the given object and the eye there are only invisible ethereal vibrations. You see from this that everything is vibration, either in the ether or in the air, and it is all a matter of degree. There are vibrations from about 32 to 32,000 per second, which are registered as the various degrees of sound. Then you go up to hundreds and thousands or millions or trillions of vibrations, until you get to a point where the eye is capable of registering them,—from about 450 to 750 trillion per second.

Everything is in vibration, and everything in the universe is interconnected—one thing with another. You cannot displace any body—without having an effect upon the most distant star,—a *slight* effect, proportionate to the weight and mass of the star and the movement of

the body. Every time a horse jumps on the earth in
the opposite direction to its revolution, the same thing
occurs;—everything in the universe acts and reacts, and
a movement of my arm and the jump of the horse carry
ether vibrations which are transmitted for ever onwards
into space. Everything in the universe is interrelated.
Therefore any disturbance in the ether or the air theoretically acts and reacts for ever thereafter.

Have you ever read Edgar Allan Poe's essay on "The
Power of Words"? If not, I advise you to read it!
He imagines two ethereal beings travelling through
space; they see certain fiery worlds and certain cold
worlds; they talk about them, and finally one of them
says, "This earth which you see, this fiery earth, *was*
a word that I uttered, and this cold world was another
word that I uttered." That is the upshot of the story,
that they actually *created* something,—the words did.
Of course that is fantastic, but the idea is that every
word you ever utter, every action you ever make, is recorded for ever on the air or the ether of space. In
this connection, we must also remember that "In the
beginning, the Word was with God, and the Word *was*
God." This divine Creative Word, the *Logos,* might
be treated at length; but for our present purposes, a
mere reference to this matter is all we need make.

Now, there is one very curious thing which comes up
in this connection. You hear a lot of talk (and a lot
of rubbish) in NEW THOUGHT teachings about the ETER-
NAL NOW. Of course, as it is commonly understood, that
is nonsense, but there is a way of looking at it in which
it is true. It takes an appreciable time for light to
travel any distance; that rate is about 186,000 miles per

second. That is about seven-and-a-half times around
this earth in one second. And, according to calcula-
tions, at that rate it would take about eight minutes
for light to reach the sun. Now, if you are looking
at the sun, you see it this moment apparently, but you
do not *really* see the sun as it is *now,* but as it was *eight
minutes ago;* and you do not see the sun as it is now
until eight minutes hence; so that, if there were a horse
galloping on the sun and you could see it, you would
not see that horse galloping until eight minutes after
he finished the race! And, theoretically, if that sun
were moved farther away, and you could still see what
was going on there, light, instead of taking eight minutes to reach us, might take a year, and then you would
see things as they were happening a year ago. Now,
some of the stars are so far away that it takes hundreds
of thousands of years for the light to reach us, travelling
at 186,000 miles a second! They calculate distances,
astronomically, by what they call "light years,"—that
is, the time it takes light to travel a year—and this is the
unit of calculation,—and some stars are half a million
light years away!

All of which leads up to this point: supposing something were happening on our earth, and a being, there
in space, were sufficiently far-away, looking at our
earth, to see what was happening here a year ago,—
that is, light leaving the surface of our globe and travelling out, would reach this point where he is in space
one year from now. All right. You perform a certain action; a year hence this person would see that
action,—that is, it is recorded there a year from now,—
or a hundred or thousand or million years from now,—

it all depends upon the distance—how far away he was placed. So, if you could get *far enough* away in space, there would always be a time, theoretically, when you could see that action, being recorded in the ether. So that every stone put in place on the great pyramid is now being put there,—at a certain distance in space. The creation of the world can now be seen in space— at a certain distance. So that there is, in one sense, an "eternal now" in the universe. That is what we call the COSMIC PICTURE GALLERY,—that is, a sort of ethereal duplication, in the astral or ethereal world, of these pictures which are created, that may be here now, with which, theoretically, clairvoyants get into touch when they perceive their visions.

There are a number of interesting experiments in this connection which have been tried in Paris. For instance, a subject was taken into a room and told to look at a perfectly blank wall. Looking at it, he thought of a picture, and then went out of the room. Another, a sensitive clairvoyant, came into the room, looked at the wall, and said that the first had been thinking of an eagle sitting in a chair,—or whatever it was! That is, it appears as though the eyesight had impressed this vision upon the wall, and the other person had "read it back" again. The whole point I am trying to make is that these phenomena are all *vibratory,*—all affect each other and are all *rhythmic;* and that this rhythm is so important that the whole ideal of the Yogi, in one sense, is to establish a connection or equilibrium between the internal rhythm and the external rhythm,—when you have poise or balance. (The great object of the magicians was to get this magical poise or balance or equilibrium.) The Kabbalah also dwelt much upon the importance of this equilibrium.[1]

One other point, before we pass on to the MANTRAS themselves; and that is the symbolism of communication between minds,—one with another.

I do not know if you have ever thought that when two people correspond with one other, or get into touch with one other,—*i.e.*, when they *know* one another's minds,—that it is entirely through a series or species of symbolism,—sounds made or actions performed or marks on paper. Apart from telepathy and other supernormal methods of communication, these are the only ways in which we can communicate,—by signs or by sounds or by writing. These are all symbolic sounds or marks which are re-interpreted. Shut your eyes for a moment. Now, as you think of it, you will find that you live inside a dark chamber called the skull, and that you are apparently inside, and that there is no means of getting out. Everything that comes must come *to you*. When you look with your eyes you apparently get outside your head and project yourself to a distance, as it were, but all the other senses are obviously receptive,—things must come *to* you. Now, living inside this dark skull, how are you going to get in touch with somebody else? How do two minds "know" each other? They must do so in a roundabout or symbolic way; and that is by creating certain vibrations in the air, which strike this person's ear-drum, causing it to

[1] "Insanity is simply a discord in the Universe—the result and evidence of a want of harmony between an individual human nature and the nature surrounding it, and of which it is a part."
— (Maudsley, *Responsibility in Mental Disease*, p. 289.)

vibrate, and it is retranslated into sound. But all that is a long way from the other individual! You never come into contact with another human consciousness *directly.* You never see a human being. There is an old saying that "No man hath seen God"; but it is equally true that "No man has seen man." You see the clothes they wear, and you see the hair and the expression and the features and the face, and so forth,—but that is all a mask. You can cut off the features and disfigure the face, but the individual consciousness would still be behind, which you can never see directly. Consciousness resides within.

I am leaving out of account, for the time being, all supernormal methods of communication—such as telepathy, and so forth,—and speaking only of the senses. Now, inasmuch as this is true, these sounds made in the air are re-translated into symbolic meaning,—they have a certain vibratory action on the air and on other people and on ourselves. And, in Yoga, we wish to study particularly the vibrations of certain sounds or certain words on the human being.

We will begin with the study of the simplest word, AUM, which is very well known today. It is usually written OM, but the correct formula is AUM. We must give it the right sound. It has a peculiar vibratory action on the spot between the eyes.[1]

The following paragraph is from O. Hashnu Hara's little book on *Practical Yoga:*

"TO PRONOUNCE AUM: To correctly pronounce AUM, the sacred word, the student should utter it in such a

---

[1] The *a* and *u* by Sandhi become O; and with *m*, form the "Pranava," or mantra OM—constituted of A-U-M.

manner that he dwells upon the final M, making it *hum* or vibrate in the throat like the hum of a bee, prolonging the sound as long as he is able to do so on the one inhalation.''

''It takes a little time to get used to this, but once the slight difficulty experienced is overcome the effect will be found instantaneous and little short of magical; but in view of the extraordinary power of this mantra students should avoid carrying the practice to excess. . . . It is principally the student himself in whom this effect is keenest. The vibration arouses every atom in the body, setting the entire system ajingle until the polarization of the body is entirely altered and reconstructed, and, of course, purification from an occult standpoint is achieved. The vibrations aroused are so powerful that they shut out all self-influences, attracting the finer, purer influences, sounds and vibrations of the higher planes and awakening all the occult forces possessed by the student, making him a new and infinitely more powerful being, for one of the results occurring from the practice of this mantra is the acquirement of *power,* the power to attract good from all things and to see good in all things.

''What the pronunciation of the sacred word will accomplish is already well known, but what students seek is how to pronounce it. . . .

''It is very injurious to one who possesses an impure mind or pursues evil connections, therefore when you attempt to pronounce the sacred word be sure your thoughts are pure and your desires are holy. I warn you that otherwise the results to yourself will be dire; whereas in a proper spirit the charm of mantra is very powerful and good for success. Whoever attains instruction in this art from the *Guru* (that is, teacher) will surely become great and powerful, succeeding in Yoga and attaining divine and supernatural powers. . . .

"The three letters of the sacred word AUM signify the principles of the creation: A—preservation; U—destruction; M—regeneration,—or, in oriental phraseology, BRAHMA, VISHNU, SHIVA, the three gods,—that is the symbolism. In the same way the three syllables represent the threefold elements throughout nature, from the great unseen forces upon which the greatest scientists can only theorize, to the simple nature with which the simplest nature is acquainted."

(I might say here that you must annihilate everything you create, in occultism.)

"The word AUM in its entire sense is simply a symbol to express the divinity, the supreme being. AUM also stands for the three substances, OBJECTIVE, SUBJECTIVE and ETERNAL. The objective substance, or matter, is symbolized by the letter 'A' and its vibrations. The subjective substance, or mind, is the unseen link connecting matter with the eternal. It is represented by the vibrations of the middle letter 'U,' and the eternal substance, or God, represented by the final 'M.' . . .

"The word stands, as I have already said, for the three realms of life in its manifestation throughout the infinite. Thus we have the natural world, which we can see, the objective,—the subjective world, or that sphere which our senses cannot perceive until they are opened to the impressions of divine things,—and finally the eternal world,—that is, the life of all.

"The word as used by the student is held to represent three states of consciousness. Spirit and thought and perfect concentration rise from the objective, the material, through subjective to eternal spirit, and as the vibrations of the world speed faster the student is carried in spirit to the divine centre of his being. The power of the vibration pierces the material nature of man, and by transition through his psychic or subjective mind reaches the eternal principle within his heart, and awakens it to life." [1]

In pronouncing this word, the "A" should start in the throat, and the "U" should be at the top of the palate, and the "M" at the lips,—and, if you notice, that is the natural way of producing it; so that you begin at the back and bring it up to the lips. If you slightly close the lips it will produce that sound.

That is the basis of all mantras. It is the sacred word, the unity, the divine presence of God. Practically all of them have that word in them. I will not give you many of these mantras, because they are not useful or intelligible. One or two, however, follow.

There is another very well-known mantra, used a great deal, and that is simply a repetition of the word AUM with TAT SAT,—"AUM TAT SAT AUM," repeating it in a sort of rhythm which you must acquire; it means "O THOU EXISTENT ONE, O!" It represents a sort of aspiration after reality, a craving. Probably the most fa-

[1] There are also many other symbolic interpretations of the word AUM: for example the mystical "Bird" or swan *Kala Hansa;* for we read in the *Rig Veda:* "The syllable A is considered to be its (the bird Hansa's) right wing; U, its left; M, its tail, and the *Ardha-matra* (half-metre) is said to be its head."

mous of all these mantras, and best known, is "AUM MANI PADME HUM"; which means "O, THE JEWEL IN THE LOTUS"—"AMEN," if you like.

Now, when Yogis say these things they usually sit on the floor crosslegged, and rock to and fro, the body being held erect, and rocked forward and backward; and, as one relaxes the mantra, another takes it up, so that you get a constant cadence and rhythm.

Arthur Avalon, in his work on *The Serpent Power,* says:

"There is nothing necessarily holy or prayerful about Mantra. Mantra is a *power* which lends itself impartially to any use. A man may be injured or killed by Mantra; by Mantra a kind of union with the physical *Shakti* is by some said to be effected; by Mantra in the initiation called *Vedhadiksha* there is such a transference of power from the Guru to the disciple that the latter swoons under the impulse of it; by Mantra the Homa fire may and, according to ideal conditions, should be lighted; by Mantra Man is saved, etc. Mantra, in short, is a *power* which is thought movement vehicled by, and expressed in, speech. The root 'Man' means 'to think.'" (Mr. Avalon gives examples of a scorpion having been killed by a Mantra, and of a fire having been lighted by the same means.) [1]

The Hindu conception of Mantra must, however, be

[1] The Hindus well know the possibilities of evil influences directed at one; also how to ward such influences off. They speak of such protective coverings as "shields" (*Grahana*); but, as Avalon says, "this Sanskrit term expresses not so much a fence to which use a *Kavacha* is put, but the knowledge of how a man may 'catch' a Mantra projected at him." (*Op. cit.,* p. 104.)

understood. According to their view, *"Thought-movement vehicled-by and expressed-in speech is Mantra."*

A Mantra, in order to be effective, has to be uttered in a certain manner—with a particular creative force behind it. It is said that the mere repetition of a Mantra will in itself have *some* effect; but to be truly effective it has to be "awakened," that is, vitalized from the conscious centre, and ensouled with creative thought. It has been said, in fact, that "the whole human body is, in fact, a Mantra, and is composed of Mantras." "Mantras are in all cases manifestations of Kulakundalini Herself, for she is all letters and *Dhvani* and the *Paramatma* itself. Hence Mantras are used in rousing Kundalini. . . . The substance of all Mantras is feeling-consciousness." One of the duties of the Guru (teacher) is to "impart to the disciple *the power of the Mantra*— a process which . . . can only be fully learnt of the Guru." (*Tantrik Texts*, Vol. VIII, p. 11.)[1]

It is also believed by the Yogis that certain Mantras contain a given number of "Letters," and that these correspond to the number of "Petals" in any given Lotus, Chakra or Psychic Centre. (*See* pp. 140–41.) Thus the six-petalled Lotus has a Mantra of six letters, etc. All this will be gone into more fully later on, however, when we come to explain the "chakras" or psychic centres, and the so-called "Garland of Letters" connected therewith.

The translations of the mantras do not mean anything particularly. They are just combinations of let-

[1] "Uttered speech is a manifestation of the inner naming of thought. This thought-movement is similar in all races." (Avalon, p. 111.)

ters producing a sound, and that sound has a certain
rhythmic vibration which is reflected in the body.
There are certain English words that are more or less
like them, but the Hindus have worked out the open,
fluent, beautiful speech which has this effect. The
Greeks and Romans also knew of the power of words in
this respect. Thus the famous line, "Atque rotis sum-
mas levibus perlabitur undas" represents the very sound
of the lapping of waves on the bow of the vessel. And
in Greek: Δαιμονίη αἰ   μὲν   ὀίεαι οὐδέ   σε   λήθω,
Daimoni | e a | ei men o | ieai ou | de se | letho
—a line consisting almost entirely of vowels, very well
represents the snarling voice of the enraged Zeus.

These mantras should be kept up for hours and hours
and hours, until, as I said before, you can fall asleep
saying them and wake up saying them. You will not
get the later developments unless you get the former
ones! For instance, you cannot do trigonometry without having first learned plus and subtraction,—arith-
metic and algebra. So that really you ought to practise these mantras and follow them up for quite some
time. All nations have their mantras; the Mohamme-
dans have several; one being: "*Ishhad lá Allah illá
'llah,*"—"There is no god but Allah,"—and so on, by
the hour. By its rhythm it will set up certain vibrations in the organism, and set the whole being into activity.

Let us take "AUM MANI PADME HUM." Try to say it
with cadence, music, so that, as some drop down, others
pick it up, and it rises and falls and swells again. It is
like a little circle or mass of word-energy.

In "telling the beads,"—*i.e.*, in prayers said by priests, ascetics, etc.,—the object is rhythmic prayer, and that prayer should be said a great number of times over and over; and there must be a means of marking-off the number of times your consciousness wanders; and that "means" must be so automatic that it does not check the flow of thought which goes with the prayer. Hence, if you count, for instance, by pressing finger and thumb together, that is automatic; it does not obstruct the consciousness, then you have something which registers the number of times our mind wanders. That is the real object of "telling the beads." Then you know that you have gone through so many thousand mantras in the course of a week or a day, or whatever it is. These you ought to practise,—these mantras and the breathing,— because they are really important.

.   .   .   .

We will now leave this subject, and pass, on, briefly, to consider the question of *incense*. The question of perfumes is most interesting. Incense is a perfume. The whole question or the psychology of perfumes has been very much neglected; the only book that gives anything like a description or analysis of it is a work in French entitled *Les Parfumes Magiques*. It is very physiological, and parts of it would have to be omitted in English translations; but it is also very occult, and when you go deeply into the subject, you will find that, in all magical ceremonies, there always are scents and perfumes. The Delphic Oracle used to prophesy over the vapour arising from a cleft in the rock. That was probably some semi-asphyxiating gas, which produced the trance-state into which the clairvoyant fell. In the temples in Greece and Rome, they used these magical perfumes to produce ecstatic states of consciousness.

Scents *do* have a psychological effect,—a tremendous emotional effect. Some will excite, some will depress, or arouse the emotions in one sense or another. A scent, a perfume, is of course an emanation from an object; it is inhaled through the nostrils, and again translated into the sense of "smell" by the brain. It is all in the brain! The sense of smell constitutes practically all taste. We only have four fundamental tastes,—sweet, salt, sour and bitter. These are the only things which the tongue tastes. Everything else depends upon the sense of smell. You find that out when you have a severe cold and you cannot breathe freely,—the sense of smell is gone, and the taste of food is also gone.[1]

The senses are interrelated one with another in a very curious way. I have referred to some cases given by Lombroso where, apparently, the sense of sight was transferred to the ear,—"transposition of senses"; and the French have studied quite exhaustively the connection between sounds and colours,—in which certain sounds call up certain colours, etc. If you strike a note on the piano, it seems red to one, to another purple, etc.

[1] See *The Sense of Taste*, p. 154: "Taste . . . is one of the senses in connection with which "synœsthesias" most often occur. Salt, for instance, is described by one observer as dull red, bitter as brownish, sweet as clear bright red, and sour as green or greenish-blue. To another observer the taste of meats seems red or brown, the taste of graham bread is rich red in colour, while all ice-creams (except chocolate and coffee) taste blue. To still another reporter the sound of the word 'intelligence' tastes like fresh sliced tomatoes, while the sound of the word 'interest' tasted like stewed tomatoes. . . ."

These are the so-called "synaesthesias." There are various theories to account for these curious facts—either the connections in the brain,—the association-fibres—between the visual and auditory centres are better than they are in other people,—or perhaps the explanation is purely psychological. In other people, there are these connections between the senses of smell and vision; between sound and sight, and even the sense of *taste* and the sensation of colour!

Oliver Bland, in his interesting book *The Adventures of a Modern Occultist* says:

"Frankincense and myrrh, and in particular, gum benzoin, possess soothing properties that affect the throat and nasal passages. . . . The *Kyphi* or Incense of Ancient Egypt was compounded of myrrh, gummastic, aromatic rush roots, resin, and juniper berries. To these aromatics were added small quantities of symbolic elements, such as honey and wine, and a portion of bitumen, or asphateum, whose purpose might be either symbolic or to serve as a binding medium for the mass.

"In addition to these, various spices and perfumes were used, cinnamon bark, sandalwood, cardarmine, and even ambergris and musk. . . . The influence of scent upon the emotions is well known, and the Egyptians favoured the use of ambra and musk as definitely aphrodisiacal perfumes. Today pure essence of patchouli is used in the Orient to serve the same end, and anybody who has ever smelt a vial of the pure oil will recognize the instant disturbance of certain nerve centres that it produces. *Kyphi* of today is recognizable as 'keef,' the popular name for the smokeable variety of the herb

Cannabis Indica. This is none other than our old friend Hashish.

"Hashish is absorbed rapidly. As a smoke, veiled by incense or mixed with tobacco, rapid intoxication results from its inhalation. This was one of the keys, perhaps the greatest of the keys, to the storehouse of those treasures of the mind which are the true Elixir, the true Gold of the Magi."

Regarding this question of "psychic perfumes," Levi says:

"*Opening the gate to soul perfumes.* Go into a room entirely free from substances that could possibly produce any odour or perfume. Take a comfortable position and enter the Silence, according to the rules given. Take one full breath, followed by a searching, purifying or cleansing breath, according to the formula given. Put in abeyance all the senses except that of smell; and then, in mind, bring before you a particular flower, or a substance that you know will emit a particular odour; rivet your attention upon this imaginary object for some minutes, and then imagine that you can smell that particular odour, and in a large per cent. of such efforts, you will be rewarded with a true materialization of the desired odour. Don't be discouraged; if you do not succeed at first, make other efforts and success will come." (*Self Culture,* p. 61.)

This is a subject which has never been properly worked out. The thing that the Hindus and the Orientals *do* know is that certain incense and certain perfumes produce emotional and physical and mental effects upon the subject, and have the effect of arousing the clair-voyant faculties. So, mantras should be performed with incense burning.

We have now discussed the initial or preparatory training for Yoga; first of all, the ASANA positions of the body. These disposed of your body; it is supposed to be quiet after that. Then you have PRANAYAMA exer-cises,—breathing, which stills the breath and produces rhythm; and that is aided by MANTRAS,—also by INCENSE, which affects the sense of smell and produces a certain emotional or ecstatic state.

.   .   .   .

Now we come to the next stage in the training, which is called PRATYAHARA, and we begin *mental* work.

PRATYAHARA means INTROSPECTION or MEDITATION,— not meditation upon an object, but turning the mind in-wards upon itself, and observing what goes on in the mind. It is a good plan to take about three minutes, close the eyes, and write down everything that comes into the mind. Then you will get the whys and where-fores of what follows more readily. Every vision, every thought, every association, every idea that comes into the mind, every sensation of the body, must be put down on paper,—everything that comes in the mind. . . .

The point is that when you turn your attention to your own body, in the relaxation exercises and in the postures, you find that the body is like a turbulent sea, in constant turmoil; and when you turn your attention to the mind, you find it is more turbulent still,—like a choppy sea breaking on the rocks. Every little sound, sensation, impression from the senses, disturbs conscious-

ness. You should observe the action of the mind. You
will see how the mind is absolutely a slave to the senses,
in the ordinary way that the mind runs along. The
object of Yoga is to enable the mind to do away with
all these thoughts which you do not want,—to pick and
choose what you do want, and ultimately to hold only
the one that you want for an hour or a day without a
break.

There are said to be two forms of Meditation—
"with" and "without seed." When the mind is fixed
or centred upon the final object of thought,—the last
link in the reasoning,—this is called "meditation with
seed." When this object has been allowed to pass, to
go out of the mind, so that it is left blank,—this is
"meditation without seed"—that is, meditation without
object, or "seed of thought." Yogis are careful to
distinguish, however, between meditation without seed,
and mere empty-mindedness. The latter is a purely
negative condition; while in the former, the mind is kept
active or alert,—ready to spring, as it were, upon the
next higher spiritual state of development reached.

The point is that we are all slaves to the five senses;
and the object of PRATYAHARA is to prove that by this
meditation and to overcome it. The convulsions of
the mind are like an enormous sea serpent, all the time
twisting and squirming about, and you have got to pour
"oil on the troubled waters," by this introspective
method,—metaphorically pouring oil on the mind. All
kinds of stimuli come from within and without,—asso-
ciations, images, thoughts, ideas, scents, visions, physical disturbances, pains in the body,—everything that
interferes with the flow of consciousness is an interrup-

tion or what we call a "break,"—a break of consciousness.

Next time we will take up "breaks" in considerable detail, and show in what they consist and how to do away with them.   Our thoughts, if we let them run along in this way, unchecked and uncontrolled by consciousness, bear a very striking resemblance to dreams,—to day dreams.   In fact, that is precisely what they *are*.

Here is a diagram which may help you:

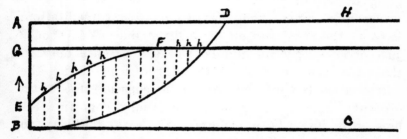

Our starting point of experience is B-C. A-H is the attainment of perfection, and the distance between these two lines is the distance we have to travel,—in the upward direction of the arrow,—through, to perfection, by training the mind.   "G" is about the average level of development that you will obtain.   "B-D" shows the degree of the control of the mind.   It begins quite slowly and rises more rapidly as you go along, until, at the top, you have perfect control of the mind.   The line "E-F," shows the degree of observation of the contents of the mind,—the degree of control in seeing what is going on within it.   You arrive at the point "F," where you can practically see what the mind is doing within itself.   The lines (h,h,h,h) represent the percentage of dissatisfaction with your own development which you have,—or should have,—as you go along. So that at the beginning, you think you are making very good progress, but after a little time you find that extraordinary difficulties come up, of a sort of which you had never dreamed. You then gain some control over the contents of the mind, and it gets better rapidly as you go along. The chart simply shows the activity of the mind and the degree of its introspective power, or the degree of your ability to perceive what is going on within the mind.

The first thing to do, then, in practising meditation, is to let the mind run on for a little time. You should just observe how the mind "works," because only in that way can you realize the difficulties. Notice the extraordinarily confused state of the consciousness of an ordinary human being, under ordinary conditions;—how it is just like a choppy sea. Note, then try to "squash," these disturbances as they come up. Any thought that rises to the surface you should metaphorically "hit on the head." Say, "No, I don't want you. Go away!"—of course aiming all the time to reach the point where you can say to *all* thoughts, "Go away!" That is a long way off yet!

If any picture comes up into the mind, or any vision, it should not immediately be sent away or put out of the mind, because it will keep recurring. If a picture or vision,—a persistent picture like a shipwreck—comes into the mind, do not try simply to banish it, because it will return. Hold it there for a moment, and endow it with objectivity; think about it until you get to the right point;—*then* banish it! It is like running away from a spectre of evil or anything else which chases you. If you face it, you can get rid of it; but the more you "put it out of" the mind the more you put it *into* it. If you put it out of the conscious mind, you put it into the subconscious; and it is like putting it into a dark cellar and slamming the lid down,—what is in the cellar causes the trouble. The thing to do is to throw it out of the window! If you want absolutely to "banish" anything, make it real first, by holding it in the mind, and *then* get rid of it.

All I wish to say in conclusion is that, only by practising these exercises persistently can you gradually acquire the mastery of the senses, to the extent that you can, to some degree, shut off the outside world and live or dwell inside your head sufficiently to begin concentration, which is the next stage, DHARANA; and the thing to do in PRATYAHARA,—meditation,—is to arrive at the point where the mind becomes more or less a tranquil blank,—so that we can put into it some object of thought with the idea of holding it there. But if you try to write your name in water it is obliterated, or if you try to write it in shifting sand; but if the sand be perfectly tranquil the name remains written.

So with the mind. You desire it to become tranquil, and then what you put in it "stays." That is the object of PRATYAHARA.

CHAPTER V

DHARANA (*Concentration*)

IN the last chapter we dealt with three topics. The first was *Mantra Yoga,* or the power of mantras or words, giving samples of them; then with *incense* and *perfumes,* —their emotional effects upon the body; and, thirdly, with what is called *Pratyahara,* which simply means meditation; and the object of that is to wipe the mind clean, like a blackboard or a slate, so that the impressions during concentration can be impressed or written on it later, when concentration begins.

So that we come to DHARANA, which is the Hindu equivalent for concentration. After the mind has been left blank, we begin to do something with it. When you come to practise concentration, you will find that all the things which you have done heretofore will be useful. Apparently useless at the time, their influence will now begin to be felt;—that is to say, the several positions, breathing and relaxation exercises, the chanting, and the meditation or emptying of the mind, —because any impingement on the mind, during concentration, will be an infringement on the unity of the thought.

Concentration is simply fixing the mind upon one thing, one thought; and that may be a physical thing or a mental or a spiritual thing, according to the object of concentration, as we shall see later.

Now, the Hindus have a definite theory of mind, and

84

I must speak of that first.   There is a theory held among psychologists which is called THE MIND-STUFF THEORY; it corresponds very closely to the Hindus' conception of CHITTA, which is "mind-stuff"; and the idea of mind-stuff is simply this; that, attached to each particle of matter, as it were, there is a little particle of mind,— in much the same way that the fog out of doors is caused by a little moisture attaching itself to each of the dust particles in the air. . . . In the same way, they say, a little particle of mind-stuff is attached to every atom in the universe, so that every atom has its own particular atom-consciousness; and when these atoms are bound together in the form, we will say, of a star-fish, then you will have a star-fish consciousness;—or if bound together in the form of a jelly-fish, you will have a jelly-fish consciousness; or in the form of a man, you will have a man-consciousness; or in the form of a woman, you will have a woman-consciousness; and so forth. So this is a sort of monistic theory, which says that every particle of matter is *alive,* and that it is only due to the peculiar "combinations" of matter which form the different "combinations" of consciousness.

This theory has been criticized by a number of our psychologists,—William James and others.   William James, for instance, has said that it is impossible to conceive these mental units being bound together unless there is something to bind them *on.*   In the same way that you cannot weave something unless there is some background on which you can weave it, as it were,—so if you take the crude material of thought, little thought-particles, they won't stick together,—there is no "gum," —as it were—and they will not adhere.   But the Hindus

think that the theory *will* work, and this is their theory
of mind-stuff,—that these particles are agglomerated or
stuck together,—forming different units of consciousness.[1]

Now then, in the human mind, these flow along; and
concentration consists in getting more of these particles
into one place,—this CHITTA, this mind-stuff; and if you
can condense them at a point, as it were, then you will
have absolute unity of consciousness at that point,—
because you have concentrated the material of the mind,
—these units,—and, just as the burning-glass will focus
the sun's rays at a point, so these mind-bits are bound
together at a point. Then you have absolute concentration. That is their theory.

I thought that it would be a good plan, before going
on to consider the practical side of concentration, to
say a few words as to what the mind *is*, according to
our conception,—our Western view,—afterwards touching a little on the Hindu view. Of course, of the *essence* of the mind very little is known. We know that
we can close the eyes and feel that inside the head there
is something, which is the thinking ''I''; and if you
begin to formulate a system of philosophy of any kind,
you go back and back and back, and you always get to
the personal element. That was the basis of Descartes'
famous dictum; he based his whole system of philosophy
on the old saying, ''COGITO ERGO SUM,''—''I think;
therefore I am.'' That was as far back as he could go,
—''I am I.'' Everything is personal!

[1] According to the Hindu teachings, when an object is presented
to the mind and perceived, the latter is formed into the *shape* of
the object perceived.

Now, what is this "mind"? At present we believe that the mind is bound up with the material brain, and with particular parts of the brain. Anatomy of the brain has gone so far that we know that certain areas of the brain correspond to the sensation of sight, other parts to the sensation of touch, others to the sensation of taste and smell, and so forth; and other parts or "areas" of the brain, as they are called, move different parts of the body,—the finger, the toe, etc.; so that it is possible, now, to put the finger on a certain spot in the brain, and say, "That part moves the big toe on the left foot," or whatever it is!

However, there are certain parts of the brain of which we do not know the exact functions; and these are the frontal areas, which are assumed to be the centres of higher thought, abstract, spiritual thought, association, reasoning, and so forth; although thought goes on more or less all over the brain. At the same time, these are the particular higher thought centres.

The mind, as far as we can see, is an immaterial thing. It is not material in the same sense that a table is. At the same time the brain is a material thing. Now, one of the greatest problems in metaphysics and philosophy has always been, how the body and "soul,"— if you choose to call it so,—how they are *connected* one with another. Apparently there is no connection between a perfectly immaterial thing—(because a thought is a "thing," as much a "reality" as a granite mountain, in one sense, because it exists,—although it is not physical)—and the brain, which is a physical thing; yet they *are* related! We know we can inject poison into a person's blood, and it will affect the mind. On the contrary, a person can read a telegram, reaching the mind directly, and it will so affect the body that he will drop dead. So there *are* these subtle connections. *How* are they connected? That is one of the greatest problems!

There are all kinds of theories. The doctrine of PARALLELISM, as it is called, claims that mind and body simply run along side by side; that they never "touch" each other, and they really do not influence each other, in one sense, at all. But this is inconceivable, because they are so intimately connected, as we have just shown, by the two examples of the poison and the telegram. It is inconceivable that two things that do not ever "touch" should so intimately be associated.

Then again there is the theory that the physical brain *creates* thought. We know that, for every thought we think, there are changes in the brain substance,—physical, chemical, electrical, and so forth, which go on here. Accompanying them in some way is a thought. Now, the *materialistic theory,* or the PRODUCTION THEORY, is that that brain-change somehow *causes* the thought, originates it, creates it, and that is why HUXLEY coined the term—EPIPHENOMENALISM. In the same way, he said, that a shadow accompanies a horse, the conscious or mental state accompanies the physical state; that, as these physical changes go on in the brain, accompanying them are the mental stages, which are, as it were, the shadows of the physical conditions. That was his theory.

Well now, in that case the physical changes in the brain would be the important things; and yet we feel that they are not so at all. We feel that the important thing, for us, is the state of our minds,—the flow of thought. So *that* theory has been given-up for various reasons.

Then there are the doctrines that mind and brain are but two different expressions of a fundamental *one thing;* that mind and matter, apparently absolutely dissimilar and separate, are really the opposite sides of the same shield, and that behind them is an "x," which is the "reality" of which they are both the expressions,— mind and matter. Apparently they are perfectly dissimilar, yet here is the reality of which they are the expressions. What is the "x"? The materialistic school says it is a form of energy or matter; the idealistic school says it is God or spirit; and the agnostic school says "We don't know!"

Then there are other theories; but I will only touch upon one more theory, and that is the plain, common-sense point-of-view,—what we call INTERACTIONISM,— that is, that there are two things, spirit and body, and that they interact one with another. If that be true, it is in accord with our own feelings and our own common-sense, up to a certain point, and it enables us, also, to account for all these psychic and occult phenomena, which the other theories do not. So let us assume for the moment that that *is* true,—INTERACTIONISM.

Now, this mind of ours works along by itself, and one of its most fundamental qualities is *memory,* and that again is a very difficult question, concerning which I want to say a few words. When we come to talk of the mind, we always have to get down to the brain behind it, because we know that it is somehow related.

Scientists did not always think that the mind was in the brain. The ancients used to think it was in the heart or lungs or spleen or in different organs. It is only within the last two hundred years or so that they have thought it to be in the brain,—but now we know it is. But it is a fact which physiology teaches us that our body is constantly changing,—being made over,—and the old saying that it is "made over every seven years" is true in a sense. The soft parts are, probably, replaced many times in seven years, but the bony parts take longer. It is true, perhaps, on the average. This being so, *the brain is also replaced;* and yet you can remember events that are more than seven years old! So that the *materialistic theory,* to go back for a moment, is this: that, just as a recording needle will scratch a phonographic record, and leave an impression upon it, so this nervous influence will leave an impression on the brain.

"Oh," you will say, "but a certain length of time after that, the brain-cell was replaced by another cell. Where has your memory gone to?" The reply to this is that, as this new cell inherits the old one, it takes on its memory too,—picks it up and carries it along. Of course, in one sense, it is inconceivable that this should be so,—and in fact BERGSON, the French philosopher, in his great book, *Matter and Memory,* attempts to show that memory could not be accounted for on this materialistic theory,—that it is inconceivable; that memory itself is a sort of spiritual storehouse, and that the brain is only a vehicle for the physical expression of these stored-up mental pictures.

Now, all these thoughts in the mind are connected with one another by *association.* They form *habits,*—motor and sensory. A word, perhaps, on HABIT would be useful. As many actions as possible, in daily life, should be made automatic; it is the best thing you can do. It is the easiest way to live, because if you have to think consciously every time you button a button, for instance, it would use up so much mental energy. The child, when it learns to walk, has to use conscious guidance. Later this becomes automatic, and we can do other things at the same time. And all through life, the more we can make automatic, by so much is the mind free to work on other things.

One other important fact about the mind, which must be touched upon. The old theory of the mind was that it was a sort of single *unit*,—a "one-thing," like a crystal ball, a sort of sphere; and, in fact, PLATO's argument for the IMMORTALITY OF THE SOUL was that it was indivisible; it could not be divided. He said that anything that is divisible is destructible, and therefore not immortal; but the mind is indivisible, therefore it is indestructible and therefore immortal! Well, that view was held for several centuries;—in fact Christianity made it a dogma, and said that the physical world was created or came into being, and the mind was indestructible, immortal,—and that dogma continued until the latter part of the eighteenth century; and then science precisely reversed this doctrine, and proved, first, the indestructibility of matter and energy,—that the physical world is immortal; and then said, "No, the mind is simply a function of the brain, dependent upon the brain for its action; therefore it is divisible and mortal and goes out like the flame of a candle." In fact it exactly reversed the whole theory. And it remained reversed until a few years ago, when a *new*

reversion took place, and GUSTAV LE BON, the Frenchman, and J. J. Thomson, in England, and others,
showed us that matter is not indestructible, but that it
is constantly coming into being and constantly going
out of being,—that it is an expression of energy; that
energy is the fundamental, real thing, and that this
physical world is the mere expression of energy. But
there is this difficulty: the mind has been shown to be,
not a single but a complex thing. It has been shown
to be like the strands of a rope,—which are held together by our conscious attention, our will, our effort;
and that, as soon as this is relaxed, the strands of the
rope tend to spread, to disintegrate,—and that is the
basis of disintegration of consciousness, multiple personality and similar cases. Then the mind has to be
woven together again, by hypnotic suggestion or by will,
or by effort, into a normal whole.

Now, most of the hysterical cases in France were in
peasant women;—dissociation was very easy, because
they did not occupy their minds,—their minds were very
plastic. Now we know that hysteria is an affection of
the mind which can be cured by hypnosis; so that our
theory of the mind is that it is a thing, which is composed of parts, but at the same time there must be a
fundamental unity in it, if it survives death. Secondly, these parts have a common memory-connection,—
as has been shown in cases of dissociated consciousness.
By an analysis of the experiments on fundamental mental states, it has been shown that there is this unity
of consciousness back of it all.

There are three *layers* of consciousness, the normal
consciousness, about which we have been talking; the

subconsciousness, which is very much talked about nowadays; and also the *superconsciousness,* of which very little is heard; but it is in this superconscious realm, strictly speaking, that all these psychic phenomena occur, —clairvoyance, clairaudience, telepathy, and so forth,— and in that realm alone.

Now, the human mind is so constructed that there is always a fundamental doubleness or duality within it. If I look at a book, I am conscious of at least two things; one is the book; secondly, *I* am looking at the book. That is, subject and object,—seer and seen,— two things.

Another point: Kant, in his *Critique,* gives a series of difficulties of thought, which he called ANTINOMIES, and two of them are: space is infinite; space is finite. Time is infinite; time is finite. Now, it is impossible for us to conceive of infinite space. On the contrary, it is impossible for us to conceive of finite space. You cannot conceive of any place where you can build a wall and say "There is no space beyond this," or "Stop here; there is nothing beyond this,"—because the mind goes on for ever. At the same time, you cannot conceive of infinite time or infinite space; so you have a state of mind where you have this difficulty presented; and this duality of mind is inevitable, because our mind is so constructed,—because always there is this difficulty, this *duality.*

Well, the Hindus say, "How are we going to overcome this?" And they say, "The only way to do so is to rise into a superior state of consciousness, where this duality no longer exists,—where you can see above these two, 'pairs of opposites,' and see that they merge

into *one;* and that is the state which we want to attain,
—where we can look down from this point of view,—
and then we shall no longer have these difficulties and
problems.''

Just to illustrate how curiously the mind works: The
famous philosopher, ZENO, invented his paradoxes, which
you may know. One of them is this: *Achilles and the
tortoise.* Achilles moves twice as fast as the tortoise.
By the time Achilles has reached the point from which
the tortoise started, the tortoise will have moved half
as far again, because it moves half as fast; and, theoretically, no matter how many millions of moves you
make, Achilles would *never* catch up to the tortoise,
because every time he moved up to the spot the tortoise previously occupied, the latter had always gone
half the preceding distance ahead. *Practically,* we know
that he *does* catch up to and pass the tortoise; but theoretically he ought not to, because every time the tortoise has been overtaken, the tortoise has moved a little
bit ahead; and no matter how tiny the distance might
be, how small, the tortoise always *should* keep ahead,—
but it doesn't!

Now, there is one other paradox, just to show this
curious jumble that the mind is always in. ZENO
proved that a *flying arrow* could never move in the air,
—because, he said, either the arrow must move where
it is *not,* or where it *is.* It cannot move where it is *not*
because it is not there to move; and it cannot move
where it *is* because, in that spot, it is stationary and not
moving! This was another paradox that remained for
centuries unsolved.[1]   The reason is that the human mind

[1] See Bertrand Russell's *Mysticism and Logic,* pp. 80–4. Here

is so constructed that we have this fatal duality, . . . two things always in mind. Like finite and infinite space, they are insoluble in our present state of consciousness. So the Hindus said, ''The only way to solve all these paradoxes and arrive at a unity, which is beyond duality, is to get into that state where all these things are perfectly clear,—seen from above,—and that state is *superconsciousness.* So that is what we want to arrive at, SAMADHI. And we arrive at it through concentration, or DHARANA,—which we now come to.

Let us consider the practical part of the subject first. To *concentrate,* you must first of all relax thoroughly. The next thing to do is to close the eyes. Then feel that the body is at rest,—that is, relaxed muscularly. Now, shut off the senses as far as you can. The senses of smell and of taste and sight are now inactive; there is only the sense of hearing, and the sense of touch. Touch is very important, but if you were seated in the ASANA position, you should be unconscious of the body.

The next thing to do is to breathe regularly, slowly. When you begin breathing you will find that you have a tendency to become tense,—when you must catch yourself and relax; sink back into the position which you occupy most comfortably,—as though into a warm bath, as I have said before.

Now then, we come to the *mental* factor,—the beginning of mental construction. Try to feel the forces, the mental powers of the head, gathered together at a point between the eyes, in the forehead.

To cultivate the power—not the actual power of con-

he says: "The finest intellects of each generation in turn attacked the problems, but achieved, broadly speaking, nothing."

centration, but the power of concentration in daily life, —there are certain exercises which you can undertake, which are very useful. I will mention a few of these. One of them which I personally have found very useful, is to take the page of a book which one does not quite understand,—philosophy or metaphysics or science, and read that page, and re-read it and re-read it and re-read it until you *do;* and that intense concentration, with the determination which is necessary to get the sense of each sentence and each word, is extremely beneficial.

Then, there is drawing or writing with the left hand— which is very valuable for several reasons. In the first place, we now know that there are two speech-centres in the brain, and only one of them is ever used. Curiously, with right-handed people it is the left-handed speech-centre, and with left-handed people it is the right-handed centre which is employed. That is understandable, because the nerve-fibres cross at the back of the neck, and the use of the right arm, when you are a baby, develops the left hemisphere of the brain, and the use of the left arm develops the right hemisphere of the brain.

If an injury occurs to the left hemisphere of the right-handed child's brain, he becomes *dumb.* If you train children in ambidexterity, when very young, both hands and both sides of the brain are developed, and this danger is prevented; and it is very important that all children *should* be so taught.

In drawing outlines of objects, look at the object for some considerable time without wavering. Then you can also look into the glass for some considerable time without the object becoming blurred,—the object in this case being yourself.

There are certain relaxing and balancing exercises which are beneficial, which the Hindus have adopted as part of their training. One is to have a glass or a bowl of water, perfectly full to the top, which is held in the hand, without spilling any of it. Or, they place it on their heads,—where it is balanced for a long time without spilling a drop.

There is one thing more, which is a good exercise for the will, that is, observing the second-hand on a watch without becoming impatient. It is extremely difficult!

All our thoughts are either positive or negative, and the positive are constructive thoughts and the negative thoughts are destructive; and the only way to get rid of the negative or destructive thoughts is to annihilate them, and supplant them by the positive ones,—replace them by positive thoughts; but you cannot do that by simply ignoring the former. I think we have touched upon that point before, viz., that you have definitely to deal with your adversary and to recognize him as a real being,—and combat him and get rid of him; and after that destructive, pulling-down work has been done, then you can fill the mind with other, positive thoughts.

We now come to objects of concentration,—or things to concentrate *upon*. Take a pencil in your hands, for instance. Now, if you look at that pencil, and take (say) thirty seconds to concentrate upon it, I think you will find that it is almost impossible to prevent the thoughts from wandering away to other things,—and thinking about the size of the pencil, or its blackness, or the fact that it is in your hand,—wandering away in a thousand directions. If you think of your finger, of course that determines the flow of blood to the part. This is one of the famous "hypnotic suggestion" experiments. Suggest to the subject to think of his finger or part of the hand,—and the blood will be determined to the part. Any physical thing can be concentrated upon in this way; but to illustrate what I mean, let us take another object.

Let us take, as a mental picture, a *black cross*. I think you will find, when you begin to hold it in your mind, that this black cross does the most curious things! Take a pencil and paper: every time, during the min-

ute you concentrate upon the cross, your thoughts wander from it, make a little mark, a little stroke. You will see, at the end of the minute, how many strokes you have! You will find that it is almost inconceivable,— the contortions which that cross undergoes!

Every break of consciousness means that the mind has wandered. This shows you, as I have said, that the mind is just like a seething, boiling sea. The object of Yoga is to get the mind into that plastic condition where you can do with it what you will,—"manipulate" it; and the first thing is to be able to hold an image— such as the black cross, or a rose, or a winged globe, or any object you like,—firmly in mind, without "wobbling." The Figure 4 may also be used as a subject for concentration.

Here are two very interesting experiments which you can try for about a minute each. Do not forget to breathe deeply during these exercises, and do not forget to relax, when you close the eyes. Think of a straight wooden ladder. Imagine that it is erected in the open, going right into the sky, like "Jack and the Beanstalk"; and begin climbing rung by rung! Go up this ladder as high as you can; your object is to keep going up without falling off, for sixty seconds.

That is one exercise. Another is descending a well; a third is flying. When you come to analyse the flow of these internal, mental states, I think you will find that they very closely resemble *dreams*. In fact, they *are* "day dreams." As soon as the control of the conscious mind is removed, the mind tends to "run along" by itself, in this haphazard, unchecked, visional sort of way; and it shows us how incoordinated and how uncontrolled the mind is, as soon as the will and attention are removed from their sphere of control.

Now, all these breaks or interruptions of consciousness are technically called "breaks"; these are the things you must watch; and, as I have said, every time the thought wanders, it must be checked by a little mark on the paper, or by some automatic action which does not distract the attention,—such as pulling over a bead. (That, of course, is the object of "telling the beads"; every time the thought wanders away from the prayer or the object of contemplation, the bead is pulled over.)[1]

[1] Says Avalon: "The Rosary with which 'recitation' (japa) of mantra is done."

Here is a classification of BREAKS which I think you will find useful; and you will notice that, as you begin to concentrate, they fall into about this order:

First: Physical sensations,—the body.

Second: The senses,—impressions through the senses. Noises. Touch sensations from the positions of the body; and so forth.

Third: Events which occurred just preceding the period of concentration,—or which happened during the day.

(The latter are very strong and insidious,—and as soon as you begin to concentrate you will find that these pictures and events begin to come up into the mind, as they do in dreams. About sixty to eighty per cent. of the dream-material is composed of the events of the day, and frequently from thoughts which came up just before falling to sleep. With these "day dreams," the events just preceding concentration, or the events of the day, are those which first tend to crowd into consciousness,—like a bubble coming up through the water and bursting on the surface.)

Fourth: Reveries or day dreams, strictly speaking. Very insistent, and very insidious.

Fifth: You will find, I think, if you introspect and try to follow intimately and minutely your own train of thought, through concentration, that the *thought itself* is active; and it will come into some such expression as this: "How well I am doing this" or "How badly I am doing it,"—an expression of itself, as it were.

Sixth: There are thoughts which are "breaks," but which nevertheless never rise into consciousness. The tendency of these thoughts is to make you forget everything, including the object that you are concentrating upon! That is to say, they annihilate everything, including themselves.

Seventh: The seventh species of break is a semi-hallucination,—in that scraps of sentences that are heard will come up to the consciousness; or scraps of visions will come before the mind.

We know that this is true in wireless telegraphy. We have what we call "atmospherics,"—that is, chance currents which are picked up and sometimes interpreted as symbols or signals. In the same way, these "breaks" are, you might say, "atmospherics" of consciousness,—cross-currents which have got tangled over the wires, as when talking over the telephone.

Eighth: A last *break* that I have been able to trace is a sort of nervous storm, which breaks within one, and is one of two things; an abnormal condition which restores you to consciousness, with a sense of exhaustion; or it may be DHYANA itself, which is the desired goal. Of course, this "storm" will only come after you have been concentrating at least an hour on an object without cessation.

After you have gone through this period of concentration, you finally come to the point where you can hold the object for a long time in thought. You have held it there, and it does not waver,—does not flicker.

In the next chapter we shall find that, being able to hold the object in consciousness, you can then outpour the mind upon the object, and become, as it were, *one* with it,—*i.e.*, hold it in the mind, and identify yourself with it; and that state is DHYANA.

CHAPTER VI

DHYANA (*Unification*) AND SAMADHI (*Cosmic Consciousness*)

DHYANA consists essentially in a unification or an outpouring of the mind on the object held in view. If the object be a mental or a physical thing, you reach the stage of DHYANA. If it be an abstract or a spiritual thing you ultimately attain the final stage, which is SAMADHI,—which is the goal of attainment of the Hindus. Then you have attained the ultimate goal along this particular line of development. It does not finish the Yoga training; but along this branch of the tree, or avenue, you have "attained."

You will thus see that the last three stages in this process,—DHARANA, DHYANA and SAMADHI,—are all bound up together, in a sense; they are part and parcel of one thing, a gradual process of development; and these three stages together are called SANGYAMA. When you begin to introspect, you will find this difficulty in quieting the mind, soothing it down. You first have the effort of quelling waves, of soothing the great internal motions, and then peace and "bliss" are attained.

Before we go further, however, I think we ought to have an object-lesson in perception,—how we "see" things. Let us take a crystal ball as an object for sense perception. Before we can understand the theory of union of the mind with the object held within it,—we must understand, first of all, how we "see" objects at

103

all; and that science of perception is known as EPIS-
TEMOLOGY,—it is the theory of sensation or perception.
Strictly speaking, there is no such thing as *colour*. *Apparently* there is, of course, but there is no "colour"
really.

What we see or perceive *as* colour consists simply in
the varying vibrations reflected from an object. In a
dark room, if the light be turned out, you would see
nothing, because there would be no light. That brings
us to the point, why we "see" anything.

Well, we only "see" a thing because the eyes and the
optic nerves are stimulated by light-rays, and either the
object itself reflects light, or it must be luminous,—
such as a candle-flame or a lamp or a phosphorescent
body, such as a firefly. When you "see" it, if it is not
luminous itself, it is only because it reflects light.

There are fifty-four octaves of vibrations known to
us—that science has absolutely measured by instruments,—and of these only one-seventh are perceived—
seven of these being sound and only one of them sight.
Thus we see what a very small little crack or opening,
as it were, the sense of sight gives us into the world.
It is just as though there were a perfectly solid wall of
vibrations, and only a little crack through which we
could see the material world around us. That is all we
ever "see." All the rest is for ever darkness and unknown to the sense of sight; so that, for all we know,—
for all you can prove by the sense of sight,—there might
be perfectly solid, substantial beings in this room,—
human beings like ourselves,—who vibrate to different
rhythms,—and hence be absolutely invisible to us! If
they did not happen to come within the particular

octaves of our sense-perceptions, we could not see them.

When we look at an object, such as a crystal ball, we perceive that it has a certain colour; or a green book,— we perceive it has a colour, green; or the red letters on another book appear to be red. Really the red is not *on* the book or *on* the letters, or *in* the crystal ball, but in the *mind;* and the reason the object *appears* coloured is that its substance is so constructed that it absorbs certain of the rays of light reaching it and reflects others. One substance absorbs some rays of light and reflects others. Another absorbs other rays of the spectrum and reflects others; and it is according to the particular vibrations that are reflected that we sense certain things and attribute to them certain "colours."

Yet we only see anything by its colour! If it had no colour at all, it would immediately become invisible to us. Then you would say, "How do I know that the book is there?" The only thing to do would be to test it by one of the other senses. Suppose that the sense of sound, the sense of taste and the sense of smell were cut off. There would only be the sense of touch left,— if your sight were taken away. "But," you would say, "although I can't see the book I can still touch it." But if you were to cut the nerves of the arm, which lead from the hand to the brain, you could not *feel* the book any more; consequently, *for you,* that book would vanish and become non existent! It is only by vibrations, travelling from the object to the brain, that we get into touch with anything in the outer world; and if those vibrations are stopped, the object immediately becomes invisible and imperceptible to us.

We now come to another point. I am looking (say)

at a crystal ball. Between that ball and my eyes the
only connection consists in ether vibrations which are
reflected from the ball. They are not material things.
You feel mentally that you could take a pair of scissors,
as it were, and cut them off in the middle and separate
the object. Now, as I look at the ball, I close my eyes,
and immediately *for me* that ball is annihilated; it is
non existent. Then what is it that I see when my eyes
are open? It is not the ball itself, because we have
found out that the colour and the other *qualities* which
that ball is said to possess are not *in* or on the thing
itself, but are, as it were, put *onto* that thing by our
minds. We construct, similarly, within our own minds,
every object that we see. In other words, *we create a
mental world which is a duplicate of the outside physical world;* we construct the world we see or hear or
touch or sense within our own brains,—a duplicate, mental world which is supposed to correspond to the external world.

Now, think what a different world this inner world
must be from the outer one! The physiological process
of sight must be somewhat as follows: light-vibrations
coming from the object strike the eye, traverse the eye,
the optic nerve, to the centre of sight in the brain.
There, by some mysterious process, they are transformed
into the "sensation" of sight. Accompanying this
sensation of sight are certain nervous changes in the
brain substance. But these nervous changes in the
brain are surely as different from the external object
as anything could well be!

We will suppose that there is a nervous change,—
some slight cell change,—in the brain which corresponds

to the sensation "crystal." Associated with that there is the sensation of "seeing" the crystal; but that nervous change in the brain is surely as different from this crystal ball as anything that you can well imagine! One is infinitely small, is a nervous, molecular change of some sort,—chemical, electrical, whatever it may be; the other is an outstanding, hard, crystal sphere,—yet they correspond one to another! There is this equivalence, this correspondence; so that what I see when my eyes are open is *something* with which my idea of a crystal ball corresponds.

Now, the point of all this is that everything we see is created within our own minds; it is a mental, duplicate world, as I have said before, corresponding with the outer world. We have constructed within ourselvs a mental world which corresponds to the outer world.

Well, how do we know that it corresponds? Of course, it is chiefly through the agreement of everybody who is normal and sound and sane. One looking at this object says "I see a crystal ball," and another says the same thing, and another says the same thing, and so forth; there is this agreement. Unless you are colour-blind or have hallucinations or are insane, every one agrees on this point.

But when you come to other questions, it is much more difficult to agree. For instance, there is the old question "What is truth?" which Pilate asked. Now, the definition of TRUTH is said to be "The perception of reality." But what is "reality," and what is "perception"? We have just seen some of the difficulties of perceiving an ordinary physical thing to which we are accustomed in everyday life; how much more difficult is it to perceive some abstract thing—such as a reality of some sort! What is that reality? There is where the philosophical schools split, on the theory of truth!

I do not know whether I have made all this clear, but if I have not it is extremely essential that we should realize that, as we look at any object, we never see the object as it really *is*. A table is apparently oblong and brown and solid, etc., but when we come to analyse it metaphysically, we find it is *not* brown, and it has *not* these qualities which we attach to it; we place those qualities *onto* the table, and if we take those away the table disappears for us,—it is no longer visible, no longer tangible, and so forth. Therefore what remains behind? The only thing we can say is, either one of two things;—either nothing, or an "x" of some kind that we do not know, but which is certainly entirely different from the table that we think we see. This table is made-up of a bundle of phenomena or outward expressions, which are all we ever come into contact with in even a material object; but the inner thing behind it, the *noumenon,* as it is called, which gives rise to those sensations, is certainly entirely different from the thing that we think we see.

Now, this is all important in bearing on the question of perceiving other things in the mind, such as mental images or visions or spiritual experiences of different kinds. It comes to the question "How do I know whether these things which I see are true?" If I pass into a peculiar psychic state and I have a vision, people will say, "Oh, well, you had a hallucination!" I say, "Oh, no! What I saw was true. I really perceived it." They would say, "Oh, no,—hallucination!" How do you know that what you saw was true? Only by *experience* can you tell that,—in these higher psychic states which, through Yoga, you attain. *If they are not true, nothing is;* because you have just as great a warrant for believing in their reality as you have for believing in the reality of a table.

A mental fact is just as much a fact as a granite mountain. True,—it is not a material thing; but it is a *fact* in the universe,—which you have to take into account.

Let us now consider the following extract from St. Theresa's EXPERIENCES. It is a little orthodox and religious in tone, but you must construe very widely her meaning of these words, because, like every one else, she laboured under difficulties of expression; she had to do the best she could!

In describing her own ecstatic or mystical state, St. Theresa said:

"For uniting oneself to God there are four degrees of prayer, which are comprised by four methods, each easier than the preceding; the first by drawing water from a well by strength of arm, which is severe labour. The second, by drawing it up with a hydraulic machine, in which way there is poured with less fatigue a greater quantity of water. The third, by conducting the water from a river or brook. The fourth, and incomparably the best, is an abundant rain, God himself undertaking the watering without the slightest fatigue on our part. In the first two degrees there are attainments in ecstasy which He sends to all persons. Thus, sometimes while reading I was constantly conscious of a feeling of the presence of God. It was utterly impossible for me to doubt that He was within me and that I was wholly lost in Him. This is not a vision. It suspends the soul in such wise that it seems to be utterly beside itself. The will roves; memory appears to be almost gone; the understanding does not act. Nevertheless it does not lose itself. In a higher degree, which is neither a rapture nor a spiritual sleep, the will alone acts, and without knowing how it becomes captive it simply gives to God its consent that he may imprison it,—as it were, falling into the fetters of Him whom it loves.

"In the third degree we come to the ecstasy. This state is a sleep of the powers, faculties, wherein—without being, entirely lost in God,—they nevertheless do not understand how they operate."

(The Fourth Degree is the completion of the operation, which is too long for quotation here.)

These experiences of St. Theresa are comparable to and agree remarkably with the Yoga teachings and the teachings of the mystics,—the object in all cases being to attain a state of mind or being which is superior to ordinary consciousness, and which enables one to get into touch with some higher mind or power than one's own.

We have just seen the difficulties of perceiving an object such as a crystal ball; and when you consider it, you will find there are certain difficulties in the way of accepting the reality of any object or thing perceived by the mind. The object of the Hindus is to hold the object in the mind, and then unify the mind with it, by an effort of will.

I have already referred, you will remember, to the fatal duality of mind, the quality of doubleness of the mind; the only way to transcend which is to acquire a higher state of mental super-vision by which you obtain a unity,—that is, you look down and "see" that these two states of mind,—self and object, seer and seen,— are delusory, and that they all ultimately merge into *one*. You want to acquire that state of Oneness, and when you have done so,—you gain a true and spiritual light, as it were. You come back to the world with intense conviction and sense of reality; and it is because of this experience (which the great spiritual leaders in the world, such as Christ and Buddha and Mohammed and others had) that they taught with the conviction they did; they felt that they *knew*. They did not theorize, but, with the conviction of knowing, they came back and were willing to suffer death, if need be,—because they felt they had the Truth.

In the first chapter, I quoted an extract from a poem; I think we are now in a position to see its meaning more than we did then. "AUM MANI PADME HUM" (the mantra), "The dewdrop slips into the shining sea." That means that this mind, or drop-of-mind, ultimately goes back to the universal Mind,—in the same way that the drop of water rejoins the physical ocean. It is the aim of the Hindus to make this drop-of-water-of-the-mind join the Universal; and the way to do that is to unify the mind with the Absolute, because that is the way of "attainment." [1]

There is a poem which gives us a vivid idea of just

[1] "The Hindu seers and the Christian mystics had agreed in seeking a unity of the self and of the Divine, wherein the nature

what the Orientals had in mind,—how completely they accept this form of unity, or monism, in their thinking, which we in the West find it difficult to accept. We always have a sense of duality, that is,—we Westerners,—no matter how we try to get away from it; and it is their attempts to prevent this which gives them their philosophy. Every one, of course, has read *Omar Khayyam,* translated by Fitzgerald; this same Fitzgerald has translated two other poems, which unfortunately are relatively little known,—although they ought to be; the first is "Sulaman and Absal,"—which is a very beautiful symbolic love story;—the second is "The Bird Parliament,"—from which I shall quote an extract. It is a philosophical treatise. The idea of the "Bird Parliament" is this: A group of birds assembled; they listened to one of their number,—the Tajida (who was a very learned bird!) who said, "Let us start out in our mystical flight, and try and reach the goal of attainment." But they said, "How are we to do it?" The Tajida said, "It is very difficult! You have to fly over great stretches of sand and desert, without water," and he enumerated all the difficulties which they would have to encounter. When they heard all this, a number of the birds refused to start, but some of the birds *did* start, and went a little way, and then dropped out and flew back again to their nests. Some of them went a little farther; and some went farther still, and some dropped out and died by the way; and it was only *thirty,* out of this vast flock of birds, who ultimately reached the Goal. The symbolical meaning of the story, of each is intimately revealed at the moment when they are nearest together."—(Royce: *Lectures in Modern Idealism,* p. 75.)

of course, being that this is the flight of the Soul to Perfection; and the physical difficulties they met on the road were the obstacles in the Path,—in the Way of Attainment.

Now, when these birds *did* reach their ultimate goal, they apparently were in great difficulty! But an extraordinary thing happened. They asked to see the Great Being who sat on the Throne behind certain Closed Doors. A Messenger first of all questioned them as to their flight; they told him of the difficulties they had gone through,—when, suddenly, the great doors flew open,—and the Thirty entered, and dared to raise their eyes to the throne:

> Once more they ventured from the dust to raise
> Their eyes—up to the Throne—into the Blaze,
> And in the centre of the Glory there
> Beheld the figure of—*Themselves*—as 'twere
> Transfigured—looking to themselves, beheld
> The figure on the Throne en-miracled;
> Until their eyes themselves and that between
> Did hesitate which *Seer* was, which *Seen;*
> Dividual, yet one: from Whom there came
> A voice of awful answer, scarce discern'd
> From which to aspiration whose return'd
> They scarcely knew; as when some Man apart
> Answers aloud the Question in his Heart—
> "The Sun of my perfection is a Glass
> Wherein from seeing into *being* pass
> All who, reflecting as reflected see
> Themselves in me, and Me in Them; not *Me*,
> But all of me that a contracted eye
> Is comprehensive of Infinity:
> Nor yet *themselves:* no selves, but of the All
> Fractions, from which they split and whither fall.
> As water lifted from the Deep again

Falls back in individual drops of rain
Then melts into the Universal Main.
All you have been, and seen, and done, and thought,
Not *You*, but *I*, have seen and been and wrought:
I was the sin that from myself rebelled:
I the remorse that Tow'rd Myself compell'd:
I was the Tajidar who led the Track:
I was the little briar that pulled you back:
Sin and contrition—retribution owed,
And cancell'd—Pilgrim, Pilgrimage, and Road,
Was but myself toward Myself; and Your
Arrival but Myself at my own door:
Who in your Fraction of myself behold
Myself within the mirror myself hold
To see myself in,—and each part of me
That sees himself, though drown'd, shall never see.
Come you lost atoms to your Center draw,
And *be* the Eternal Mirror that you saw:
Rays that have wandered into darkness wide
Return, and back into your Sun subside."

You must acquire that point-of-view. They were different aspects of the underlying Essence,—which is the *One Thing* back of all. All manifestations, all good, bad, everything, are merely different aspects of the one underlying reality. The one thing *you* must do to attain this state, the ability to realize the One Reality, is to unify yourself *with* it. When you can do that, you see the whole universe. *You attain Cosmic Consciousness.* Cosmic Consciousness is attained when you achieve the ability to unify your mind with the Universal Consciousness,—and from that higher standpoint you can see, not only that everything is good, but you actually have all the wisdom, all the knowledge, all the power,—everything that the universe contains! That is the object of the Yogi!

One more extract,—regarding this question of cosmic consciousness,—to give you an idea of how it feels, when it comes upon one. This extract is taken from Dr. Bucke's very interesting work entitled, *Cosmic Consciousness*,—wherein he gives an account of his attainment of this state,—how it came about. He enumerates many other cases of famous spiritual teachers or literary or poetical or artistic persons who had consciously or unconsciously attained this state of cosmic consciousness.

Dr. Bucke says:

"I have in the past three years collected twenty-three cases of this so-called cosmic consciousness. In each case, the onset or incoming of the new faculty is always sudden, instantaneous. Among the unusual feelings the mind experiences is a sudden sense of being immersed in a flame or a brilliant light. This occurs entirely without worrying or outward cause, or may happen at noonday or in the middle of the night, and the person at first feels that he is becoming insane. Along with these feelings comes a sense of immortality,—not merely a feeling of certainty that there is a future life,—that would be a small matter,—but a pronounced consciousness that the life now being lived is eternal, death being seen as a trivial incident which does not affect its continuity."

(In other words, man does not "have" a soul or "attain" immortality,—he *is* a soul and *is now* immortal.)

"Further, there is annihilation of the sense of sin, and an intellectual competency,—not simply surpassing the old plane but on an entirely new and higher plane. The cosmically conscious race will not be the race that exists today any more than the present is the same race that existed prior to the evolution of self-consciousness. A new race is being born that will, in the near future, compass the earth.''

Regarding his own particular experience of illumination, Dr. Bucke writes as follows:

"I had spent the evening in a quiet city with some friends, reading and discussing poetry and philosophy. We had regaled ourselves with Wordsworth, Schelley, Browning, and especially Whitman. We parted at midnight. I had a long drive in a hansom to my lodgings. My mind travelled under the influence of the ideas, images and emotions called up by the reading and talking. I was in a state of mind of most peaceful enjoyment, not actually thinking but letting images, ideas and emotions fleet of themselves, and spread throughout my mind. All at once, without warning of any kind, I found myself wrapped in a flame-coloured cloud. For an instant I thought of fire, an immense conflagration somewhere close by, in that great city. The next moment I knew that the fire was within myself.''

This is very illuminating,—because the idea of *light* always plays a big part in psychic development and psychic phenomena. Christ said, "If thine eye be single, thy whole body shall be *full of light*"; and it is a curious fact that all spirits talk of mediums as being "*lights*"; and of one being "the light of the world," and so forth.

Regarding the question of the eye being single, we will come to that later. It deals with the "third eye,"

—the Eye of Shiva. But the point now is that *light* is the important psychic factor; and it is a very curious thing that, in the case of material or physiological sight, —any activity of the nervous system is connected with phosphorescence, or phosphorus,—which is a very high constituent of the nerves,—and of course phosphorescence is a phenomenon accompanied by light; and there are many psychic factors which could be collected, bearing upon this question of light.

This internal light which comes to one who has experienced Cosmic Consciousness is one of the very striking phenomena connected with it; and it is a tangible mark that you have attained a certain stage of development.[1]

Two other factors enter into it. Time and space are obliterated. "Spirits" say that, in the spirit world, time and space, as we perceive them, *do not exist,*—and they do not exist in our dreams. When we dream, we enter a world in which time and space, as we conceive them, *are* not. There is one whole school of philosophy which says that time and space are purely subjective or mental; that they do not have objective existence at all, but that they are purely subjective.

Well, that is a very big question, of course, upon which hundreds of volumes have been written, and we cannot solve it now. But I will only say this,—that in one sense they *are* illusory and in another sense they are

[1] In Yoga, again, this question of *Light* is very frequently discussed. Thus, in Hatayoga the contemplation of "Light" is particularly prescribed. "Fiery Sparks" are seen, during development (as with our mediums), but "after seeing the fiery sparks they see the light."

not. If you conceive time and space as real things, in the sense that a crystal ball is a real thing,—then, of course, they do not exist; but if you conceive them as real mental states, then they do exist,—they have actual reality. Also, it can be shown that they exist objectively, *in a certain sense.* Time and space are only arbitrarily related to our life and its flow. Take time; it is measured by the ticks of a clock or a watch, or a metronome; or the earth, turning on its axis, gives us an artificial period which is a certain length of time,—divided by us into hours, minutes, seconds, and so forth.

A propos these units of time and space, you have all had the experience of feeling how quickly an hour has gone or how long it has been, and that shows you that an "hour" *to you* is not an hour, but a certain mental period through which you have passed,—long or short as the case may be.

Let me give here one little instance,—an experience I had some years ago, which throws some light on this question. I was experimenting at that time with a mixture of drugs, hasheesh and mascal and two or three other things,—the object being to watch the psychological effects upon my own consciousness. The second time I took this drug,—after four hours of very intense and beautifully coloured visions which ensued,—the sense of time and space left me completely. I know we were walking up Sixth Avenue about four in the morning, four of us,—all rather "wobbly,"—and that we went into a restaurant. We had a sandwich and some coffee. In the middle of the sandwich, I put it down on my plate, and said, "I won't finish that!" The others said, "Oh, yes; go ahead! We will wait for you." And I said, "Oh, no! No! No! I couldn't do that! It would take *years* and *years* to finish that sandwich!" They laughed, of course, and said, "Go ahead; it will take only a little while." To me it seemed that between each "chew" hours elapsed,— hours and hours of time,—and they could not induce me to finish the sandwich,—it would take too long!

So we went out; the elevated railway station was about a block and a half away, but miles and miles up the street I saw the station! We started to walk to it. We walked and walked and walked,—hours and hours, apparently,—before we finally arrived at the station! On the way I had this very curious experience: between the time my foot hit the pavement and the *sensation* of my foot striking it, *hours* elapsed,—although, of course, it was but the fraction of a second. If I took out my watch and noticed the second-hand, between every second, hours and hours and hours would again elapse.

This only shows that my sense of time had completely "gone to smash";—in other words, a mental change had taken place in myself, in which my time and space-senses had been completely upset,—for me they had all changed,—as they often do in dreams, in delirium and in other states.

Now, if there be another sphere of consciousness, different from our own,—different from this purely artificial sphere in which we live,—it is conceivable that our time and space senses should fundamentally change there. We do not have to be delirious. I was perfectly wide awake and perfectly sensible, but just my

sense of time and space had gone. Now, spirit-com-
munications,—granting that they are true,—are more or
less unanimous in asserting that the time and space relations, as we call them, *do not* any longer exist,—and
that, of course, the material world, as we see it, does not
exist either. Let us now apply this to our Yoga practices.

The object of these exercises (DHYANA), is to attempt
to unify the mind with an object,—to induce unification
with the object and the annihilation of the ego. Holding the object clearly in mind, it must be concentrated
upon; and then an attempt made to unify that thing
with the mind, so that, as I have said before, a sort of
"click" takes place in the mind; an extraordinary experience is undergone; and the "thing" joins itself
to "you" by a curious internal phenomenon,—you are
one with it; the sense of duality has vanished, and you
have this sense of unification.

In the words of the Kularnava Tantra, "Dhyana is
that form of concentration in which there is neither
'here' nor 'not here'; in which there is illumination
and stillness, as of some great ocean, and which is the
void itself." For further details, consult Avalon, *The
Serpent Power.*

This all relates to an attempted unity with a physical
thing, or with a mental image; but when you try to con-
template a spiritual thing or an abstract idea, and when
you seek to become one with *that,* or unify yourself with
it,—then you attain that state which the Yogi tries to
reach,—SAMADHI. This is a greater unity than the previous DHYANA. It is one with the Supreme Mind,—that
is, Cosmic Consciousness is attained, and the ultimate

attainment of the Yogi is thus reached along that particular line.

We in the West have attempted to do more or less the same thing by the processes of *mysticism*. I do not want to touch on this mystical teaching now, as it is usually associated with certain religious experiences. There are many books on mysticism which will show the curious analogies—(perhaps not curious, because they are based on fundamental truths)—but the analogies between mystical training and the ultimate attainment of Yoga.

These inner experiences bear a close analogy, in many cases, to *dreams*. In dreams we apparently meet and talk to people. In our daily life we meet and talk to people. In dreams we pick-up and handle material objects. In daily life we pick up and handle material objects. In dreams we have arguments with people,— sometimes even duels. In daily life we have arguments and mental or physical duels. And so forth; the analogy exists. How, then, are you going to differentiate between your dream-experience and your daily life? Every test that you can think of, to apply to ''reality,'' here in this daily life, you can apply to ''reality'' in the dream world, and it will be found to yield exactly similar results.

You may say, ''Oh, well, I can pinch myself; thus I can show that I am really here,—it hurts.'' But if you have attained a certain control of your dreams, and in your dream-state you say, ''Now, to prove that I am really here, and that this life is a fact, I am going to pinch myself'';—in your dream you will find that you can pinch yourself and that it hurts; so that *this* test is fulfilled. Every test that you can think of, as applied to the dream-body, is the same as if applied to the physical body,—so that it is impossible, from this point-of-view, to distinguish between the two.

That being the case, the question arises: "How do we know that this life is not all a dream? How do we know that the dream world is not another state of consciousness,—this world just another state, and that they are *both* dreams; that when we die we wake up, and then we find that we have simply had a period of alternating personality, one in this world and another in another world?" How do we know?

The Hindus claim that that *is* true; that there is a sort of higher mind, that this life *is* all a dream, and that the dream-world is also a dream; they are both dreams; they are inter-related,—and that, when we die, or wake up into the final, actual reality,—then we perceive that they *are* both dreams.

Personally I do not believe this to be true. You have all read *Alice in Wonderland* and *Alice Through the Looking-Glass*. Alice had encountered Tweedledee and Tweedledum in the forest, if you remember, and she found the Red King asleep there; and Tweedledum said, "What do you suppose he is dreaming about?" And Alice said, "How could I know that?" "Why," he said, "of course, he is dreaming about *you*." Alice said, "How do you know?" Tweedledum said, "Well, you are *here*. That shows you are being dreamed about. You are just a thing in his dream. If he stopped dreaming about you, you would go out like a candle flame." Alice said, "Oh, nonsense." He replied, "Of course.

You are just a dream-image,—a figure in his dream.
If he stopped dreaming about you, you would go out altogether." Alice said, "You are talking rubbish,"—
but she could not *disprove* it.

It is the same with us. All these theories,—that the
world is a dream, etc.,—we *feel* to be rubbish, but we
cannot *disprove* them. I think there is one test, however, which you *can* apply, which will show a difference
between these dream figures and the figures that we
meet in daily life,—that is, each other. If we meet
a person in a dream, and we have a conversation with
that person, we feel that there is no "centre of consciousness" in the person that we are talking to; that
we have created it; and in this daily life we feel that
that person *has* a "centre of consciousness" of his own,
which continues to exist whether we are asleep or awake.
But the dream-person has no such "centre of consciousness" which continues to exist after we are awake; it
"goes out,"—just as Tweedledum said to Alice. I think
this test distinguishes between the dream-figures in the
dream-life and those encountered by us in the physical
world in which we now live.[1]

We come to a final question. This state which is attained in SAMADHI—many people feel they would not
want to acquire! They say, "No, I have built-up my
personal consciousness as the result of work and effort,
and if this is all going to be annihilated or swept-off into
the 'ocean of consciousness,' I don't want it; I would
rather stay where I am!" Well, that is very reasonable in one sense. We certainly do work hard to get

---

[1] I have devoted a chapter to a discussion of this question, in
my book, *Modern Psychical Phenomena*.

what we now have, and we ought to keep it. But the
Hindus teach this also, which is not really appreciated
by us Westerners, viz.,—at the time this unification
takes place, you also keep your own consciousness *in a
sense.* You are lost, but you are there. I have mentioned before that during those moments in which we
experience a very great intellectual climax, or experience a very keen emotion of any kind, we are really
swallowed-up in that emotion; we do not feel *"I* am
existent,'' *"I* live,'' *"I* feel so and so''; but simply feel
the emotion itself. You are lost *in* that emotion, *in*
that state.[1] And that is what the Hindus mean; when
you become *one* with the Universal Consciousness, you
are the Universal Consciousness,—with all its powers,
all its potentialities, all its qualities; but at the same
time you exist as a separate factor. Dr. Bucke stated
that fact, and dwelt upon it particularly in his statement of his brief experience of ''cosmic consciousness.''
The gist of it was that, while he experienced this sensation and lost himself in the higher state of consciousness,—Cosmic Consciousness,—he was also aware of himself at the same time.

.   .   .   .

Samadhi has been defined as ''the identification of

[1] See Edward L. Thorndike: *The Elements of Psychology*, p.
108:—"Think, for instance, how one feels when half dozing in the
summer sunshine or when swimming lazily, or when in the agony
of whooping-cough, or asthma, or when beside oneself with rage,
or when absorbed in the smell of the woods. One is then swal-
lowed up in the sensation, is lost in the feeling, for the time being *is* it, one does not 'think' or have 'ideas' or notice 'things.'
One simply feels the warmth, the water and the sky and one's
bodily movements, the pain, the rage, the odorous air.''

Manas and Atma, as salt and water"—that state in which all is known as one (equal) and the "nectar of equality" (oneness). Even in Samadhi there are said to be various degrees of perfection. The most perfect state is said to be symbolized, on our earth plane, by the sexual crises—and Samadhi would consequently represent a perpetual state of "bliss" corresponding to this condition. "This, the most intense form of physical delight symbolizes the Supreme Bliss arising from the union of Shiva and Shakti in the spiritual plane upon which it is enacted " (*op. cit.*, pp. 248–49). From this it will be seen that Samadhi is far from being the empty, vacuous state of "nothingness" which most people imagine! And it is further said that "Refreshment, increased power and enjoyment, follows upon each visit to the Well of Life." There is, of course, much erotic symbolism in all the Hindu teachings,—just as we find close connections between sex and religion here in the West.

In arriving at this point of attainment, the Yogis have also independently developed certain psychic powers, by certain methods; and the next chapter will deal with these psychic powers and how they are gained, during the process of attainment. They are "offshoots," as it were,—like the branches of a tree. We have been following the main trunk,—up to the top, where the bird perches; but, branching from this "tree" are big and little branches,—and these psychic powers are developed by the awakening of the *Kundalini,* and by other methods which we will discuss in the next chapter.

QUESTIONS AND ANSWERS

Q. When you had that peculiar sense of loss of time and space, you did not really lose the space sense,—you had a different conception of it, did you not? *A.* Yes, I lost the ordinary, traditional, conventional sense of space,—that a mile was a mile. There was *a* sense of space, but it did not represent the same space that we usually know.

Q. That was the effect of the drug upon certain brain and nerve centers? *A.* Yes, doubtless; it all has a physiological basis. I think that even the most illuminated spiritual state has a physiological basis. In a little book which deals with these practices it says: "The way of attainment or genius or Godhood, considered as a development of the human brain."

Q. I have sometimes dreamt that I was dreaming. How do you account for that? *A.* It is a dream within a dream. There are many such cases, on record. It is like a reflection of a reflection. Probably there is some duality of consciousness in that state. The mind is made up of layers or strata, and there are fluctuations going on all the time between these different layers,—from one to the other, a deeper or a lesser depth of consciousness being reached in the dream-state.

Q. If it be true that we use such a very small percentage of the brain cells,—that even the very greatest minds use a small percentage,—perhaps these Yogis have learned to use more of their brain cells,—in attaining that higher plane? *A.* Possibly.

Q. *(Continuing)* Because, being an old race, they may have developed them through the centuries? *A.* Yes. There is a good deal in connection with the brain that remains unknown; in a future Lecture we will deal with the brain and its blood-supply and other things, and the occult teaching in connection with it. In Mrs. Piper's trances, the spirits said that they used certain unoccupied portions of Mrs. Piper's brain; and it is probably true that all these experiences develop in fallow ground.

Q. Will you tell us how the Yogis use their will in these practices? In an ordinary way? *A.* There are *two wills*. The conscious will, which can be trained; and the subconscious will, which few people know they possess. It is upon the exercise of this subconscious will that certain psychic experiments, such as "astral projection," depend. It is led up to by a series of occult exercises and practices.

Q. Don't they say that telepathy is the next faculty that will be developed,—that is, to be reduced to a science? *A.* Yes. My own theory is that it is merely an extension of faculties which we already possess. For instance, what is called hyperaesthesia, —the extreme sensitiveness to nearby objects and people, and their auras, etc.,—leads into psychometry, or the perception of the influences which objects carry; and from psychometry to telepathy and to clairvoyance, is a mere step; they are all graded.

Q. Is "cosmic consciousness" the ability to unify yourself with the universe? *A.* Not quite. It is the attainment of that state of consciousness which enables you to perceive from a cosmic point-of-view. But the *state itself,*—which you attain in this way,—is that consciousness which is omnipotent, omniscient, omnipresent,—in short, a God-consciousness.

Q. When you attain this consciousness, do you think you can *do* things which are beyond the normal or ordinary? *A.* Certainly,—because you only attain that consciousness after you have passed through all the stages of development. Now, my giving these talks does not enable you to attain cosmic consciousness. You must experience it yourself, by practising these exercises and methods; and, in the process of attainment, you acquire certain powers, which enable you to do the things you speak of. That is what the Hindus do. One who has learned *this* secret can become invisible; one who has attained *this* state can fly in the air; one who has attained *this* one is now immune from disease, —and so on and so forth. Some of this may appear fantastic, but I think there is a great deal of truth in some of the claims.

Q. You were speaking of the unreality of the table. Mrs. Eddy, in her book, says there is no reality in matter. *A.* Yes.

Q. It seems to apply here. *A.* Yes. That raises a very interesting point. In speaking about the table I mentioned the fact that matter,—as it exists, as we perceive it,— does not exist; the point is now raised that this coincides with Christian Science. In one sense that is true. There is a great similarity between the two ideas. There is a doctrine in philosophy which is termed "Idealism," which says that, inasmuch as we do not see a thing as it *is*, but only its qualities or attributes, there must be a thing, an "X," behind these phenomena, behind these qualities; and that "X" is something *mental;* otherwise the mind would be incapable of perceiving it, because the mind can only perceive something which is akin to itself. *Idealism* says, therefore, that the universe, at basis, is mental. Mrs. Eddy came along, and said "Yes. . . . That is a fact. That being the case, *your body* is mental. So the only thing you have to do to cure yourself is to perceive that the body *is* mental at basis,—as *Idealism* has taught since before Plato,—and apply it in daily life,—*think* your body whole and you *are* whole."

To my mind,—and there is, of course, great latitude of opinion here,—the difficulty in applying this doctrine of *Idealism* to daily life is that between theory and practice. You may believe theoretically that this wall does not exist, and you could prove by a series of abstractions that the wall is composed of atoms, which are composed of electrons, which are manifestations of ether or electricity—which are possibly mental in origin; but for *practical daily life* we have to live *as if* that wall existed; and for practical daily life we have to live *as if* we had a physical body. Not that the mind does not exert an enormous influence on the body; but I do not think it is *all*-inclusive, as the Christian Scientists believe. That is the distinction. I have discussed this question at some length, however, in my book *Modern Psychical Phenomena.*

CHAPTER VII

THE KUNDALINI (*Secret Energy*) AND HOW IT IS AROUSED

THE last chapter dealt with the attainment of the ultimate stages of consciousness desired by the Yogi,—the attainment of SAMADHI through DHYANA,—the unification of the mind with the Absolute.

Every one is, however, interested in *phenomena*. I have always noticed that in a lecture, accompanied by demonstrations, most people tolerate the lecture for the sake of the demonstrations! And I suppose it is the same with Yoga,—although, as a matter of fact, all through these practices,—which one undertakes in Yoga,—one obtains all kinds of phenomena of an interesting psychological character,—not spiritistic and not supernormal invariably,—but interesting psychological, inner experiences which are *real*. We now come to an offshoot of these experiments, so to say,—in which we shall delve more particularly into the direct experimental production of phenomena, by means of the Yoga methods.

Before doing so, it will be necessary to say a few words regarding the constitution of man, according to the Hindu conceptions.

The ordinary Western view of man is that he has a physical body, and that somewhere inside this is concealed a "spirit" or "mind" or "soul," or something,

129

—a very vague idea,—and that this mind works, and thinks, and constitutes the real man; and that, beyond this, there is some spirit or vapour or shadow or wraith, which he calls a "soul," which somehow inherits the "Kingdom of Heaven"; but what the connections between mind, spirit and soul are have always been very vague in our Western minds.

Now, the Hindu idea is that man is made-up much more complexly than this. To begin with, man has seven bodies, and the lowest of these is the physical body, —the "gross" body, they call it; that above this there is the "etheric" body (this is also, of course, the Theosophical doctrine, which is borrowed from the Hindus) and above that there is the "astral" body, and then the "mental" body, and so on, through the higher planes above the mental. Each of these bodies acts as a sort of link or intermediary between the one above and the one below. For instance, the etheric constitutes the link or connection between the astral and the physical; and the astral constitutes the link between the mental and the etheric; and so on.

I have already mentioned very briefly the subject of *insanity,*—the fact that there is a connection or link between the mind and the body, and that many forms of insanity are due, not to fundamental diseases of the body or to fundamental disorders of the mind, but to the *link* between the two being out of order.

These bodies, then, all function on their own particular *planes,* and there are as many planes as there are bodies,—or, rather, there are as many bodies as there are planes,—each functioning in its own plane; the physical body functions on the physical plane, the mental body on the mental plane, the etheric body on the etheric plane, and so on.

Now, the Hindus have an idea that energy, as it were, plays down on matter from above,—which I also believe to be fundamentally true,—although matter in a sense is alive, in the sense that it is in constant motion, rapid motion; also that it has a sort of innate consciousness of its own. There is also another consciousness which is added to it when that becomes organized or bound together, and that this is due to the fact that there is a playing-upon that material substratum of this energy from, as it were, *above*.

The Hindus have worked-out a very elaborate theory of evolution on this principle, the "outpouring of the divine breath," and other things, which we cannot go into now. At any rate, this fact that we can draw on an inexhaustible supply,—a source of mental and physical energy,—seems experimentally demonstrated to us by our practical daily lives and by common experience.

For instance, a woman of my acquaintance took some morphine for a minor operation, and under the influence of this morphine, read through in one day three books of a heavy character, and remembered practically every word of those three books.

Take another drug (cocaine), and you experience extraordinary happiness. But the happiness you experience is not *in* the cocaine,—it does no exist *in* that little white powder,—it is *in* the human being, and the drug simply brings it up to the surface. So that you evidently have these extraordinary latent capacities for happiness, of memory,—for all these extraordinary powers within yourself, and they have to be brought to the surface, by some artificial means, in order for you to acquire them.

Hypnotism does this; it brushes away the obstacles of thought, and all body suppressions,—all those factors within ourselves which keep repressing us all the time, —and it allows these inner inexhaustible stores and possibilities to come to the surface.[1]

William James has an essay entitled "The Energies of Men," and he shows in this very illuminating essay that we use only a small fraction of the energies within ourselves. There is also this curious physiological fact which very few people know, viz., that the baby, even before it is born, possesses as many brain cells as it ever will! We do not add brain cells; we merely develop them, or bring them into useful activity, layer on layer, as we go through life; and, no matter how far we may develop our minds or our brains, we never get to the point where we use all those cells,—so that you need never be afraid of exhausting your own powers; we always have a reserve, physiologically.[2]

These extraordinary mental heights, these mental powers, these latent energies, this happiness and joy and "bliss" (as the Hindus are always saying), ex-

[1] The body is a vast magazine of power (Shakti). The object of the Tantrik rituals is to raise these various forms of power to their full expression." (Avalon, p. 72.) This is done through Prana.

[2] "It would take a model as large as St. Paul's Cathedral to make all the neurones in the brain visible—a man counting at the rate of 50 a minute, working 12 hours a day, would take probably over 700 years to count all the nerve-cells in one man!" (E. B. Thorndyke, Elements of Psychology, p. 151.) There are well over ten thousand million of them in the body.

pressing combinations of emotions and feelings and thoughts,—can thus be attained artificially, through drugs, or by experimental methods such as hypnosis; and can also be attained by a species of mental work within oneself,—in these Yoga practices; and when you attain this state of SAMADHI, you arrive at that state in which you experience this "bliss." Then you unlock automatically all these energies and powers within yourself, and you attain them at the moment of attaining COSMIC CONSCIOUSNESS.

The Hindus, however, make a very clear distinction between the *kinds* of liberation, or ecstasy, which may be produced by means of drugs, on the one hand, and meditation, on the other. Thus we read: *"Ananda* (Bliss) of a kind may be secured through drink or drugs, but no one supposes that this is liberating bliss." This shows us how thoroughly the Hindu Psychology took such states of being into account, and studied them.

The SPIRIT OF MAN is divided by the Hindus into five categories; and symbolically they always use elements to express them, in much the same way that the alchemists did.

There is the Pure Spirit of ATMA. Then they say there is the "air," which is MANAS;—*i.e.*, the mind or thought faculty; Fire, which is BUDDHI,—the discriminating faculty; "water," which is CHITTA, or thought-stuff; and "earth," which is AHANKARA, or "egoity,"— you might say.

There are, you will see, certain qualities of spirit,— believed in by the Hindus,—which are very similar,— namely, MANAS and CHITTA,—that is, thought and thought-stuff. How do they differ? The Hindus say they differ in the same way that water differs from the motion of water. One is a quiescent state; the other is the same thing in motion. Incidentally, I may say here that, in the West, there is great controversy as to whether a "thing" is the same "thing" at rest as it is in motion. For instance, the human mind, the consciousness,—is it a *thing* or a *go?* Is it an entity, or is it something which only exists while it is moving, in action? And when that action stops, does the thing itself go out of existence? Another school says, "Anything that moves must be something,—something *to* move." And so on.

To return, however: This internal instrument of the mind has five SHEATHS or KOSAS,—namely, the Body of Bliss, the Thought-Sheath, the Consciousness-Sheath, the Fire-Sheath, and the Body-of-Nourishment. This last is supposed to feed, or draw nutriment, from the five TATTVAS or ETHERS. (In addition to these there are also the three LOWER BODIES,—the Causal Body, the Subtle Body and the Gross Body.)

The Hindus write a great deal about these TATTVAS or ETHERS; but before going into them, I must say a word regarding our Western conception of ether. Most of us think of the ether as a vague, tenuous, vaporous thing, which is *so* thin and *so* tenuous that no instrument has ever registered it,—which is a fact. Some people even doubt its existence. On the contrary, Sir Oliver Lodge believes that it is so enormously dense and solid that platinum and gold are as nothing to it. In his book, *The Ether of Space,* he defends this view. The sun and the earth, he says, or the earth and the moon, by the force of gravity, exert an enormous pull on each other; there must be *something* which keeps them apart. "What is that something?" "It must be the ether." And he has calculated, for instance, that the pull of the earth on the moon is something like five million-million pillars of steel, each a square foot thick, —which would be equivalent to the force which the ether transmits between these two bodies.

On the contrary, Haeckel, in his *Riddle of the Universe*, thought that the ether was the traditional gas, so to say, and calculated that a globe or sphere of ether the size of the earth would weigh about two hundred and fifty pounds! So there is a great difference of opinion; and, as I have said, some physicists are even inclined to believe that the ether does not exist at all! This is the new school of RELATIVISTS,—who hold the DOCTRINE OF RELATIVITY. Just a word regarding this may be of interest,—because it has caused quite a stir in the scientific world. It means, primarily, that everything is *relative,* and that, as you are moving, and everything else is moving, there is nothing stable in the universe from which we can get a stationary point of observation, as it were. The analogy which has been used is that you are on a moving ship, and you observe some one walking on another moving ship. You cannot calculate his *actual* motion because, in addition to all the motions of the boats, etc., the earth is moving on its axis, and the axis of the earth "wobbles," and the earth is moving through space, around the sun, at a definite rate,—about nineteen miles a second,—and the whole solar system,—our sun and all,—is travelling through space at a certain rate, towards a distant star; and perhaps all this is moving further into space; so that you can never get to a final point of "stationary-ness,''—everything in the universe is moving, and, that being the case, this doctrine of RELATIVITY says that everything is *relative*. There is, of course, much more to be said of the doctrine than this; but the above will serve our present purposes.

Now, this ether, according to modern science,—Western science,—is thought to be one thing, one ether (whatever it is), which conveys light-rays; and this is why it has been called "luminiferous" ether,—because "lumen" = light. Sound, however, is thought to be conveyed through the *air;* and, whereas sound travels, at ordinary temperatures and pressures, only about 1,100 *feet* a second, light travels at the rate of electricity,— 186,000 *miles* a second!

The Hindus believe that there are numbers of ethers, and that there is an ether for each of the senses. They have these names; LUMINOUS ETHER, conveying light; SONORIFEROUS ETHER, for conveying sound; TANGIFEROUS ETHER, for conveying the sense of touch; GUSTIFEROUS ETHER, for the sense of taste, and ODORIFEROUS ETHER, for the sense of smell.

We know that in a vacuum, where there is no air, sound is not conveyed and heat is not conveyed, and so we think that air is the medium for conveying heat and sound, and that no ethers at all are connected with touch or with taste; but the Hindus *do,* and they account for these things by various subtle theories which we cannot enter into here. However, these TATTVAS or ETHERS are thought to be modifications of the "Great Breath," which is a sort of fundamental, primal Energy which the Hindus believe in; and this acts upon the PRAKRITI. The Great Breath flows in five streams,—the different

TATTVAS. These tattvas or ethers have different *shapes*. Some of them are in the form of triangles, some in squares, some in loops, some are like scallops, and some take other shapes. They also have different movements.[1]

Says Avalon: ''Prana in the body of the individual is a part of the Universal Breath or the 'Great Breath.' An attempt, therefore, is first made to harmonize the individual breath . . . with the Cosmic or collective breath. . . . Strength and health are thereby attained. The regulation of the harmonized breath helps to the regulation and steadiness of mind, and therefore concentration.'' (*The Serpent Power*, pp. 212–13.)

Now, the PRANA, which we discussed in our chapter on PRANAYAMA, is the energy of *our universe;* this is the state of tattvic or etheric energy in which our universe dwells. There are currents of this running north and south, and east and west, throughout the universe, and there are also currents of this PRANA in the body. These currents are inhaled and exhaled and circulated throughout the body in our breathing exercises—when we practise PRANAYAMA; and we must learn to absorb this PRANA, retain it, and send it through the body,—and particularly to certain centres in the body where we wish to utilize this energy for vivifying purposes.

This is a very important point, which the Hindus have dealt with and dwelt upon; and it is the *crux* of their whole experimental system,—this direction of the prana or energy to certain centres. The seat of the prana is said to be the heart or chest,—as it were, pervading the

---

[1] The special operation of each of the Tattvas is located at its individual centre in the microcosm.

whole chest from the heart, and thence it spreads all over the body.

There seems to be a sort of uncertainty, or vagueness about the Hindu teachings, as to whether this prana is spread by the nerves as we conceive "nerves"; but, in any case, they call these prana-carriers the NADIS; and later we will come to something which is called the VOICE OF THE NADA,—which is very mysterious!

Here is a quotation from a Sanskrit writer, showing the doctrine regarding these NADIS:

"From the heart ramify the Nadis. Of these there are 101 principal ones. Each of these branches into 100, and each of these again into 72,000. Thus there are 10,000 branch Nadis and 727,200,000 of the smaller ones. Altogether, taking into account other main Nadis, which we will come to, there are 727,210,201."

If you take a knife and dissect a human body, you do not find these "Nadis"; you do not find all the various centres we will come to later on; but it must be remembered here that the Hindus were always supposed to be a psychic nation,—were supposed to possess psychic sight,—a certain amount of clairvoyance,—and they say: "No. This matter which is talked about, these psychic centres, these ramifying nadis, are *astral* matter,—not physical matter; therefore you won't find them by the aid of a knife; yet they exist; they are part of the body."

Says Avalon: "The term 'nerve' is used for default of another equivalent. These Nadis, called Yoga-nadis, are not, like the nadis of physiology, gross things, but subtle lines in which the life-force works in bodies. . . . Some are gross nadis, such as the physical nerves, veins

and arteries, known to medical science. But . . . they
exist in subtle forms, and are then known as Yoga-nadis.
The latter may be described as subtle channels of Pranic
Energy.'' (*The Serpent Power*, pp. 115; 130.)

Enormous importance is attached by the Hindus to
processes of *cleansing* the Nadis, by proper pranic
breathing exercises, etc. As Avalon says: ''Months
or years may be spent in the preliminary process of
cleansing the Nadis.''

So we come, now, to the heart and root of the whole
Eastern doctrine of the development of psychic powers.
It depends upon a very secret and ancient doctrine
which has been given only in the Sanskrit, and never
written out in detail, but always passed on by word of
mouth from master to pupil; it is the most secret of all
the teachings of the Hindu school; it is the doctrine of
the KUNDALINI; and it is upon the awakening of this
sacred KUNDALINI, or secret energy, that all these powers
depend.[1]

In order to understand how this operates, we must
understand still further the inner constitution of the
body. Up the interior of the spine—in the marrow, as
it were—there is said to exist a tube, a hollow tube,
which is called the SUSHUMNA; and it is up this SUS-
HUMNA that the KUNDALINI passes. The KUNDALINI itself is symbolized by a snake, having three and a half

[1] Writing of the Kundalini, Mme. Blavatsky says (*The Voice of
Silence*, p. 12), ''*Kundalini* is called the 'Serpentine' or the
annular power on account of its spiral-like working or progress
in the body of the ascetic developing the power in himself. It is
an electric fiery occult or *Fohatic* power, the great pristine
force, which underlies all organic and inorganic matter.''

coils. From this you will now see the importance of keeping the spine *straight,*—as we so often insisted, in speaking of *Asana,*—bodily posture.

The object, of course, is to awaken this Kundalini,— this serpent of fire, of life, and to send it, direct it— (the energy, that is)—through certain centres of the body—one after the other, in turn. These centres in the body are called CHAKRAS or LOTUSES. The Hindus are very fond of the lotus, and they say that these CHAKRAS look like lotus-flowers, having a certain number of petals; and, in the ordinary human being, these psychic centres are stationary,—that is, immovable. They are also variously coloured.

With their awakening or vivification, however, you acquire *clairvoyance* and *clairaudience,* and numbers of other psychic powers to be enumerated later. When they are awakened, they will begin to glow with a certain colour or colours, and also to spin, like a spinning-wheel.[1] These Chakras have a certain number of petals. Speaking of these petals, Mr. Avalon remarks:

"In the Indian system, the total number of the petals correspond with the number of the letters of the Sanskrit alphabet; and the number of the petals of any specific lotus is determined by the disposition of the Nadis around it. These petals, further, bear subtle sound-powers, and are fifty in number, as are the letters of the Sankrit alphabet. . . ." (*Serpent Power,* p. 43.)

[1] Mr. Arthur Avalon has criticized these views of Mr. Leadbeater's, and pointed out that they do not accord with the traditional teachings of the Tantras. (See his *Serpent Power,* pp. 34–38.)

We now come to a very difficult and subtle question—namely the so-called Sanskrit "letters" on the petals of the various lotuses—the "Garland of Letters." If one studies the illustrations of the chakras, one finds that, upon the petals, are certain Sanskrit letters,—a letter on each petal. (In the centres are also geometrical figures, animals, etc.,—purely symbolical.) Now, these letters are not supposed to be really *there*, in the sense that they are physically written upon the petals, because the petals themselves, as we have seen, are not physical, in that sense. The letters, and the sounds they typify, are purely *symbolic;* but just what this symbolism means it is often extremely difficult to discover. Arthur Avalon, in his work, *The Serpent Power,* has examined the various theories at length, and the student is referred to his book for details. Suffice it to say here that the letters may be said to represent *Powers*, which powers are qualities of the lotuses, and that these powers are represented by the letters, standing for Mantras, connected with the chakras. "They represent only the ideas of men."

These centres correspond *in the physical body* to the principal nerve-plexuses—the cardiac, the solar, etc.—while the chakra between the eyebrows corresponds to the pineal gland in the brain. It must be emphasized, however, that this correspondence is only symbolical, as the centres themselves are not physical, nor in the "physical" body.

It must always be borne in mind that these Chakras, or centres, are *not physical things*—though they are often spoken of as though they were. Mr. Leadbeater speaks of them as composed of astral or etheric matter, while the traditional Hindu teachings seem to indicate that they are more nearly psychic centres, pure and simple. Thus: "The lotuses are . . . centres of universal consciousness. . . . These Chakras are differing centres of consciousness, vitality and Tattvik energy. Each of the five lower Chakras is the centre of energy of a gross Tattva,—*i.e.*, of that form of Tattvik activity which manifests . . . sensible matter. The sixth is the centre of the subtle mental Tattva. . . ."

The *first* is the MULADHARA CHAKRA, which is situated at the base of the spine. This lotus has four petals, and it is here that the Kundalini sleeps, in three and a half coils, curled up. Its tail is in its mouth,—a sacred symbol,—and it remains at rest at the entrance of the *Sushumna,* but it does not penetrate it or arise through it until awakened. When it does, it passes up the Sushumna, or the spine, to vivify the various Chakras. Till then, it has remained at rest.[1]

Now, on either side of this Sushumna, or tube, are two other tubes, known as IDA and PINGALA,—which lie, as I have said, on either side of the Sushumna tube.

A great deal has been said and written to prove that the mystical TREE OF LIFE, spoken of in the book of Genesis, is connected with this Kundalini,—because, when it is awakened, you then have psychic powers— and it was in this wrong awakening of the power of life, —this extraordinary energy, and the knowledge that it brings,—which was wrongly awakened by some being called ADAM.

That accounts for the legend of the Serpent, which is

[1] *At rest*—that is, in the form of *static potential energy.*

this serpent-fire,—Kundalini. The whole Genesis legend, according to the Oriental view, is merely a way of symbolizing the awakening of the Kundalini force.

In *Le Compte de Gabalis* (a mystical treatise) is a paragraph dealing with the allegory of Eve and the serpent, and its relation to the Kundalini force:

"ALLEGORY OF EVE AND THE SERPENT

"The Primordial electricity or Solar Force, semi-latent within the aura of every human being, was known to the Greeks as the *Speirema*, the serpent-coil; and in the Upanishads, the sacred writings of India, it is said to be coiled up like a slumbering serpent. In the Third Chapter of the Book of Genesis it is symbolized as the serpent, 'more subtil than any beast of the field which the Lord God had made.' Eve, when this force stirred within her, was tempted to its misapplication. Directed downward through the lower physical centres for generation, unhallowed by a consciousness of responsibility to God and the incoming soul, the serpent force or fire brought knowledge of evil; directed upward through the brain for regeneration, the formation of the deathless Solar body, it brought knowledge of Good. Hence the dual operation of the solar force is symbolized as the Tree of knowledge of good and evil.

"The curse of the Lord upon the serpent . . . makes reference to the fact that, during a certain period of human evolution, man shall remain in ignorance of the law governing the serpent (Solar Force) which shall manifest in man's lower or earthly vehicles misgoverned by the human mind.

" 'And I will put enmity between thee and the woman, and between thy seed and her seed; it shall bruise thy head, and thou shalt bruise its heel.' During the above mentioned cycle of evolution, in his ignorance of the Law governing the Serpent Fire, man shall continually direct it downward or bruise its head, while the serpent fire, thus misdirected, shall bruise man's heel,—heel being a euphemism for that part of man nearest the earth,—that is to say, the body, lower emotions and mortal mind. . . .

"And the Lord said, 'Behold, the man is become as one of us, to know good and evil; and now, lest he put forth his hand, and take also of the tree of life, and eat, and live for ever. . . .' Here the tree of life symbolizes the upward play of the solar force for the creation of the deathless or Solar Body. Hence the meaning is lest man should learn the law governing Solar Force, and, directing it upward, become immortal. . . ."

Now, this energy,—this extraordinarily fundamental energy in the body,—is very closely connected with the creative energies, the sex-energies of the body; the body is vivified by this energy, and it is utilized for certain purposes. The doctrine of our Western church is based largely on ASCETICISM, but I think it has become twisted-up by a perverted view of the older teachings. Scholars went to the East, and they saw certain holy men who performed remarkable feats. They also saw that these men were ASCETICS; and they said, "Ah! He is an ascetic! He can do these wonderful things. He is a holy man. Therefore asceticism is the cause of this." And they taught it. But they did not perceive or know that this energy was utilized or directed into certain channels,—psychic channels,—and that unless this *is* done the whole point of asceticism is lost.[1]

You must either use up the sex-energies of the body in healthful exercises and activities, *or* in their normal channels of expression; *or* through these psychic avenues; and if you do *not* expand them in any one of those three ways, then you have curious mental and physical troubles, perversions and abnormalities, and so forth. The mediaeval ascetics had a twisted view of the whole subject.

A propos this energy, there is an interesting analogy of which I have often thought; it is that, in many spontaneous psychic cases,—POLTERGEIST cases, we call them (in which furniture is thrown about, bells rung and crockery broken, etc., without apparent cause), nearly always a girl or a boy between twelve and fifteen years of age is the author of the phenomena. The spontaneous outburst of these phenomena is, I am sure, associated with the awakening of the sex-energies at that time,— which find this curious method of "externalization."

For example: there lived a girl in Paris, about the middle of the last century, Angelique Cotton, who was called the ELECTRIC GIRL. Wherever she went in the house, the furniture followed her about and fell over; and of course the family called in the local police, the

---

[1] Says Avalon (*The Serpent Power*, p. 213): "The force which, under the influence of sexual desire develops into gross seed, is made to flow upwards. . . . This force ascends and comes back as the nectar of Shiva-Shakti. . . . It is consumed as a form of subtle energy, and rises to Shiva along with Prana." There is a good deal upon this subject in the *Shiva Sanhita*.

police investigated and tried to stop the manifestations,
—threatened her, and so forth. However, the phenomena developed, and kept up for nearly a year. They
finally stopped, and nothing more was heard of them.
In nine cases out of ten, you will find that these spontaneous POLTERGEIST cases are connected with young
people of about that age; and I am sure that there is a
definite energy-connection between the two.[1]

To come back to the MULADHARA lotus or chakra, at
the base of the spine,—the first of the seven:[2]—in Muladhara is also said to dwell a sun between four petals,
which exudes a poison; and this is said to be the sun-
fluid of mortality, or death; and this flows upwards,
and ultimately arrives at the right nostril, where it
mingles with the moon-fluid of immortality,—which goes
to the left nostril or PINGALA; and we have the sun and
moon there united in a form of symbolism which we shall
come to presently,—in discussing another of the chakras.

The Muladhara chakra is said to be the centre of the
body, in the sense that it is the *subtle* centre—the centre
of its psychical and spiritual power. On its four petals
are, of course, four Sanskrit letters, one on each petal,
and in its centre a form of Tattva, or etheric energy.
Like all the chakras, it hangs head downward, until
aroused or vivified by the Kundalini passing through it,

[1] There is, of course, a great deal of occult knowledge extant
concerning the relations of psychic force and the sexual energies;
but the pupil must be far advanced to obtain this.

[2] Avalon, and some of the Tantras, speak of six, and not seven,
Chakras. The seventh, *Sahasrara*, is omitted. It is difficult to
see why this should be so, however, and I can see no valid reason
for so doing. I shall, therefore, continue to speak of the seven
Chakras, or centres, in this volume.

when it turns upwards, like a flower to the sun. This, and all the other centres, it must be remembered, are *in* the Sushumna, and not in the body proper. And the Sushumna is in the spinal cord—to the extent that it can be said to be "in" space at all.

The *second* chakra is called the SVADISTHANA CHAKRA. It is situated at the base of the sexual organ; it consists of six petals, and is blood red.

The six letters on the six petals of this lotus are "like lightning." Water is the Tattva of this chakra. While said to lie "at the base of the sexual organ" it is of course in the Sushumna, like all the other chakras.

The *third* chakra is the MANIPURA, and is located in the centre of the body, just below the solar plexus; is of a golden colour; has ten petals,—or sometimes twelve (according to the different authorities), and is called the CITY OF GEMS. When this centre is awakened you become clairvoyant. (*A propos* this, it is very curious that many clairvoyants claim that they can see with the "stomach," or the solar plexus, which is where this chakra is situated.) [1]

It is said that by raising Kundalini Shakti to the Manipura centre, power may be acquired over fire— and Arthur Avalon, in his book, *The Serpent Power* (p. 104), gives an instance of fire having been kindled in his own house, merely by the power of Mantra. On the other hand, immunity from fire—such as the me-

---

[1] Lombroso has quoted some cases where letters were put on the "pit of the stomach," as he calls it, and were read; and, of course, according to this teaching, this is due to the independent functioning of this chakra, which has been accidentally aroused, independently of the others.

dium D. D. Home apparently enjoyed!—is accounted
for, by the Hindus, by the process of uniting the Prana
with the Tejas Tattva in the navel.

The Manipura chakra is said to be "lustrous like a
gem," and is the seat of the "Lord of fire."

Fourth, we have the ANAHATA CHAKRA, which is situated in the heart. It is blood red, has twelve petals,
and is the seat of the Prana. The Hindus have a saying that "He who has awakened this chakra can walk
in the air"—that is, he experiences levitation. The
mystics are supposed to have aroused this centre, hence
their ability to "levitate."

It is in the Anahata chakra that the "sound" is heard
—the Pulse of Life. In this centre is the "Tree which
grants all desires" and beneath it the "Jewelled altar." This chakra is the critical point in Yoga development.

The *fifth* chakra is the VISHUDDHA CHAKRA. This is
situated in the throat, just below the larynx; is of a
golden colour, has sixteen petals, and is the seat of the
AKASA TATTVA.

In the Vishuddha chakra is the moon, "the gateway
of the great liberation." Here, it is said, "the three
forms of time" are perceived.

The *sixth* chakra is AJNA, which is situated between
the eyebrows. This has a connection with the pineal
gland—which subject we will go into later. It has two
petals, and is supposed to possess three mystical principles.

In the Ajna chakra the subtle Tattvas of the mind
reside. After this centre has been awakened, the Yogi
thenceforth receives his powers "from above" instead

of "from below." He is no longer subject to this world. In this centre is the great mantra AUM. An inverted Yoni is also situated here. Here, the tattvas of the sun, moon and fire meet. The Yogi, by meditating on this centre, gains great psychic powers. It is here that the Yogi places his Prana at death, before leaving his body.

The *seventh* chakra, which is the SAHASRARA CHAKRA, is known as the sacred thousand petalled lotus. There is some difference of opinion among Hindu students as to where this is located; but it is usually said to reside within the brain, or outside the body altogether; and this shows you how independent of the physical body, in a sense, their physiology is. It is connected with the "aura." In the centre of this chakra is a YONI, with face looking downward. In the centre of this Yoni is a mystical moon,—continually exuding an elixir or "dew." It is the moon fluid of immortality, and flows through Ida.[1]

The Sahasrara chakra contains on its 1,000 petals *all* the letters of the Sanskrit alphabet, repeated twenty times. Herein is achieved the Great Bliss. Shiva himself dwells therein. The Yogi who has aroused Sahasrata is no longer subject to reincarnation—he is free from all but past Karma. Herein is the Supreme Light —the ultimate Goal of Yoga.

[1] Sarkar (*Hindu Achievements in Exact Science*, p. 60) has suggested that the six lower chakras correspond to the six vital sympathetic plexuses in the body; and that "yoga or contemplation means control over the functions of these plexuses." Also, according to Hindu physiology "the soul has its seat within the *Brahmarandhra* above the foramen of Monro and the middle commissure, but traverses the whole cerebro-spinal axis, up and down, along the sushumna."

In addition to these great or major chakras, there are also certain minor chakras, of lesser importance. We may briefly mention the *Lalana* chakra, a red lotus of twelve petals, situated above the Vishuddha, at the root of the palate; the *Manas* chakra, having six petals, closely connected with certain sensations, dreams and hallucinations; the *Soma* chakra, having sixteen petals, whose powers are "good," etc. I need not go into further details regarding these centres now, for fear of confusing the reader. Interested students can find much additional material of interest concerning them in Avalon's *The Serpent Power.*

Now, after the Kundalini is awakened, it flows up the Sushumna, darts and turns through all these various centres or chakras,—animating them, causing them to glow, causing them to spin,—and if the operation has been performed successfully, you see a star before the eyes, which is the sign that it has been awakened properly.[1]

Mr. C. W. Leadbeater says that one or two things may happen wrongly. In the first place, you may awaken these chakras in the *wrong* order; then you have trouble! Or it may take a downward turn and animate three lower chakras or centres, which are known only to black magicians.[2]

This idea—that the chakras can be aroused in any other order than from the lowest upward shows, as Mr. Avalon points out, "a misunderstanding of the specific

[1] Avalon says "it is manifested as a light between the eyebrows" or "in the form of a sharp flash of lightning."

[2] According to Mr. Leadbeater. Mr. Avalon asserts that there is "no lower centre" known to the Yogis. (*Serpent Power*, p. 38.)

character of the Yoga.'' It would be physiologically
impossible for Kundalini to arouse Centre 3 without
first passing through Centre 2 *en route,* etc. Therefore,
in all cases, operation must begin at the *lowest* centre,
and proceed upward, as each is aroused in turn.

The Kundalini, after it rises to the throat, passes
down through what is called the HOLE OF BRAHMAN; and
this plays a very important part in Yoga functions or
practices. The Kundalini passes up through this, to the
right side of the AJNA lotus, then to the left nostril,
where it is called the GANGES,—the SWIFT FLOWING
GANGES, or IDA. By a modification in the opposite direction, it goes to the left side of Ajna, and then to the
right nostril,—crossing over there,—where it is called
PINGALA; and the space between these two is called
BENARES,—the Sacred City.

Probably you all know the great import that the Hindus attach to the river Ganges and to Benares, the
sacred city situated on its bank; and you had thought
this just a curious custom,—a sacred city built on a
sacred river. But it is more than that! It is bound-up
with this doctrine, known only to the Hindus, and not
to the ignorant missionaries who go there. It is all a
purely occult doctrine,—this sacred Benares which is
the great centre of attainment, symbolized in their city;
and the Ganges,—this river,—which is the secret, sacred
energy which has been finally aroused, and is flowing
through them like a river of fire,—a river of energy.[1]

---

[1] "It is because the Orientalist and missionary know nothing
of occultism, and regard it as superstition, that their presentment
of Indian teaching is so often ignorant and absurd." (*The Serpent Power,* p. 105.)

Of course, as a matter-of-fact, the real Ganges is a filthy, dirty, germ-infected river,—in which natives with all kinds of diseases bathe, and later-on drink, and thus spread plague and other diseases all over India. That is the *fact;* but the point is that, symbolically, it is bound up with this occult doctrine; and to the Hindus, of course, it is a very sacred river because of that.

There is much symbolism in all this Hindu terminology. Thus, the "Jewelled Altar" is in the eight-petalled lotus below Anahata; the "Isle of Gems" is a state of Cosmic Consciousness—or Supreme Ecstasy; while the so-called "Ocean of Nectar" is the Infinite Consciousness Itself.

In order to save this precious energy, then, which is thus generated within the system, the Yogis endeavour to prevent the constant dripping-away of this fluid,—this "dew,"—which drips down through the Hole of Brahman. What they endeavour to do is to stop up this hole in the back with the tongue; and their great object is to train the tongue so that they can bend it back and insert it there; and if they do this, and plug-up this entrance, then they think they have gained great power. And the Yogis perform all kinds of curious practices in order to lengthen the tongue and make it more pliable,—even cutting the thread underneath, and rubbing it with salt every day, and pulling it out with the fingers,—all kinds of curious practices to make it long, so that they can bend it back and tuck it up this "Hole of Brahman"; and thus prevent the dripping-away of this sacred energy, this "dew." This is utilized in the body, and directed to the awakening of the psychic centres.

These sacred energies, which are thus preserved, are called OJAS, and are supposed to be the most sacred of all energies.

On the other hand, mind force is concentrated by the yogi under the name *Vogabala,* and in oriental Black Magic, this is concentrated on the lowest centre, according to the ritual of the infamous *Prayoga,* with the result of inducing sexual hallucinations. In the so-called white or mediumistic magic, the centre of energy is by the third centre (the navel) for materialization phenomena, and the fifth or base-of-the-throat centre for clairaudience. Those who can reach the sixth claim the power of astral voyaging.

Now, for awakening the Kundalini, and getting it to "perform" properly, you have to begin with certain MUDRAS, as they are called,—which are a combination of the various exercises, that is, ASANA and PRANAYAMA, coupled with all the mental exercises. And there are various MUDRAS. They are called the YONI MUDRA, the MAHA MUDRA, the MAHA BANDHA, the MAHA VEDHA, the MULA MUDRA, the KHECHARI, the VAJROLI MUDRA (which last is said to be the most secret and the most sacred of all) and many others.

These MUDRAS consist of a combination of certain physical postures,—in which the legs and feet and hands and arms and head and all parts of the body are in a certain position,—with breathing exercises, coupled frequently with mantras or chants, and of course intense meditation and concentration, on those points where the centres are located. The breathing intakes the psychic energy or prana. The attitude facilitates the sending of it to certain points in the body; and then, by will, this prana is directed to a certain spot or point,—one of the chakras,—until it is vivified and aroused,—when it begins to glow, it begins to spin, and you have that chakra aroused by the action of the Kundalini power or force.

Just an example of one or two of these MUDRAS. (I) Fix the gaze on Ajna, between the eyes, with the tongue tucked up in the epiglottis. Then contract the throat and press the chin onto the breast. (II) Sit on the left ankle; stretch out the right leg, and take hold of the toes with the hand. Contract the throat, and press the chin firmly against the breast. Now, draw the breath through the Sushumna. After holding the breath as long as possible, it should be exhaled very slowly (so as not to expend the Prana).

In the celebrated *Yonimudra,* the Yogi closes the eyes, ears, nostrils and mouth with his fingers. He then forces the lips to take the shape of the beak of a crow, and inhales, concentrating in turn upon the chakras.

Shaktichalana Mudra is performed by contracting the rectal muscles until a peculiar sound is heard in the Sushumna. This is usually preliminary to the Yonimudra.

The *Khechari Mudra* consists in turning back the tongue into the throat, as previously described, with the mind fixed on Ajna.

The so-called *Bandha* are really "bindings," and represent certain physical methods of controlling Prana. A number of these processes are described at length in *The Serpent Power,* to which the reader is referred, for further particulars.

These Mudras, then, if practised, arouse the Kunda-

lini, awaken the chakras, and as they are awakened and
aroused, certain psychic powers result, such as:

ANIMA, which is the power of assimilating oneself with
an atom. Or—

MAHIMA, which is the power of expanding oneself in
space; or—

LAGHIMA, which is the power of reducing gravitation, or
"levitating"; or—

GURIMA, which is the power of increasing one's weight,
—apparently adding to gravitation; or—

PRAPTI, which is the power of instantaneous travelling,
—that is, "astral projection," as we here say; or—

PRAKAMYA, which is the power of instantaneous realization; an irresistible will; or—

ISHITA, which is the power of creating by thought;
or—

VASHITA, which is the power of commanding and being
obeyed by beings, by animals and by matter,—so that
one can move objects without contact.

All these, of course, depend upon the awakening of
the Kundalini; these powers are mere offshoots of that.

It has, of course, been pointed out that these various
centres or chakras correspond, in a very striking manner, with the various nervous plexuses—cardiac, solar,
lumbar, epigastric, cerebral, etc. This is a very striking fact. It must never be lost sight of, however, that
while this *analogy* or *correspondence* may be present,
the centres themselves are not located *in* these various
bodily plexuses, *but in the Sushumna,*—at a point cor-

responding to them.   Arthur Avalon points this out and
insists upon it over and over again, in his work, *The
Serpent Power*.   He says: ''Here in the spinal column
they exist as extremely subtle vital centres of Prana-
shakti and centres of consciousness.''   One of the Tantras also speaks of the lotuses as being strung on the
Sushumna like beads on a thread.   In speaking of the
lotuses as being ''in'' these centres of the body, therefore, this meaning or symbolic interpretation of the language must always be borne in mind.

Now, this Kundalini force, as it exists at the base of
the spine, is supposed to inhabit a three-dimensional
world,—that is, a world like that in which we live; but
when it enters the Sushumna, although it enters a definite ''space,'' as we know it, it is supposed to enter a
fourth dimensional space.   This is a very curious con-
tradiction, apparently; but there is an odd biological
analogy which seems to bear some relation to this point;
and it is this.   One of the great ''miracles'' of science
is the nutrition of the body,—how it is that a potato
or a chicken which is running about,—or a carrot, or
a slice of bread,—can be little Mary Jones *tomorrow*,—
can somehow be *turned into* little Mary Jones,—a part
of her living body.   The miracle of it is—*how?*   We
know that this process of *metabolism*, or food-change
and cell-growth, goes on all the time in the body.   What
happens to make this matter, supplied to the body in
the form of food, become *alive*,—part of the living
body?   We do not know, but we *do* know this: that, if
you examine the centre of a cell with a high-powered
microscope, there seems to be a double flow of material
from the outside of the cell to the centre, and then out

again, in the form of an ellipse; it starts from the outside of the cell,—this matter,—as pabulum or food; that it reaches the centre, and at that centre some change takes place whereby it becomes *living*. As it travels back, it becomes *body*. In this "centre," there seems to be a well of energy,—welling up from nowhere, constant, like a fountain, which comes from no discernible source, and yet is always present; and it is this energy which vivifies matter. It is "in" space,—and yet it seems to be spaceless. It comes from "nowhere."

"Seizing upon foreign matter is an outwardly directed activity, assimilation is an inwardly directed activity or return current; cell division and multiplication is an outwardly directed operation, co-ordination is inwardly directed, and so on. . . . This outflow and inflow is a common Tantrik notion." (Avalon, p. 278.)

You see, then, there is this analogy between an interesting biological phenomenon and the Kundalini force, which, while *in* three dimensions, is said to enter four, as it passes into the Sushumna.

Just here we encounter the doctrine, on the one hand, of the fourth dimension; and, on the other hand of more practical ways of awakening the Kundalini,—the particular methods used; both of which subjects will be taken up in the next chapter.

CHAPTER VIII

THE KUNDALINI (*Continued*); "THE FOURTH DIMEN-SION," ETC.

THE last chapter ended by stating that the Kundalini power, when it enters the passage in the spinal column, —called *Sushumna*,—enters into a fourth dimensional sphere of activity; and we shall find that this fourth dimensional sphere is a sort of spiritual sphere, although, in a certain sense, it may be said to be *in* three dimensions, too. As this fourth dimension figures so largely in our own psychic literature as well as in Hindu literature, I think it may be well to obtain as clear a conception as possible of what the *fourth dimension* really is before going further.[1]

If you take a point, that point is defined by Euclid as "That which has no parts and no magnitude." It is supposed to be an infinitesimal point of departure, and occupies no space in itself. Now, that point, acting in a certain direction, generates a line,—a line being said to be "a number of points laid on end,"—*one* direction, *one* dimension. (A direction is a dimension, strictly speaking.) Through this same point, if you draw another line at right angles to the first, you have a second

[1] I must once again emphasize the fact that I am merely stating theories or teachings—and not necessarily my own views—in what follows. For a critical discussion of the theory of the Fourth Dimension, the reader is referred to Robert T. Browne's book, *The Mystery of Space.*

direction or dimension,—*two* dimensions. And there is a *third* way in which you can draw a line at right angles through that point,—at right angles to the other two,— and that is at right angles *to the paper or blackboard,*— because on a flat surface, or a two-dimensional surface, you cannot draw the line *on* it. These three directions, according to geometry, are the *only* three dimensions there are,—the only ways in which you can draw a line at right angles to other lines through a given point.

Take a square,—two dimensions, length and breadth. If you add a third dimension, *viz.,* height, you have a cube of three dimensions, generated by moving at right angles to itself.[1] Now, it ought to be possible to move in *some* direction at right angles to these three, into a *fourth* dimension; in the same way that the second dimension is at right angles to the first, the third dimension is at right angles to the second, the fourth dimension should be at right angles to the third! Theoretically, there should be a fourth dimension, just as there are the traditional three.

1 The cube, opened out, becomes—very curiously—the Cross.

We know that, in algebra, it is easy to "create" a fourth dimension. We can write X^{-1}, first dimension, X^{-2}, X^{-3}, etc., and it is just as easy to write X^{-4} or X^{-n}— (to the nth)—as it is any other number or power. In mathematics, we can deal with four dimensions, or any number of dimensions, but in geometry it is difficult to do so. Moving at right angles to itself, a square would generate a cube, and that cube, moving at right angles to itself, should generate a *hypersolid* or *tesseract,*— which is a fourth-dimensional figure,—generated by the movement of the cube, in the same way that a cube is created by the movement of a square, or the square is generated by the movement of a line.

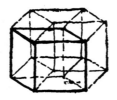

Each higher space is generated from the one lower; and we have calculated exactly what a "tesseract" should possess. It should have sixteen corners, thirty-two edges, twenty-four square faces and eight bounding cubes; and it may be of interest to state, in this connection, that the geometry of the fourth dimension has been worked-out so accurately that there is a large book, by Prof. Manning, dealing with "Geometry of Four Dimensions," and explaining it in great detail.

Probably you have heard a great deal regarding the connection between the fourth dimension and clairvoyance. The clairvoyant power (a certain kind of clairvoyance) enables you to see into the interior of a solid object. For instance, a person brings you a box and asks, "What is in there?" A clairvoyant can tell. You say, "How? It is impossible to see into a box or anything which is sealed up in all directions." We can tell by analogy how that is possible.

Let us suppose that a piece of paper is a flat world, having two dimensions,—a flat surface; and that there are beings living on this two-dimensional world who do not know anything about height, or the third dimension,—only length and breadth; they are two-dimensional beings; in their consciousness a third dimension could not enter. This square—"A" is a room of theirs;

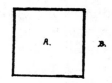

and an individual would live inside it. Another individual, B, outside the square would never be enabled to see inside, unless there were a door made for him to enter,—because he could never see that person from an elevated or higher space; because it does not exist for him,—a third space. But *we* can see this "person" by looking down on him from above,—into what, to the two-dimensional being, would be a closed space,—the interior of a hermetically sealed room. *We* can see that person from outside, because *we* can look down on him from above,—see him from a third-dimensional viewpoint.

To make the analogy clearer, I see rings in a box because I look "down" on them from above; but if I could not look down on them from this upper height or space I could never see them. By analogy, from the fourth dimension, one could see down into the interior of what is *to us* a sealed space or room or box. In the same way that *we* see into a two-dimensional space from the third, the fourth dimensional being could see into a (to us) hermetically sealed room in the third.

We can demonstrate many curious facts in connection with the fourth dimension. Take (say) two pieces of paper, cut in the form of triangles. Now, no matter how you move these triangles about, you cannot make them coincide in space. No matter what "angle" they take, you cannot make them coincide. But if you take one of them and *turn it over* in space,—and place it *onto* the second,—you get the coincidence, because you move it into a third dimension.

Take a left-handed glove. No matter how you turn it about, you cannot make a right-handed glove out of it. Yet you can turn this glove inside out, and make a right-handed glove out of it. Theoretically, it is possible to turn a hollow rubber ball inside out without tearing it, in the fourth dimension, in the same way that you turned the glove inside out in three.

Here is another very curious fact. Take a piece of string. You will find that, as long as it is kept on a flat or two-dimensional surface, it is impossible to tie a true knot in it. In order to tie a knot in the string, you have to lift-up one end *over* the other, and that is taking it into the third dimension,—which you are not entitled to do! As long as it is *flat*, kept in two dimensions, you cannot tie a knot in any string.

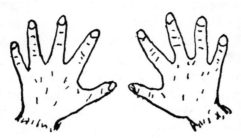

Prof. Zöllner, of Leipsic, sealed the ends of a piece of cord onto his table, the rope being free from knots; the lights were turned down, and, in the presence of Slade, the medium, a number of knots were found to be tied in the cord,—which would be impossible to account for, so long as the two ends of the cord were sealed.

In our space, when you hold the two ends of a cord, you cannot tie a true knot in the string. You can tie a loop, but that is not what we want. You cannot tie a true knot in any piece of string when the ends are held. But Zöllner said, "it is possible for the *spirit*,—being a fourth dimensional being,—to take that rope into the fourth dimension, and in some way turn ·it over, and produce a knot in it,—in much the same manner that *we* can produce a knot by lifting this piece of string into the third dimension when tying it." On the basis, largely, of these experiments, he wrote his famous work on *Transcendental Physics*.

If this fourth dimension really exists, it enables us to account for many psychic facts,—because it would permit us to attain a higher point of view,—from another dimension,—which would allow us to look down into this world of ours from a higher state of mind,—in the same way that *we* can look down on a two-dimensional world from a higher plane of consciousness, and see what is inside it; in this way we can account for clairvoyant diagnosis.

A clairvoyant can look at a human being and say, "Your liver is out of order!" How does he look at the interior of the body? Fourth-dimensional sight!

There is one other point in this connection which is

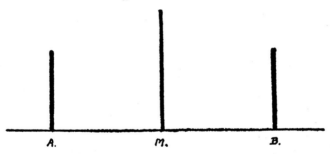

A.   M.   B.

interesting. You have just seen that a glove can be turned from a right to a left-handed glove by turning it inside out. The "astral world" is said to be, in one sense, a fourth-dimensional world, and to possess properties which that world possesses. It is also a mirror-world. Look at a mirror; we stand in front of it, and it reflects our image, but the right and left hands are reversed, and all the movements of the body are reversed in the reflection. The distance an object is this side of the mirror appears to be the same distance on the other side of the mirror. If you hold "635" up to the mirror it appears "536." If you have ever obtained "Mirror Writing,"—which is sometimes produced automatically,—it has to be held up to the mirror to be read.

In *Through the Looking-Glass*, Alice walked through the mirror and found herself in a looking-glass world; and she found that everything was being done backwards. If she wanted to walk to the right, she must begin by running to the left as fast as she could, and she soon found herself on the right, where she wanted to be! Everything was in that curiously reversed state,— just as everything would be in a mirror world.

Mr. Steiner has informed us that the astral world, which one might say is in some essentials a looking-glass world (until you know how to "read" it) has to be interpreted backwards. There are many other interesting facts which could be brought out in connection with the fourth dimension. But for our present purposes I want only to bring out the point that it has a distinct relation to psychic phenomena, because it enables us to define certain powers,—such as clairvoyance,—which we are not able fully to understand without the fourth-dimensional space or sphere of activity.

Of course there are other theories of the fourth dimension,—such as *Time,* as Mr. H. G. Wells postulated; on the other hand, it has been objected that time is not four-dimensional but *one*-dimensional,—it has only length and nothing else! [1]

[1] Einstein, however, in his theory of Relativity, has revived this idea and given it an added plausibility. (See *From Newton to Einstein,* by B. Harrow, p. 63), etc.

The theory has been advanced that *life* is a fourth-dimensional thing, and that it is *"Throughth"*—it passes *through* the world of matter, manifesting in various degrees and phases; that is, a fourth-dimensional activity; because it comes from a higher sphere of being, and thus manifests itself in different degrees.

If you take a triangle, and you make it pass through a plane or flat surface,—as it passes through, you will see the different "qualities" which that triangle would manifest to a two-dimensional being; it would seem to enlarge and get bigger, and then smaller and smaller until it would finally disappear.

Now, that is like life. It begins with a very little point, and increases in breadth and power up to maturity, and then gradually diminishes, down to the point where it becomes extinguished. But it has not gone into "nothing"; it is in the fourth dimension still. So the fourth dimension has been defined as *"Throughth,"*— that which passes *through* a plane, or a certain flat film of activity, such as our world. That was the definition given by William James Sides, in his lecture at Harvard University. He defined the fourth dimension as *"Throughth."*

·   ·   ·   ·   ·   ·   ·   ·

Let us now apply this to our Yoga Philosophy. The Kundalini power, when it passes into the Sushumna, is said to enter a "mental" world,—this fourth-dimensional world; and although it is existent *in* the three-dimensional world, in one sense (inasmuch as it is definitely connected with a three-dimensional body), its activities are supersensate, superphysical, or fourth-dimensional; and of course the chakras are, as I have said before, composed of vital substance.

Speaking of this point, Avalon says: "They (the chakras) can be the objects of immediate perception only to Yogis. . . . Chakras proper, which as subtle, vital, and conscious centres in the spinal cord are invisible to any but a Yogi's vision. . . . The Yogi 'sees' the chakras with his mental eye (ajna). . . ." (Pp. 80, 177.)

This Kundalini power, then, after passing up the Sushumna, and awakening the various chakras or psychic centres in turn, is said to create or generate or beget a *New Universe* of activity, in the sense that it calls it into being. It brings into play, into activity, a new world, which has not existed until then; this is in a sense a "creation" of a universe by the mating or union of matter and spirit,—and this is what has symbolically been called the *Celestial Marriage;* it is the arousing of the Kundalini and its action on our material world.[1]

When we came to the practical part, *viz., How to awaken this Kundalini power,*—we saw that there were certain practices, called *Mudras,* which consist in assuming a certain bodily position, *Asana;* practising *Pranayama,*—getting, so far as possible, rhythm and harmony and balance, and concentrating definitely upon certain centres within the body,—these centres being the chakras. That being done, the Kundalini power is awakened, vivifies the chakras, and you have all these

[1] Professor Mukhyopadhyaya has suggested that the Chakras are aroused indirectly, by a sort of psychic *induction*—but I can see no valid reason for supposing so.

Siddhis, or psychic powers, which automatically come of themselves, as it is awakened.[1]

Regarding the awakening of the Kundalini, Swami Vivekananda, in his *Raja Yoga,* says:

"After practising this first breathing for a few days, you take up a higher one. Slowly fill the lungs with breath through the *Ida,* the left nostril, and at the same time concentrate the mind on the nerve current. You are, as it were, sending the nerve current down the spinal column, and striking violently at that last plexus, the basic lotus, which is triangular in form, the seat of the Kundalini. Then hold the current there for some time. Imagine that you are slowly drawing that nerve current with the breath through the other side, then slowly throw it out through the right nostril. This you will find a little difficult to practise. The easiest way is to stop the right nostril with the thumb, and then slowly draw in the breath through the left; then close both nostrils with thumb and forefinger, and imagine that you are sending that current down, and striking the base of the *sushumna;* then take the thumb off, and let the breath out through the right nostril. Next, inhale slowly through that nostril, keeping the other closed by the forefinger; then close both, as before. . . . It is well to begin with four seconds, and slowly increase. Draw in four seconds, hold in sixteen seconds, then throw out in eight seconds. This makes one *Pranayama.* At

1 In the Vedas it is said: "How can there be any Siddhi (psychic powers) for him who knows not the six chakras, the sixteen adharas, the five Ethers, and three Lakshas, in his own body?"

the same time think of the triangle; concentrate the mind on that centre. The imagination can help you a great deal. . . . The next breathing is slowly drawing the breath in, and then immediately throwing it out slowly, and then stopping the breath out, using the same numbers. The only difference is that in the first case, the breath was held in, and in the second held out. The last is the easier one. The breathing in which you hold the breath in the lungs must not be practised too much. . . . One day, if you practise hard, the Kundalini will be aroused.'' [1]

Now, as you are practising *Pranayama,* and the necessary concentration to awaken the Kundalini, certain forces will begin to develop,—certain phenomena will begin to be observed. One of them is the peculiar internal sound which you will notice; this is called the *Voice of the Nada.* The Hindus claim that this sacred ''Voice of the Nada'' is heard internally; that it is the ''Voice of the Silence,'' or the ''Soundless Sound,''— of which so much has been written, and so much mystery has been made. It is this voice, or this sound, which is soundless to an outsider, but which is distinctly heard by the person himself.

Says H. B. Blavatsky (in *The Voice of the Silence*):

''He who would hear the Voice of Nada, 'the Soundless Sound,' and comprehend it, has to learn the na-

[1] The familiar Caduceus of Mercury is said to be a symbolical expression of the Kundalini; the central rod is the Sushumna —interlaced by Ida and Pingala; the two wings at the top are the two lobes or petals of the Ajna Chakra, while the little ball at the top of the rod is the pineal gland.

ture of *Dharana*. . . . When to himself his form appears unreal, as do on waking all the forms we see in dreams; when he has ceased to hear the *many*, he may discern the ONE—the inner sound which kills the outer. . . . For then the soul will hear, and will remember. . . . And then to the inner ear will speak the VOICE OF THE SILENCE. . . . And now thy *Self* is lost in SELF,—*thyself* unto THYSELF,—merged in that SELF from which thou first didst radiate. . . . Behold! thou hast become the Light, thou hast become the Sound, thou art thy Master and thy God. Thou art THYSELF the object of thy search; the VOICE unbroken, that resounds throughout eternities,—exempt from change, from sin exempt, the seven sounds in one, the VOICE OF THE SILENCE. *Om Tat Sat*. . . ."

These sounds or phenomenal acoustic manifestations have been classified.[1]

Madame Blavatsky, again, in *The Voice of the Silence* (pp. 10–11), lists them as follows:

First: a nightingale.
Second: the sound of a cymbal.
Third: the ocean spirit in a shell; sound of rushing waters.
Fourth: the Chant of Vena,—(an Indian stringed instrument like a lute).
Fifth: a bamboo flute.
Sixth: a trumpet blast.

[1] These nada "sounds" usually proceed from the region of the Heart, but are said sometimes to be heard in the right ear. In the eighth or *Laya* state, we arrive at the "soundless" condition.

Seventh: dull thunder rumbling.

Eighth: you pass through all those and you attain *Silence,* which is the silence we wish to attain, the "Pearl of Great Price," which has been obtained after passing through these ordeals, in order to obtain these phenomena. Then you arrive at this supreme attainment.

Other writers have said that you hear buzzing sounds, the sounds of a lute, of a harp, of a bell (*a propos* this, you will remember the "astral bell" which Madame Blavatsky produced); the sound of waves, of thunder, the hum of the bee, of a metal drum, and finally *Silence.* This drum-sound is generally heard in the Ajna chakra, between the eyes.[1]

Now, if you were frankly to ask me what degree of objectivity I should attach to these sounds,—what they signify,—I should be inclined to think that they have a physiological basis, and they are due to two causes. One is the pressure of the blood, which, as we know, will produce singing in the ears and other sounds; and the second and more important is the fact that by the intense practise of *Pranayama,* tiny air-bubbles find their way into the blood, and, travelling through the circulation, produce these extraordinary sounds. Of course, I think that, *associated* with these sounds occur, very often, extraordinary psychic phenomena; but personally I should be inclined to think that these sound-phenomena have not any particular spiritual signifi-

---

[1] The *nada* is held to be "the first produced movement of the ideating cosmic consciousness leading up to the Sound—Brahman."

cance, but rather are the result of certain physiological phenomena going on in the body.

To return to the point: How to arouse the Kundalini power, Swami Vivekananda, in his *Raja Yoga* has a paragraph on this, and, in fact, he has been criticized quite extensively for giving so much information,—because, some said, it would cause harm! I have always felt that many people are great cowards, when it comes to matters psychic; for in the same way that you never make any definite advance in physics or chemistry or any other science without *experimenting* and trying things out, in the same way you do not make any advance in psychics—unless you experiment.

When I was working in Yoga systematically, people would say to me, "Oh, it's all right; you'll become insane! You'll have trouble with your lungs and your mind by following these Pranayama exercises; you'll become insane eventually!" And I would reply, "All right; I *will* become insane. But I am going to do these exercises!" And I *did* do them, and I don't think I am insane. At least, I hope not!

The point is, I think there is very little danger in giving these exercises to people, because practically no one has the persistence to follow them out! It requires great practice and concentration, for months and months, to obtain enough results to be detrimental to anybody, and by that time you have had enough experience to do them properly.[1]

Swami Vivekananda says:

[1] "Every man is either a fool or his own physician at Forty." (Proverb.)

"*Prana* means the vital forces in one's own body. *Yama* means controlling them. There are three sorts of Pranayama,—the very simple, the middle and the very high. The whole of Pranayama is divided into two parts. One is called filling; the other is called emptying the lungs. When you begin with 12 seconds in the lowest Pranayama, when you begin with 24 seconds in the middle Pranayama, that Pranayama is the best which begins with 36 seconds. That Pranayama in which there is first perspiration, then vibration of the body, then rising from the seat and joining of the man's soul with great bliss,—is the highest Pranayama. Fixing the mind on the lotus of the heart, or on the centre of the head,—this is called DHARANA."

(As a matter of fact, Dharana is not limited to that. You can concentrate on other things.)

"*Dhyana* is spoken of, and a few examples given of what to meditate upon. Sit straight, and look at the tip of your nose. Later on, we will come to know how that concentrates the mind, how, by controlling the two optic nerves, one advances a long way towards the control of the arc of reaction and so to the control of the will. These are a few specimens of meditation. Imagine a lotus upon the top of the head, several inches up, and virtue as its centre, the stalk as knowledge. The eight petals of the lotus are the eight powers of the Yogi. Inside, the stamens and pistils are renunciation. If the Yogi refuses the external powers, he will come to salvation. So the eight petals of the lotus are the eight powers, but the internal stamens and pistils are the extreme renunciation, the renunciation of all these. Inside of that Lotus, think of the Golden One, the Almighty, the Intangible. He whose name is OM, the inexpressible, surrounded with effulgent light. Meditate on that. Another meditation is given. Think of a space in your heart, and in the midst of that space think that a flame is burning. Think of that flame as your own soul, and inside that flame is another space, effulgent, and that is the soul of your soul, God. Meditate upon that in the heart. . . ."

Of the two great sources of information concerning these inner, mystic practices of the Yogis, the *Shiva Sanhita* is strangely silent. It gives almost no information of value regarding the awakening of the kundalini. The *Hatha Yoga Pradipika,* however, is more precise. Here we read:

"As Ananta, the Lord of Serpents, supports this whole Universe with his mountains and forests, so Kundalini is the main, support of all the Yoga practices. When Kundalini is sleeping, it is aroused by the favour of the *Guru,* and then all the lotuses and Granthis (knots) are pierced. Then Prana goes through the royal road, Sushumna. Then the mind remains suspended, and then the Yogi cheats death. . . . He who, with upturned face and tongue closing the hole in the palate, contemplates upon Kundalini, and drinks the clear waves of the stream of nectar, flowing from the moon in the head into the sixteen petalled lotus (in the throat), through the control over prana, during the Hatha Yoga practice,—this Yogi is freed from all diseases and lives long with a body soft and beautiful as the fibres of a lotus stem. . . . The Kundalini is de-

scribed as being coiled like a serpent. He who causes
that *shakti* to move is freed, without doubt. . . . You
should awaken the sleeping serpent Kundalini by taking
hold of his tail. Between the Ganges and the Jumuna
there sits a young widow inspiring pity. He should
despoil her forcibly, for it leads one to the supreme seat
of Vishnu. Ida is the sacred Ganges and Pingala the
Jumuna. Between Ida and Pingala there sits the young
widow Kundalini. . . . Seated in the *Vajrasana* posture,
firmly take hold of the feet near the ankles and slowly
beat with them the *Kanda.* Assuming the *Vajrasana*
posture, the Yogi should cause the Kundalini to move;
he should then perform the *Bhastrika Kumbhaka.* Thus
he will soon awaken the Kundalini. He should then
contract the sun (near the navel) and cause the Kundalini to move. Even though he be in the mouth of death,
he need not fear it. (Contracting the stomach contracts
the 'sun.') By moving the Kundalini fearlessly, for
about an hour and a half, she is drawn upwards a little
through the Sushumna. By this process Kundalini certainly leaves open the mouth, and the Prana goes naturally through it. . . . Only a Yogi leading the life of
a celibate and observing a moderate and nutritious diet,
obtains perfection in the manipulation of Kundalini
within forty-five days. Having set the Kundalini in
motion, he should practise the Bhastrika Kumbhaka
constantly. The person perfected in Yama, and practising this, need never fear death. . . .''

Arthur Avalon, in *The Serpent Power* (pp. 240–41),
says:

''The principle of all the methods to attain Samadhi
is to get the Prana out of Ida and Pingala. When

this is achieved these Nadis become 'dead,' because vitality has gone out of them. The Prana then enters Sushumna, and, after piercing by the aid of Kundalini the six chakras in the Sushumna, becomes Laya or absorbed in the Sahasrara. The means to this end, when operating from the Muladhara, seem to vary in detail, but embody a common principle,—namely, the forcing of Prana downward and Apana upwards (that is, the reverse of their natural directions) by the Jalandhara and Mulabandha, or otherwise, when by their union the internal fire is increased. The position is thus similar to a hollow tube in which a piston is working at both ends without escape of the central air, which thus becomes heated. Then the serpent force Kundalini, aroused by the heat thus generated, is aroused from her potential state called 'sleep,' in which she lies coiled up; she then hisses and straightens herself, and enters the Sushumna, when by further repeated efforts the chakras in the Sushumna are pierced.''

The whole sum and substance of the *mudras*, as a matter of fact, is simply this: That one must, while sitting in *Asana* and practising the *Pranayama*, concentrate on the chakras, in turn, beginning with the lowest and meditating on that, and then on the next, and then on the next above it, and so on,—until the seven have been passed through. The first stage is to endeavour to *feel* the position of the lotuses in the body,—to become as sensitive and receptive as possible, and then to feel, if possible, *where* that centre *is*. As the centre of consciousness is shifted, you begin to feel a stirring. You should then hold it there, meditate on that spot, and then *will* that that centre shall be aroused, by this psychic energy which is being directed to that particular centre.[1]

The point is, you should not try to develop purely telepathy, purely clairvoyance, purely astral projection, purely physical phenomena,—but rather to arouse the Kundalini by certain methods of life,—mental and physical, psychic and spiritual; and when *that* is awakened, automatically all these psychic powers will come to you. As proper progress is made in awakening this power, these other psychic phenomena will come of themselves, —of their own accord; then you will find that you are able to levitate yourself, or project the astral body, to read other people's minds, to control animals, or to become invisible, or any of the numerous things which you have read about.

The process of arousing the Kundalini may, then, be summarized thus:

Physical and mental exercises, of a specific character, arouse this power; and the power, once aroused, vivifies in turn the various chakras. Sitting in the prescribed Asana, the mind is steadied by a suitable Mudra, and Pranayama is begun. The air is inhaled and retained (Kumbhaka), being forced downward, in the body, against the lower pranic currents, which are at the same time forced upwards, by contraction of the anal muscles. Concentration, during this early period, has so far been upon Ajna; but it is now shifted to the Heart centre,

[1] "The *order* (of arousing) is, first, meditation on them, next awakening the Kundalini and Her passage to the Brahma-lotus and then her return therefrom . . ." etc. (*op. cit.*, p. 3).

and the thought (image) of a flame is held in the mind, existing in this centre.   This is now mentally projected downwards to the lowest centre (Muladhara).   Internal heat or "Fire" is thereby generated, which arouses Kundalini.   Thereupon she becomes active, pierces the opening into the Sushumna, and proceeds upwards to the second centre, which she vivifies—and so on, until all are finally aroused.

The mere awakening of the centres, however, does not in itself insure "liberation."   Even when Kundalini has reached and vivified the topmost chakra—Sahasrata, —this is not insured.   There is a constant tendency on the part of the Kundalini to return to its starting point, and work must be incessant.   Only when Kundalini takes up her *permanent abode* in Sahasrara is liberation attained.   It is said that great psychic powers are insured to the Yogi who can hold Kundali Shakti in this centre for three days and three nights steadily.

Great care must be taken to guide the Kundalini safely back again, at the close of Meditation; to its centre at the base of the spine.   For, as Avalon says, "the return of Kundalini is the setting again of the Tivatma in the phenomenal world of the lowest plane of being after it had been raised therefrom in a state of ecstasis, or Samadhi" (p. 251).   The Kundalini is therefore, as a rule, led back to Anahata (the heart centre), retained there during a period of meditation, and then led down again to the lowest centre, whence it started.   The ease with which this process is accomplished depends partly upon the will of the Yogi and partly upon the purity of the Nadis.[1]

[1] One of the distinguishing characteristics of ecstasy aroused

It must not be thought, however, that the object of arousing Kundalini is merely to produce or induce psychic phenomena. On the contrary, its prime object is to attain Cosmic Consciousness thereby—"the rousing and stirring up of Kundali in Kundali Yoga is a form of that merger of the individual into the universal consciousness which is the end of every system of Indian Yoga." It is said, indeed, that the form of union so attained is more complete than any other, and that Samadhi attained through Dhyana—pure meditation, without arousing the Kundalini—is not so perfect or so "Blissful." The Kundalini is the individualized expression of the great Cosmic Power, and the reunion or merger of the microcosm into the macrocosm represents the goal of attainment.[1]

In one sense, of course, the Hindu philosophy is a *selfish* philosophy,—simply the development of self.

But is not all religion—Christianity included—selfish in the last analysis? As Edward Carpenter says: "Religion and Morality, under the commercial régime became, as was natural, perfectly selfish. It was always: "Am *I* saved? Am *I* doing the right thing? Am *I* winning the favour of God and man? Will *my* claims to salvation be allowed? Did *I* make a good bargain in

by Kundali Yoga is the extreme *coldness* of the body. This is, of course, also characteristic of many psychic phenomena, and may be noted in the cases of materializing mediums, etc.

[1] Says Avalon: "It is to be noted that, in the Estimation of the practitioners of I undali Yoga, it is the highest Yoga, in which a perfect Samadhi is gained by the union with Shiva of both body and mind" (p. 200).

allowing Jesus to be crucified for me?'' (*Pagan and Christian Creeds,* p. 190.)

And we read that ''doing good to others is the supreme duty'' in the primary stages of Yoga.

The whole aim of Yoga is to arrive at this state of harmony,—of internal balance or adjustment,—which is also the great aim of magic and mystical practices,—to equilibriate the forces within the body to those without,—to adjust the vibrations, the general forces within the body to the external Cosmos; and when that has been brought about, then you have harmony and happiness.

There are many people who, when you mention ''Samadhi'' or ''Cosmic Consciousness'' will say: ''Oh, that is all hallucination! You are in a morbid, abnormal state, through these concentrations, breathing exercises, and so forth! You get into a sort of semi-anesthetic condition, where anything appears real to you,—in which state you deceive yourself,—as in dreams.'' But the Hindu says, ''No, it is a true state; it is as real as anything in the world, and if you do not believe it, *experience* it yourself; and then you will believe it.'' The psychologist says, ''No! I cannot experience this. I want an objective, outside proof.'' And the Hindu says, ''You can't have that objective, outside proof. *Experience* it. Then you will know.''

So there is this irreconcilable conflict between the two schools,—the objective and the subjective. One says, ''You must know from inner experience''; and the other says, ''I must know from outside experience''; and you cannot settle this argument unless you have enough of the inner experience to know that what the Hindu says is true.

Of course the Hindus, like all Orientals, are flowery

in their language. They are bombastic. They claim a great deal, and they say many things which appear to us rubbish,—and a great many things which doubtless *are* rubbish,—such as living for ever, and "He who does this is immune from all disease," and so on. Nevertheless, they possess great knowledge and know great truths.

This brings me to my last point, which is this: There are three schools of psychic development in existence—the *Yoga*, which we have been discussing; the *Occult;* and the purely *Mediumistic* or *Psychic.*

Yoga Philosophy we have now studied and know a good deal about; the mediumistic or psychic you probably know a good deal about also. Mediums depend upon becoming receptive or passive, and allowing influences to play through the organism and assume control. I have given a fairly complete account of these methods in my book: *Your Psychic Powers: and How to Develop Them.*

The Occultists,—the representatives of the Occult school,—say: "That is wrong! This extreme passivity,—this extreme receptivity to influences,—is *not* a good thing for the human Ego. It allows influences to play on and through you which are not helpful. You don't know what they are. It is to be discouraged!" In that I think they are very largely right. I think extreme mediumistic and psychic development is not helpful, and that the occultist is often correct in that point-of-view. You should retain a consciousness of self,—a control of the ego,—during psychic experiences; and this control can be obtained by Yoga practices which, as you see, are a sort of "halfway house" between the Eastern and Western schools.

It is hard to say just what is right and what is wrong in all these three methods of development; but in the same way that, in observing an exciting event, you become lost in the excitement and in the event, and in a certain sense *lose self,* yet in another sense you do *not* lose the sense of self, so, in the same way, in Samadhi, —in cosmic consciousness,—you experience this mystical state,—become one with the Superconsciousness,—but at the same time you retain your own consciousness,— experiencing the one without losing the other. This is hard to explain, but theoretically there should be a merging into the higher consciousness while retaining the "self" as a background,—without the *feeling* of self.

CHAPTER IX

"The Guardians of the Threshold"

In the present chapter, I propose to dwell, first of all, upon the ethical side of the teachings of the Hindus,— before passing on to the more practical or experimental side of the subject. Let us consider the little treatise called *Light on the Path*, which has been acknowledged to be one of the best books written on this subject. It is a series of sayings or "aphorisms" which must be taken symbolically, and the instructions which are given must be accepted, not on their face value, but with a certain inner meaning, and the ability to interpret them results from a prolonged study of Hindu and psychic science. For instance, take three sentences, such as the following:

"Desire only that which is within you. Desire only that which is beyond you. Desire only that which is un- attainable."

Apparently paradoxes! Solution:

"For within you is the light of the world,—the only light that can be shed upon the path. If you are un- able to perceive within you, it is useless to look for it elsewhere. It is beyond you, because when you reach it you have lost yourself. It is unattainable, because it for ever recedes." . . .

Of course the great founder of the Yoga system,— was PATANJALI, and *he* had a series of sayings or "aphorisms," as they are called, which outline the instructions to be followed in Yoga. He did not outline the specific exercises so much as the philosophy; and for this reason, if you read Patanjali's *Yoga System,* hoping that you will get specific instructions as to how to awaken the Kundalini, you will be disappointed. If you want that kind of information, do not get Patanjali! An illuminating Exposition of these Aphorisms will, however, be found in Mabel Collins' little book, *The Transparent Jewel.*

We now come to the question of KARMA, about which a great deal has been written. Practically, for our purposes, KARMA means CAUSE AND EFFECT,—the result of certain actions,—the consequences of deeds. KARMA is not a sort of fluidic substance which runs after a person like a dog,—as many people think,—but it is simply the result of your own actions, your own thoughts, your own emotions, your own life. In other words, it is, as I have said, cause and effect.

But KARMA is more than a physical law; it is something which is intimately bound-up with a person and his life or lives,—and follows him, as it were, from one life to another life. Of course, in that case, as you see, it is intimately connected with the doctrine of REINCARNATION,—because the Hindus contend that this life which we are now living, is but a "drop in the bucket,"—an infinitely small speck in the whole span of existence, and the doctrine of KARMA extends not only to this life —but to the *whole* of life,—as seen in its vast extensions. Therefore, in a sense, there is some truth in this doctrine that a man's life is controlled by his karma, but it is not the ordinary acceptation that most people have of it; and when you come to consider the doctrine of

REINCARNATION you will find that there are several difficulties within the problem which certainly require solution.[1]

First of all there is the old question: Why do we not remember our past lives? People say, "If I have lived before, why don't I remember my past lives?" The answer to that is that the *total* self,—of which we in this life are a mere infinitesimal expression,—is existent in a sphere of activity which is unreachable in the present life; and that we are incapable of bringing over into the physical brain our thoughts, our experiences, of past lives; and the reason for this is because there is a break between the material and the immaterial worlds, as expressed in the manifestations of consciousness through the brain.

When you come to think of it, very few of us can remember what we did today last week or even yesterday. So it is only natural to suppose that even if we had lived a previous life—with the extraordinary disconnection resulting at birth,—it would be extremely difficult, if not impossible, for the majority of people to carry-over their mental experiences and memories into this life.

Another thing: this "personality" which we now know, Theosophists believe to have been built up, as a result of our actions in this life; it is the result of our present growth,—of our environment, our reactions to

[1] See my earlier work *Your Psychic Powers: and How to Develop Them* for a discussion of this question. I again emphasize that, in what follows, I am merely stating theory or teaching, and not necessarily my own views. Each reader must form his own conclusions from the existing *data*.

it; it is the product of this life.   But the basic principle
behind it, the soul, the "X," of which we are the expression, is that vast soul of which we here are but a little
spark or offshoot; and when we die, we add to that great
soul the experiences of this life.   We supply additional
material to our *total* life,—gathered from this life; and
every life furnishes new *data* and new material with
which we supply the total self,—of which we are the
expression.   Such is the teaching.

I do not know whether I have made this clear; but the
point is that from each life we gather certain experiences, and we add these experiences to the total self,
and we consequently become richer and more experienced and more advanced with each life that we live.

Many people *can* apparently remember incidents in
their past lives.   I have met several who claim that they
can do so; and who certainly offer remarkably good evidence of the fact.   On passing into certain psychic
states, they remembered scenes,—incidents which had
previously occurred to them; and in answer to those
who would say "Merely hallucination," they say "No!
When I went to a certain place I knew beforehand what
would happen there, and what that place would be like.
I could tell that there had been a door cut in this wall
which is no longer existent; and on inquiry it was
shown that a door *had* existed in that spot";—and
many similar instances of that character,—seeming to
show that a memory of past lives is possible with certain
people who claim it.

This doctrine of KARMA, then,—to come back to that,
—contends that a man is the result of his actions, and

all that he suffers is the result of his actions; and that implies the doctrine of FREE WILL,—so in order to understand KARMA properly, we must understand this problem of FREE WILL. It is a metaphysical problem and a very difficult one, but I think it can be made relatively clear.

FREE WILL means merely that we have free choice in our actions,—which, of course, everybody who has not thought about it extensively believes. Common sense and our own inner feelings tell us that if we go out of a certain house we can turn to the right or to the left, as we choose; but those who do not believe in Free Will, —the DETERMINISTS,—say "No! Every action, every choice you make in this life, is the result of previous education, environment, mental, moral and physical upbringing; and every action you perform,—every thought you think,—is the result of previous training, and you could not possibly have thought or acted otherwise!"

For example: If you were to place a man on the edge of a precipice, and he had the tendency or the temptation to commit suicide, he might leap off the precipice and commit that act,—if certain previous stimuli in his life caused him to do so; and the DETERMINISTS say, "If you lined up a hundred men along that bank, and their previous mental and physical and moral training had been *exactly* alike, *all* those men would jump off into the river, and none of them could possibly have been able to restrain themselves! In other words, our actions are determined." That is the basis of *Determinism.*

And, the Determinists say, it must be true for this

reason: accompanying every thought there is a physical change in the brain; there is a perfectly-connected link; if you introduce *will* into this universe of ours, as a determining factor, you introduce something new,— some outside influence, into our closed system or circle, —and *that* scientists are not willing to admit! They say "No! The universe is a perfectly closed system; and it is impossible to introduce anything into it from outside,—because everything *in* it exists already. You may convert one thing into another, transform or transmute one thing into another, but everything is *there*. And they will not allow FREE WILL, because it adds or superadds an energy which we are not entitled to do. So that the great argument against FREE WILL is drawn from the doctrine of the CONSERVATION OF ENERGY.

We cannot now go into this long-disputed question of FREE WILL, because many hundreds of books have been written upon the subject, for and against, and it is improbable that we can solve it now! But I think there is a distinct tendency in philosophy and in metaphysics to support the common-sense doctrine that there *is* free-will in the world; and that is also supported, in my judgment, by certain psychic experiments recently undertaken, which show that the human will is an actual energy,—and that instruments can be definitely affected by the exertion of this will,—showing that the will is a *real force;* and if that be true, if it is an energy, a real "thing," capable of influencing our material world,— the whole objection to the doctrine of free-will vanishes! I think that one day these psychic phenomena will solve the problem of free will,—in the same way that psychic phenomena will solve the problem of the soul,—simply by facts,—by phenomena, by scientific proof.[1]

These doctrines which have been handed down to us from the East, through Theosophy, through Rosicrucianism, through the secret doctrines of all the ages,—have come to us, it is claimed, from a very old civilization,— older than Egypt,—and that is the civilization of *Atlantis*. Probably most of you know the story of Atlantis, which Plato has narrated very beautifully; but in few words it is simply that there existed in the centre of the Atlantic Ocean a vast continent, named "Atlantis," on the northern coast of which were the "Gardens of the Hesperides,"—and that it possessed a very high culture and civilization. This whole continent, after its inhabitants rose to a great pinnacle of culture, and conquered a large part of the then civilized world, sank beneath the Atlantic Ocean in an enormous cataclysm, and was entirely swamped by the waves, in the year 9600 B. C. or thereabouts; and the only parts of Atlantis which now exist are the Azores islands, which were the highest mountain-peaks of the Atlantian continent.

For hundreds of years this doctrine of Atlantis has been ridiculed by scientists; but lately there has been a great deal of scientific evidence brought forward in its favour. Professor Termier,—who is one of the official geologists of France,—has published a Report in the Smithsonian Institution, in which he says that there is a great deal of geological evidence pointing to the existence of a real Atlantis; and, apart from this, there are

[1] See my *Problems of Psychical Research*, for a discussion of this question, with the facts as to experiments, etc., undertaken.

many other evidences of the existence of some land bridge between the American and the African and European continents.

For instance, certain species of butterflies and moths and beetles and ants, and even mammals, are found to exist in South America and in China, or in South America and South Africa; and these are so far separated that, either you have to assume that there was an absolutely parallel evolution in the two continents, developing identically the same insect or beast,—which is almost inconceivable; *or* that there was some land-connection by which they could migrate, because the present stretches of water are certainly too great for any such creatures to have passed over them; and you *do* find these creatures and these insects in two different parts of the world, now widely separated, and impossible of being reached in any direct manner. So that there is a certain amount of evidence, lately brought forward, in favour of the existence of *Atlantis*.

.   .   .   .

All this ethical and religious teaching is one end of the scale of psychic practice which exists in India; the highest rung of the ladder; and on the lowest rung you find the wandering fakers, who perform miracles for a few cents, and who perform tricks which many people believe to be genuine, but which are certainly, in ninety-nine cases out of a hundred, tricks pure and simple.

These tricks consist for the most part in simple conjuring tricks,—such as growing a shrub from a seed, or causing certain balls to disappear from under little cups, or placing a boy in a basket and running the basket through with a sword—and the boy is found to have disappeared and is found up a tree in the distance; or eating coloured threads and drawing them out of the mouth; or dropping dry sand into water and putting the hand in and lifting up the sand perfectly dry;—and feats of that character. Now, these are all tricks. For instance, the "mango-tree trick" is performed in various ways, one of the most common being that the mango seed, which is about two inches long and an inch broad, is scooped out hollow, and the mango shoot,—a small branch of the tree,—is treated and watered carefully, and then rolled around itself and tucked into this hollow seed; and that seed is substituted for the genuine seed, which has been examined; and the prepared seed is placed in the ground, and covered with a cloth. The magician then places his hands underneath the cloth and manipulates the seed, working a little bit of the greenery out, and shows it; then a little bit more, and showing that, until finally the whole branch is disclosed; and when that point has been reached,—under cover of the cloth, which has been removed every time to show the little seed sprout,—he introduces a very large branch,—the fifth or sixth time, under the cloth,—the last branch being two feet high.

The dry sand trick,—just to take another example,— is performed by carefully preparing the sand in grease, —frying it, so that each individual speck of sand is covered with a little coating of grease; and when this is lumped together and dropped in cold water, the magician puts his hand in; the oil has prevented the sand from becoming wet, consequently it is still "dry," apparently, when lifted from the water. And so on.

There remains one trick which the Hindus are said to perform,—very well-known,—and which is somewhat of a mystery. That is the famous rope exploit. The magician is said to throw a rope into the air; a boy climbs up, disappears in the clouds, and his arms and legs fall down. Then the magician pastes these together, and the boy gets up, whole as before!

That is the story, which is certainly staggering enough! When first published, it was backed-up or supported by a series of photographs which were published in the *Chicago Examiner* years ago, and it was claimed that the whole thing was the result of hypnotism,—that when the camera was exposed, "which cannot be hypnotized" (as the audience was supposed to be), it showed that nothing of the sort took place. But the so-called "photographs" produced to back-up this story of collective hypnotism proved to be *woodcuts*, and not photographs at all,—so that the whole incident was a newspaper trick,—a newspaper story,—and the problem of that rope trick still remains,—whether it has really ever been performed or not. I have spoken to very many people who have lived years in India, who have tried to see this feat performed and were never able to do so; and I doubt very much whether it has ever been shown. If so, there is possibly some basis of hypnotic "glamour" in it; but it is exceedingly doubtful whether the trick, as described, has ever been shown in India, though various simpler modifications of it can certainly be seen.

Those who may possibly be interested in this subject can consult a little book of mine, called *Hindu Magic,* in which all these feats are explained.

Incidentally, I may say that the Indians,—the Hindus,—*have* certain psychic powers, of course,—even the lower class of "psychic practitioners"; and these men possess power over animals or over other human beings, and possibly are able to project their own astral bodies, —and feats of that character,—powers of telepathy and clairvoyance, leading up to the great Adepts.

. . . .

India is not the only country which practises Yoga. Every country in the past has had its system of Yoga philosophy,—Egypt, Chaldea, the Hebrews, Japan, China,—all the Oriental countries. There is a Chinese Yoga, a Japanese Yoga, a Christian Yoga,[1] and so forth; but they all are on different lines, and as this work is limited to Hindu Yoga we will not go into them.

If you will but remember that the word *Yoga* means simply a graduated system of ascetic religious practices,—coupled with scientific experiments,—you will see that it is quite possible for any country to have its own doctrine and its own system of Yoga,—along its own clearly defined lines,—all of which are more or less different.

I may also point out that it is rather a curious and interesting fact that the *type* of psychic phenomena and the *type* of ghosts in each country is entirely different. The type of Japanese ghost story, for instance, differs as widely as possible from the Zulu ghost story or the English or American ghost story; it is quite different. For instance, the Japanese ghosts are nearly all solid,

---

[1] For a good account of the Christian Yoga Practices and Doctrine, see A. K. Mozumda: *The Life and the Way:* Christian Yoga Metaphysics, 1911.

material beings,—who come back and live with humans for a period of a few hours or days or weeks; and then dematerialize one morning,—and are gone! They are quite different from our phantasmal, fleeting creatures!

A word or two, however, may be of interest regarding Persian Yoga or Magic, because it bears more or less intimately upon this subject, and also upon a subject we will consider later-on in this chapter.

After the Persian Yogi has gone through a certain number of mystical or psychic practices, he arrives at a certain state of attainment, and then he experiences a certain set of visions or psychic phenomena which it is his duty to record. The visions, which come before his eyes during the practice, will frequently be very wonderful; and after a time he will find actual "persons" before him,—such as "a radiant angel of light with a beautiful face, *El Ganee.*"

When the student is pure enough to stand the dazzling splendour of this vision without fainting, "then all knowledge of earthly matter will be given to him, for the angel will take him by the hand and lead him forth, showing to him the wonders and terrors of the world. Everybody is not strong enough to stand that terrible journey, when the evils and horrors of man are laid bare, and all the wickedness which is continually being perpetrated,—all the cruelty and misery which is hidden from civilized society unrolls before his eyes, and the bowels of the earth are open before him!"

"Then, from here, the angel takes him to other worlds or other spheres, where bright beings of celestial radiance dwell, and the secrets of the Most High become clear and definite to his intelligence. At first he will remember only part of what he sees, but after a time he will remember more and more, until his mind is able to retain all that he has seen, and all that has occurred to him in his travels."

El Ganee corresponds very nearly to the *Adonai* mentioned in *Zanoni.* That is to my mind an interesting passage, because it deals with the question of the "Guardian of the Threshold," to which we shall come a little later on. That is a mystical Being which meets the neophyte at a certain stage of his initiation or progress, and conducts him on a mystical journey, through which he mentally passes and experiences certain events. To this mystical being,—to this question of the Guardian of the Threshold,—we shall come later on in this chapter.

The Persians are largely fire worshippers, and I have thought that a few words regarding their views on *fire* might be interesting. In *The Message of Zoroaster,* there is a chapter devoted to this subject: "Why do we hold fire sacred?" It is for five or six reasons, which the author summarizes as follows: "The *first* fact we notice as we look at the fire is that it soars up,— it never burns downwards but always upwards. The *second* fact we notice as we look in the fire is that it is the most living of the four elements. The *third* fact we notice as we look at a fire is its coalescing tendency. The *fourth* fact we notice as we look at the fire is that it purifies all that it touches. Nothing can ever pollute fire. On the contrary, if fire be kept continually burning, no matter how impure or how polluted the thing may be, its scorching burn will ultimately burn-out all this impurity. The *fifth* fact we notice as we look at the fire is that by its ceaseless movement, as well as by its continually changing the nature of all that it touches, it visibly manifests the eternal change that pervades the universe. Then, *finally,* look at the fire as a symbol of God. Of all the symbols that have stirred the heart of man, is there one that can be worthily placed by its side?''

Says another author:

''God is a consuming fire. The universe is burning up. Everything is ablaze. Our bodies are ablaze, being consumed in the mighty fire of the All-Fire, GOD. It is this fire which is the cause of all motion in the cosmos.''

That sentence will be clear when we understand what fire is. *Flame* is a species of combustion; but *heat* is increased vibration; and as you increase vibration you get more nearly in touch with higher planes of activity, which function on a plane itself having an increased vibration. When you place a poker in the fire, the reason that it gets red hot is that the molecules of the poker vibrate more rapidly; and if you increase the heat, those molecules vibrate so rapidly that finally the poker won't stay solid any longer, but becomes liquid and finally gaseous,—and goes off as vapour; and the higher you go in the scale, the greater the vibratory activity and the more nearly we approach that plane of activity which has these higher vibrations. That is one of the reasons why fire, symbolically, is considered so

sacred by the Persians and these other fire worshippers;
—a very logical doctrine.[1]

Fire is also one of the tests through which the Initiate
must pass. In the past he went through certain trials
or initiations,—trial by water, trial by fire, trial by
other elements, as we know; and in the middle ages they
had these *actually*,—they caused the person to place
his hand in the fire, or placed him under water,—as
they did with the witches; if they drowned, if they
sank, they were innocent; if they floated they were
guilty! They were doomed in any case! If they
floated they were guilty; then of course they were
killed. If they sank they were innocent, but then they
were dead,—drowned. In much the same way that alchemy has an exoteric or physical or obvious interpretation,—as we shall see in a later chapter,—and also
has an inner, esoteric meaning,—so, these tests by fire
and water did not mean burning or placing a person
under water at all; but were *mental* and *spiritual* tests,
through which the neophyte must pass. (Our material
Fire corresponded, of course, to Spiritual Flame or
Light, of which I have already spoken.)

In order to make this clear, the following little story
may be illustrative. It is a "test by water" through
which the narrator, a woman, passed,—and to my mind
it is quite illuminating.

She found herself in a boat. In this boat was an in-
distinct figure whom she felt to be one who could help
her, and on whom she could depend; and she felt that
if this figure deserted her, she would be in great peril.

[1] See Clymer: *The Philosophy of Fire*, for further details regarding this interesting topic.

They floated down the river in this boat. She was, of course, afraid; she depended on this "figure" for her support. Writing of her experience at this time she says:

"I will say here that I never saw this being distinctly, and part of the time he was invisible, but I could sense his presence. Sometimes he appeared as being of light; sometimes dim. . . . Sometimes I was very conscious of his presence and of his thoughts, and at other times I was not sure that he was with me until he spoke. While he was working with the life tides he seemed to be at my head, but I could not see him; now I could hardly sense his presence and could not see him. 'Take hold of my hand,' I said, 'and do not leave me,' becoming possessed of a fear of losing him in this strange country and then be lost myself. I had lost God and that was what made me afraid, and felt that things were not right. If I could have sensed God in all this, even if I had been afraid, it would have been a different kind of fear. . . . There was a feeling that at any moment he might vanish and I be unable to find him. It was so beautiful there that I wished for more light, but instead it grew darker and the mirror-like surface of the water became ruffled and the boat began to rock a little. The shadows on the banks took strange shapes. Then a light began to grow high up on the left bank; the shadows parted on either side of the light and I beheld the crucified Saviour on the cross. Then the shadows closed again. . . . It was dark now and the water growing rougher; it was sad among the shadows, but now we seemed to have passed from the river to a wider and

wider expanse of water, and waves loomed out of the
darkness. A dreadful foreboding took possession of
me. Was it the valley of the shadow of death we had
entered, and were we out on the ocean now where it had
grown wilder, until we were wrecked? The boat lurched
dangerously, but no word was spoken by my companion.
. . . The waves grew higher and higher and a great
storm raged, and presently I found myself in the water
and sinking down, down, down. . . .

"All through this dreadful experience I appeared to
be alone; there was no consciousness of the presence of
my companion. . . . Just at the instant I said to myself, 'Yes, I am ready to die; God save me!' there was
a pause, and instead of losing consciousness I was re-
lieved, and the storm ceased. . . . Oh, joy! There was
my friend seated in the boat, calmly looking out over
the river just as when we first started. . . . And then I
recalled his words given me probably for my comfort
almost at the beginning of the dark time, 'We are never
to be separated!' How quickly I had forgotten, and
imagined I was alone! . . . The boat grazed on the white
beach, and we stepped out on to solid land. It was
such a relief to find that the *trial by water* was
over. . . ." [1]

That is an experience of an inner, mental, or psychic
character, which narrates the sort of initiatory passage
through which the soul must pass,—its various descents
and experiences. These trying and harrowing experi-

[1] "Little Journeys into the Invisible"—"A Woman's Actual
Experience in the Fourth Dimension" by M. Gifford Shine. Some
interesting experiences of this kind (tests by fire and water) are
to be found in "The Dreams of Orlow" by A. M. Irvine.

ences are common to all mystics and people who go through certain Initiations; and this most trying period, —before we see the Light,—the mediaeval mystics spoke of as the "dark night of the soul,"—where apparently no hope was to be experienced,—nothing to be gained, —everything had been trampled out of the life which had been healthful and hopeful, and nothing hopeful had yet come into it. "It is darkest just before dawn"; and in these mystical experiences this is very marked.

Those who may be interested in this subject of mysticism, and these inner experiences, will find many of them narrated in a book by Mr. J. C. Street, entitled *The Hidden Way Across the Threshold,*—also in various published books on Mysticism.

．　　．　　．　　．　　．　　．　　．　　．

We come now to one very interesting topic in connection with psychic development, and that is a discussion of the PINEAL GLAND and the PITUITARY BODY, and their occult functions. The pineal body is physiologically a ductless gland,—one of several glands in the body which do not lead out into the external environment, and are hence called "ductless"; but they have a profound effect upon the nutrition of the body, on the circulation of the blood, on growth, on sex-life, and on other inner functions of the body. These functions of the pineal gland are fairly well-known now, from the physiological point-of-view; but, apart from these, there are certain mystical and occult phenomena connected with the functioning of the glands, which have been taught in occult science for a very long time. Both the pineal gland and the pituitary body are situated in the brain—the so-called "Cave of the Mind"—the pituitary body being in the lower fore part of the brain, and the pineal gland near the centre.

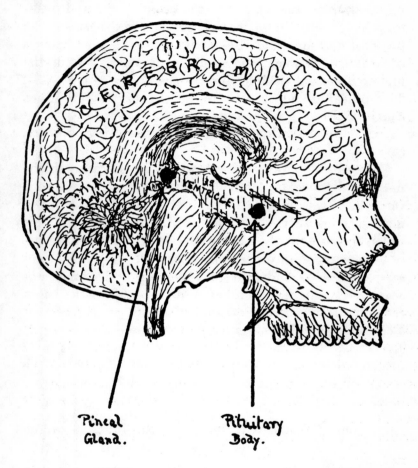

Pineal Gland.

Pituitary Body.

From the occult point-of-view, the pituitary body is the seat of the *mental principle,* and through this body or centre, the will is energized,—and it 'is, in a sense, the bridge or connecting point between the physical world and the spiritual world. Inasmuch as the blood is thought to be a stream of life force—prana—on the physical plane, these glands—the pineal gland and pituitary body—are the doorways, so to speak, between the physical and spiritual life—ATMA. . . . They are points of contact between the brain-consciousness and the higher Spiritual Self, leading to the Supreme *One*. . . . The pineal gland is said to be the organ for Inner Spiritual Feeling or Sensation.

Dr. William H. Dower, in his *Occultism for Beginners,* says:

"Molecular motions in the pineal gland cause spiritual clairvoyance, but to make this clairvoyance illumine the field of the Universal, the fires of the Pituitary body must unite with the fires of the Pineal gland, and this union means that the sixth and seventh senses have become as one, or in other words that the individual consciousness is so indrawn that the magnetic sphere of Manas—the highest mentality—and Buddhi—the highest spiritual sense, are conjoined. This is the highest Yoga, *the Divine Marriage of Matter and Spirit,* or of *Love and Wisdom.* . . . Hermes, or wisdom, is now united with Love,—Venus or Aphrodite, and on the psycho-physical plane there results an entity of perfect balance—the Divine Hermaphrodite, or the Androgyne."

Madame Blavatsky, in discussing the function of the pituitary body and its interaction or connection with the pineal gland, says:

"When a man is in his normal condition, an adept can see the golden aura pulsating in body centres, like the pulsations of the heart, which never cease throughout life,

This motion, however, under the abnormal condition of effort to develop clairvoyant faculties, becomes intensified, and the aura takes on a strongly vibratory or swinging action. The arc of the pulsations of the pituitary body mounts forward more and more until, just as when the electric current strikes some solid object, the current finally strikes the pineal gland and the dormant organ is awakened and set all glowing with pure *akasic* fire. This is the psycho-physiological illustration of the two organs on the physical plane which are, respectively, the concrete symbols of the metaphysical concepts, called *manas* and *buddhi* (the lower mind and higher mind). The latter, in order to become conscious on this plane, needs the more differentiated fire of *manas,* but once the sixth sense has awakened the seventh, the light which radiates from this seventh sense illumines the fields of infinitude; for a brief space of time man becomes omnipotent,—the past, future, space and time disappear and become for him the present. If an adept, he should store the knowledge he thus gains in his physical memory, and nothing save the crime of indulging in black magic can obliterate the remembrance of it. If only a *chela* (that is, a pupil), portions alone of the whole truth will impress themselves on his memory, and he will have to repeat the process for years, never allowing a speck of impurity to stain him, mentally or physically, before he becomes a fully initiated adept." [1]

[1] Captain Ronald Strath (M.D.), medical examiner for the British and Canadian Recruiting Mission, in New York, 1918, told me that he has made many *post-mortem* examinations of the brains of Hindus, and found that the pineal gland is, in nearly all cases, nearly twice as large, in the brain of the Hindu, as the average European.

The pituitary body is situated near the centre of the brain, and the pineal gland further back; and between the two there is a sort of bridge or connection,—that is, crossing over this bridge, a vital, magnetic current is supposed to act,—which connects the two, and sets them going in the mystical manner described.   And, as you will see, it is very closely akin to the awakening of the psychic centres or *chakras* by the *kundalini*.[1]

.   .   .   .

We now come to our final question, viz., the Meeting with the *Guardians of the Threshold*,—a mystical term employed to symbolize the encounter between the pupil seeking Initiation, and certain beings whom he encounters at one stage or another of his internal, mental progress or spiritual growth.   (The Guardian of the Threshold is also known as ''The Keeper of the Secret,'' ''The Wall,'' and ''The Destroyer.'')

Lately much has been said regarding psycho-analysis, —the analysis of dreams by a perfectly scientific psychological process which enables us to get at the real meaning and ''content'' of dreams directly.   What we remember of a dream is what is called the *manifest content*, but that is only a very small percentage of the *whole* dream; it is but the top expression, as it were, of the whole dream, which is called the *latent content*,— that is, the underlying reality of the dream, which we never normally reach or remember.   The way to reach

[1] Concentrating upon the Pineal Gland is one of the methods employed to facilitate the projection of the Astral Body. See, in this connection, two valuable articles by Oliver Fox, in the *Occult Review*, April and May, 1920; ''The Pineal Doorway,'' and ''Beyond the Pineal Door.''

the latent content of a dream is by hypnosis or by psycho-analysis,—dipping down deeply enough into the mind to get at the lower strata and reach the real dream itself,—when you will find that the dream always has meaning, always is consecutive, always expresses a certain thought, and, as Freud says, is usually some "suppressed wish."

Why, then, do we not remember the *whole* dream? The reason, psychologists say, is that there is a *censor* which represses or suppresses the dream in its entirety. What is this censor? All psychiatrists and those who deal in abnormal psychology, write very flippantly about the censor,—what it does, its functions and its actions,—but no one has had the courage to ask what the censor really *is*.

I propounded this problem to Dr. Morton Prince, of Boston,—editor of the *Journal of Abnormal Psychology,*—and the most noted exponent of this science in America,—and he replied that he really did not know, but that he supposed that the Censor consisted of a "complex" or group of thoughts and emotions which had somehow constituted themselves into a body or a being, as it were,—which took upon itself the function of censoring our dreams!

It is inconceivable, in a way, that one "star in the firmament" should be thus empowered when all the others have not those faculties at all! From the occult point-of-view, we believe that the psychologists have only half the truth,—and that what they call the "censor" is but the feeble, undeveloped manifestation of the First Guardian of the Threshold,—which acts in much the same way as the censor does. The Lesser or First Guardian of the Threshold is a being which is created by our thoughts, our emotions, our *lives,*—and is, in a sense, one might say, a *thought-form* which is brought into being by our own mental activities.   We endow it with life.   It is a mental Frankenstein,—and that mental Frankenstein, when sufficiently endowed with life,—when it has accumulated sufficient personality,—is the thing which we encounter in certain of our mystical experiences,—when we have progressed to a certain extent and travelled sufficiently far.

Steiner, in his book, *Initiation and its Results,* has given quite a detailed account of the meeting of the student with the Lesser Guardian of the Threshold, and narrated the exact words that this Lesser Guardian of the Threshold will speak to the student.   Doubtless much that he says is imagery and symbolism,—although he claims that it is actually true,—but he has exaggerated a great deal that he says, I have no doubt.

The fact remains, however, that the Guardian of the Threshold is, in a sense, an astral form which is awakened and revealed to the higher sight of the occult student, and it is this superphysical meeting with this form which constitutes the meeting with the Guardian of the Threshold.

Annie Besant speaks of three kinds of "Guardians of the Threshold": *First,* elementals, which strive to bar the astral plane against man.   *Second,* thought-forms of our own past,—which are the Guardians we have been considering.   *Third,* we have the most terrible forms—which come into being when a man has steadily identified himself with the lowest part of his being.   A curious change then takes place in him; the higher part of man withdraws itself from the lower; and at death, the highly vitalized astral and mental bodies, belonging to the dead physical body, attach themselves to the new physical body,—forming a constant and ever-present menace or Nemesis—a terrific form of astral being, which, in such cases, might rightly be called a Dweller on the Threshold, rather than a "Guardian"!

Says Steiner:

"It is one of the lesser magical performances to make the Guardian of the Threshold visible on the physical plane. To make this possible, it is necessary to produce a cloud of smoke consisting of fine substances by means of some frankincense, which is compounded with a number of ingredients of a special sort and mixed. The deeper power of the magician is then applied to mould the smoke into shape, and so animate this substance with the still unbalanced karma of the individual. He who is sufficiently prepared for the higher vision no longer requires this phenomenal sight, but he who sees this still unbalanced karma without adequate preparation, as a visible, living creature before his eyes, exposes himself to the greatest danger of falling into awful byways. The Guardian of the Threshold has been romantically depicted by Bulwer Lytton in *Zanoni*."

Now then, this lesser Guardian of the Threshold, this being, when encountered, draws the Veil, which hides the inner life of the student, and there he can see two paths before him, the right and the left,—that which leads to the good and that which leads to the evil,—and he can choose which he will follow. That, of course, is symbolic, but I have no doubt that the symbolism is an expression of truth. Of course, in our dreams, we have very much the same experiences.

This Being, which is thus created, can, it is said, be made objective or real by a magical ceremony of the kind mentioned. In fact, one of the latest scientific theories of materialization is that put forward by Professor Morselli, of Genoa,—''The Psycho-Dynamic Theory,''—and it is practically the same idea stated in other words. He simply says that the subconscious mind of the medium, in trance, is enabled to picture a form and project it into space,—and then this thought-form is capable of clothing itself, or enshrouding itself, with etheric matter to the extent that it becomes visible to the senses of those forming the circle; and Prof. Morselli has published this theory in a book which gained wide credence among scientists in Europe, shortly before the war started. So that this thought-form,—granting that it can be created,—which we will discuss in the next chapter,—might quite conceivably be objectified or rendered visible through these magical processes.

After you have passed through this first Initiation of the meeting of the Lesser Guardian, you come to the more mystical encounter with the Greater or Second Guardian of the Threshold, and about that very little has been said which is concise. The only thing Steiner says about it of value is this:

''When the individual has recognized all those qualities from which he has to free himself, his way is stopped by a sublime and luminous form whose beauty it is quite impossible to describe in human language. This meeting occurs when the organs of thinking, feeling and willing have so far loosened themselves in their physical connections that the regulation of their reciprocal relations is no longer managed by themselves, but by the higher consciousness, which has now entirely separated itself from the physical conditions. The organs of thought, feeling and will have then become instruments in the power of the human soul, which exercises its controlling power over them from superphysical regions. The soul, thus liberated from all the bondage of sense, is now met by the Second Guardian of the Threshold, who addresses him as follows:

" 'You have freed yourself from the world of sense. You have won the right to settle in the superphysical world. From this you can now work. . . . Hitherto, you have but freed yourself, but now you can go forth as a liberator to all your fellows. It shall be open for you to unite yourself with my form, but I cannot be blessed where there is yet any one unredeemed! . . . With those powers you have already won, you can stay in the lower regions of that world; but before the gates of the higher regions I stand as one of the Cherubim with fiery sword in front of Paradise, to hinder your entrance, as long as you have powers that remain unapplied to the world of sense. If you refuse to apply your powers in this way, others will come who will do so; and then will a lofty superphysical world receive all the fruits of the sense-world, but to you will be denied the very soil in which you were rooted. The world ennobled will develop itself beyond you, and you will be shut out therefrom. Then would your path be the black path, while those from whom you have severed yourself go forward on the white way.' ''

You will observe that, just as in discussing the Kundalini power, we found an interpretation of part of the story of Eve, the Serpent, and the Garden of Eden; so now we discover yet another link in our chain of interpretation—the inner, mystical interpretation of the story of the expulsion from the Garden,—and of the Cherubim who stood with fiery sword, guarding the gate of Knowledge. Viewed esoterically, mystically, it will thus be seen that the whole story narrated in Genesis is a mere exoteric account of certain inner strivings of the soul, in its upward path of development.

The Christian conception of the "Trinity" is also a symbolical conception, borrowed from the older Hindu writings. Avalon says: "There is one Spirit, which appears threefold as a Trinity of Manifested Power (Shakti). As so manifesting, the One becomes twofold, and the relation of these two makes the threefold Trinity common to so many religions." (*Op. cit.*, p. 190.) We must also remember that Ida and Pingala when they reach the space between the eyebrows make with the Sushumna a plaited threefold knot called Triveni,—and proceed to the nostrils. Here again we have a symbolic Trinity.

Those who have read Bunyan's *Pilgrim's Progress* will probably remember it as a *story;* but if you were to read it again, from the point-of-view of Initiation,—and psychic, spiritual development,—I think you would find that it is extremely illuminating, and will throw great light on all these questions.

CHAPTER X

THE RELATION OF YOGA TO OCCULTISM

WE have now given a résumé of Yoga Philosophy and of the main Yoga teachings. Of course, a great deal more could be said in this connection. For instance, a whole book, entitled *Nature's Finer Forces,* is devoted almost entirely to the so-called Tattvas, or ethers; and two or three books are devoted to breathing. Many other works would extend these Yoga practices into an Encyclopedia of volumes,—if one chose to devote that much space and work to them. But I think that in the preceding chapters I have given a fair résumé and outline of the main Yoga teachings and doctrine; and we shall now endeavour to see how these Eastern teachings connect with or dovetail into our Western ideas of science and philosophy and "psychics."

As I have said before, there are three main schools for psychical training in the world,—the *Yoga,* which we have considered at length; the mediumistic or *psychic,* —that is, our traditional training here in the West, which will be found fully described in my former book, *Your Psychic Powers: and How to Develop Them;* and the *occult,*—which is a sort of "halfway house" between the two,—inasmuch as it contends that the extreme passivity and negative conditions said to be necessary for the development of psychic and mediumistic states, are not necessary and are not beneficial;—and in that I think occultism is largely right. Like Yoga, occult-

ism and magic seek to *control* the phenomena studied.
First of all, it will, I think, be interesting to see how
the Yoga practices connect with the occult school; and
to give an outline of the occult teaching and magical
practices, and the various factors in connection therewith; and in the next chapter we shall see how these
Yoga practices connect with our psychic facts, and we
shall study, briefly, their production.   In the last chapter I propose to give a detailed explanation of the methods of "astral projection,"—that is, how the astral
body is actually projected from the physical body,—
and of all that has been written, and is known up to
the present, in connection with that.

Occultism has a perfectly definite outlook on the
world.   It has a religious school; it has a philosophy, a
theology and a science all its own.   There is an occult
philosophy, science and sociology, ethics, esthetics, science; and those of you who may be interested in this
side of occultism will find a very excellent résumé of
what the occult school teaches in a little book by Dr.
Papus, entitled *What is Occultism?*   As you know,
Dr. Papus was considered the most learned and probably the leading occultist in the world at the time of
his death.   From his book I abstract a sentence or two
which will give you an idea of what he taught:

"Occultism is the sum-total of the theories and practices, the paths of realization, that are based on occult
science.   Occultists regard man as consisting of three
principles, harmonized into a general unity.   These
principles are,—first, the physical body, regarded solely
as the product and support of the other elements; sec-

ondly, the astral body, doubly polarized, and uniting the lower (the physical) to the higher (the spiritual); thirdly, the immortal spirit.''

You will see from this that the astral body connects matter and spirit, as I have said before, in a little different way than the theosophical students conceive it, but on the same general principle.

Another author has said:

''By occultism is meant a knowledge of the finer forces of nature. The finer forces of nature are those not generally perceptible to the five senses of man. There is no sharp line between the inner, finer forces and the outer, grosser forces; likewise between the outer, material senses and the inner, spiritual senses; they merge gradually one into the other.''

At this point I must call attention to something which has not, perhaps, been sufficiently understood by the average layman, and that is that all the forces in this world are invisible, intangible—we can never sense *directly* any of the energies in the world. Even chemical energy, apparently the best known of all of them, is quite unknown in its essence,—in its inner nature.

We see only the *effects* of these forces, in our world,— the outer manifestations or the phenomena; and what we call the *noumena*,—the inner essence of the thing,— we never see. Just as we never actually see matter, or we never actually see the spirit of man,—his ''soul,''— in the same way we never see any of these energies; and all the noumena of nature are, and must necessarily be, to us invisible, because behind these manifestations is the invisible world, of which they are the expression. Therefore we can never see reality,—and the invisible is the real! All that we ever *see* is the expression of the invisible,—that is, through the five senses. There are, however, ways of perceiving reality directly and truly, —*viz.*, by superphysical vision, by higher sight or by clairvoyance. When we come to clairvoyance, we will find that it does actually see the essence of the phenomena going on before us,—in other words, the "hidden side of things," which we never see in our daily lives.

We hear much of "physical forces" in comparison with "unknown forces," so-called; but, as a matter-of-fact, there are no *known* energies in the world. Nobody knows anything about the innermost essence of even the most common energies,—chemical affinity, gravitation or magnetism. Take electricity; there is a great dispute as to the nature of electricity. We know much of its manifestations. We can control it. But the innermost nature of the thing itself is never known directly.

Occultism, then, has a perfectly definite scheme of the universe. It deals with the invisible world; but it deals *directly* and scientifically;—in the same way that our scientists, by the microscope and by the scalpel and balance, investigate the phenomena of nature,—the outer expressions,—occult scientists, by their occult "microscope" and "balance" and "knife," investigate the innermost essence of nature. Certain senses, which can be developed, can explore the innermost side of the hidden world about us. This practical side of occultism, this work in connection with occult science is *magic;* so that you will see from this that magic, *as such,* is not something terrible,—not something horrible,—not necessarily "black magic," but is the scientific investigation of the superphysical world. A *mage,* one who practised magic, was not necessarily a black magician, but a *sage.* Originally he was a wise man. Those who practised "magic" were scientists. But, of course, they earned the reputation of being "magicians" because they could perform wonders, which the mediaeval, ignorant mind could not understand.

Emile Boirac, writing on the relationship of "Science and Magic" in his *Psychology of the Future,* pp. 291–3, says:

". . . It is perfectly clear that the word 'magic' is for the scientific researcher but the provisional denomination of certain human faculties which have not hitherto been sounded. . . . It is very regrettable that science and magic are regarded as being opposed to each other, whereas in truth they complete each other advantageously. It is only in working in the two directions that one can be convinced of this; for on the one side the regularity of the magical phenomena will be recognized, while on the other will be seen the progressive magical advancement of natural science. . . . *Magnetism is the key to physical magic; mono-ideism, or the exercise of thought, joined to volition, is the key to psychological magic.*"

A very good illustration of the difference between the outer and the inner expressions of nature is to be found in *alchemy.* Our chemistry is a direct outgrowth of the mediaeval alchemy, and those who have read books on alchemy have doubtless come across the experiments which the mediaeval alchemists performed. They had various aims in view. One was to find the "elixir of life,"—one, the "philosopher's stone." Another was the "fixation of mercury," and another the single element which was at the basis of all matter.

Some of these results have now been established scientifically by our modern physical and chemical methods. For instance, we can freeze mercury solid, so that it is "fixed" for the time being, and can make a hammer-head with the frozen mercury, with which we can drive a nail. Modern chemistry has practically come to the conclusion that all our various chemical elements are but the different manifestations of one underlying element; and Sir William Crookes proposed, more than fifty years ago, the name *prothyl* for this single, underlying substance.

The philosopher's stone, which changes everything to gold, and the elixir of life, we have yet to find! If we look through the alchemical records, we find that many of the alchemists were, of course, chemists. They were exploring this realm of nature. And that, to the ordinary reader, was what alchemy meant. But to the initiated all these experiments which were described by the alchemists did not mean investigations in chemistry or in physical matter at all. Esoterically interpreted, they meant the discovery and progress of the soul, through certain initiations and practices. In the same way that mystical experiences enable one to find oneself, to develop the inner nature, so this "alchemy of the soul" aimed at the same thing.

Mr. Redgrove, in his work on *Alchemy,* points this out very clearly at the beginning of the book:

"According to this view (this is, the esoteric view), the phenomena of the transmutation of the base metals into gold symbolized the salvation of man,—the transmutation of his soul into spiritual gold, which was to be obtained by the elimination of evil and the development of good, by the grace of God; and the realization of that salvation or spiritual transmutation, may be described as the 'new birth,' or the condition of being known as union with the Divine."

Here, you see, we come very closely in touch with mysticism,—with all occult training in various schools. The aim is, however, concealed throughout, under symbolic language.

In another little treatise, entitled *The Riddle of the Sphinx,* we find a statement, and at the same time a very excellent summary, of the main alchemical symbolism:

"To him who shall read this book and ponder its symbols understandingly, will have come great fortune. Having sacrificed the animal, conquered the goat of Mendes, possessed himself of the powers of the Trident, plucked the rose from the cross, solved the riddle of the universe, seen the phoenix rise from its ashes, performed the Great Work, built the temple without hands and the sound of hammer, achieved the transmutation of metals, become possessed of the philosopher's stone, placed the stone which the builders rejected but which became the head of the corner, solved the problem of perpetual motion, cast a horoscope of all being, squared the circle, and, having become master of the Great Art, he will have solved the mystery of time, space and form, and all that which is behind and in, and through time and space and form. He will have ascended to the high place in the Mount of Olives,—whence he will have recovered the Lost Word, and thence be enabled to pronounce the ineffable name of the Deity."

What does all that mean? Extremely symbolic language. "Sacrifice the animal" means the animal nature of man. What is the "goat of Mendes"? Man is represented as a pentagram, his feet on the ground and his head squarely placed in the zenith above, the two arms extended. This figure reversed is the head of the goat, and signifies that the animal is paramount over the spiritual. To "conquer the goat of Mendes" is to triumph over the animal, by reason of the spiritual nature.

What is the "power of the trident"? Life, love and intelligence,—three-fold. "Pluck the rose from the cross"; what does that mean? All sentient life is upon a material cross. When the spiritual part becomes the ruling factor, in its nature, it has lifted itself above the burden of the earthly conditions, and therefore of the cross.

The sphinx represents the mystery of existence. The "phoenix arising from its ashes," of course, typifies the traditional legend of the phoenix,—but also is intended to symbolize the raising of the immortal soul of man from the ashes of the body.

The "Great Work" is the building of true character.

"The building of the temple without hands" signifies the building of the spiritual, from within. The "transmutation of metals" is the transmutation of character, from the grosser metals into pure gold. "The philosopher's stone,"—truth,—the love of that which is just and right for its own sake, is the wonderful stone which reveals all life. The "stone which the builders rejected" is the spiritual nature of this stone.

"Perpetual motion,"—life is an eternity of motion. To understand this fact is to solve the problem of perpetual motion, for life is eternal. The "great art";— he who overcomes earthly desires, to the extent that he dominates them, has achieved the greatest art.

The "Mount of Olives" is the place of peace, within one's own soul. The olive throughout the ages has been the true symbol of peace. To "recover the lost word" is to realize the oneness of the individual self with the all-self,—to know what unity is, and that there is nothing outside it.

"To pronounce the ineffable name of Deity" is to become so completely at one with *the One* that there is no shade of inharmony." [1]

These few mystical interpretations will give you an idea of the inner symbolism of alchemy,—what they were writing about throughout the middle ages. It enables us to see that the mediaeval alchemists were trying to accomplish the same things as the Yogis, as the occult-

[1] "The 'end of the world' comes to him who has passed from the 'lower' or 'world consciousness' into the state of spiritual enlightenment from whence his view of being is changed from the 'without' to that of the 'within.' To such an one the 'millennium' has dawned, and the 'transfiguration' has taken place."

ists, as the mystics of all ages,—the saints and seers,—all endeavouring, by different routes and different means, to achieve the perfection of self, the cultivation of the spiritual domination and the attainment of cosmic consciousness.

Unfortunately, of course, magic became degenerate,—in the same way that everything good can be abused; and then we merge into black magic and grey magic,—which is a little less than black,—as distinct from white magic, which is the pure and unalloyed.

BLACK MAGIC set about attaining certain worldly desires by magical means, by practices. Magicians sought —what humanity has always sought—love and money; and they had various devices to achieve these two ends. To attain the love of another, they concocted certain "love-potions" or "filters,"—called the *Powder of Sympathy* and other names. I give here a formula of one of these preparations, a love potion.

"The wise men of old knew well the value and power of love potions; and in the middle ages we find signs of their uses and virtues; but today their virtue seems to be lost sight of,—it has become a 'lost art,' like Egyptian mummification, and only here and there do we find a man who, living hermit-like, has preserved the ancient wisdom in all its perfect glory. From one of these men, wise in the occult wisdom of the East, we have procured the following formula (all this is from an old book):

"To compound an effective love-potion, the following substances must be gathered, in complete silence, by the light of the full moon, high in the heavens:

"Three white rose leaves.

"Three red rose leaves.

"Three forget-me-nots; and

"Five blossoms of Veronica.

"If they can be picked fresh, in this way, their charm is of great strength.   If you live where you cannot pick them, and can only obtain them at second hand, they should be procured as fresh as possible, then opened by moonlight and sprinkled with water, in which has been placed three drops of some perfume.   Having obtained your leaves and flowers, you must place them in a glass vessel, and pour over them 295 drops of clear Easter water,—that is, water gathered from a river or pond on Easter morning; then place the vessel over a spirit-lamp and allow the water to come to a boil.   Boil for the sixteenth part of an hour.   When it has boiled the requisite time, remove the glass vessel, pour the contents into a clean flask and cork tightly.   Seal it so as to prevent any air from getting to the contents for at least twenty-four hours.   At the end of that time uncork it, and administer three drops to the person whose heart you desire to secure.   The effect, if rightly performed, is unfailing!''

But, of course, when you come to figure out "the sixteenth part of an hour,"—for it is extremely essential that it should be boiled exactly that length of time,— you will find it necessitates boiling so many minutes and seconds, and a small fraction of a second, and of course that renders it practically impossible for you to boil it *just* the right time; and if the formula fails, they say, "Oh, but you did not give *precisely* the right time to boiling!''

We now come to WITCHCRAFT, which is a sort of off-shoot or branch of magic,—and which flourished, as you know, for several hundred years throughout Europe and America.

Witches were supposed to be beings whom the devil had touched, and with whom he had a compact. Witches had the power of making other people ill,—causing them actually to wilt and die, by putting "spells" and "curses" on them, and by other diabolical methods. They also had the power of leaving their physical body, and travelling, on a certain night every year, to a rendezvous, which was called the *Witches' Sabbath*. The Witches' Sabbath was held at the junction of four roads; all the witches being gathered together, the devil appeared in person and the Sabbath began. You can find in many mediaeval books a description of this physical orgy. The "Sabbath" was described minutely by many of the witches, even under torture; and they swore, in their last moments, that they had really visited the Sabbath, and that the things described really took place, —from which we can hardly doubt that they really *thought* that they had been there. This does not say that they had actually been there;—in fact, their physical bodies had frequently been proved to be lying at home in bed; but the doctrine put forward was that some "devil demon" had entered their bodies while their spirit had travelled to the Sabbath!

In order to secure this trance-like condition, enabling the astral body to leave the physical, the witches rubbed themselves over with a special preparation known as *The Witches' Unguent*. It doubtless contained drugs, which, when soaked into the pores of the skin, induced insensibility and hallucinations,—these being coloured by the times in which they lived and the beliefs current at that particular period.

I have a formula of one of these witches' unguents. It is said to be made of "poisonous lettuce," hemlock, nightshade, mandragora (Mandrake), poppy, henbane, serpent's blood, and the blood of unchristened children! This formula is taken from the *Romance of Leonardo da Vinci*. A certain incantation had to be said, after this was rubbed on the body,—which was this:

> "Emen hetan, emen hetan, palu baalberi astaroth,
> "Help us!
> "Agora, Agora, Patrisa,—
> "Come and help us!"

After which they were supposed to fall insensible and visit the Sabbath.

The methods of "bewitchment" which were employed at that time were curiously similar to those which have prevailed in all ages; and if you will read the history of witchcraft in Ancient Egypt, in China and Africa,— all over the world,—you will find that the methods for "bewitching" are more or less the same.[1] The chief method of bewitching is to construct a little waxen image or figure, representing the person you desire to bewitch; then slowly to melt this figure before a fire, or stick it full of pins, and as this effigy is melted or pierced through with pins, the person it represents is supposed to become ill and die. That you will find all through the ages,—even among the Bushmen of Australia, who

[1] In Hayti and Africa and the Southern American states, among the negroes, we find Voodoo—a terrible form of "Bewitchment," about which much could be said.

were totally disconnected for hundreds of years from all other tribes by the stretch of water between Australia and the mainland.

Other very similar methods which were used for ''bewitching'' were: to work on a picture or portrait or photograph of the person you desire to bewitch (these methods are used now), or by a reflection in the mirror, or the shadow of the person. This shadow method is one which is said to be much used in India, by the lower class of Hindus.[1]

As an offshoot of this black magic,—that is, the evil side of magic and occultism,—we have the practice of Satanism,—devil worship,—resulting in the Black Mass, which is said to be practised in Paris, in Malay, in India, in New York and in London.

In this connection, I will narrate a rather curious story, which was told me by a friend who attended one of these black masses in Paris, and who contends that it is absolutely true. He was led, blindfolded, through a number of underground tunnels, and there,—when he reached the sub-subcellar of a house which he did not

[1] Methods of countering these spells have been devised: Banishing Rituals; Blessings; Prayer; exorcism; charms and Amulets; various occult practices; the employment of certain Herbs —such as Laurel leaves, garlic, etc.; burning powders and incense,—of which the following formula is said to be especially potent:—

Pure spirits of wine—90% pure alcohol: coarse rock salt, dissolved in the alcohol—one teaspoonful to each 8 ozs.: Frankincense and Myrrh, also stirred in and dissolved. This compounded mixture must be burnt in an *iron* vessel, and the incense—like smoke inhaled by the exorcisor, as well as allowed to fill the room. It will be found highly stimulating in its properties.

know,—was a long table spread, and around it a number of men in evening clothes, with masked faces. They were all standing around the table. Suddenly, at the far end of the room, the black portières were parted; a man issued forth, held up his right hand and said, "He is here!" At that moment my friend experienced a blinding flash of light, and lost consciousness! He recovered several hours later, and found himself on the floor. No one else was in the room; he had no sensation of pain,—no knowledge or feeling that he had been attacked or stunned in any way; but the fact remained that he had suddenly become unconscious, for no apparent reason, at that moment, and remained unconscious for a long time. He finally found his way out of these passages into the light, and escaped.

Those who may be interested in all this can find records of experiences of this kind in a book by A. E. Waite entitled *Devil Worship in France;* and one, in French, by M. Lancelin, entitled *My Experiences with the Devil.*

We now come to one rather curious side of occultism, and that is the occult interpretation or significance of blood. You remember that when Faust signed his compact with Mephistopheles,—in *Faust,*—he signed it with his own blood,—and that is true of most of these occult agreements. Many "pacts" which are signed between people,—perhaps from motives of superstition,—are signed in the same way.

However, occult science says that there *is* a real, occult principle within the blood, that it is not a mere chemical compound, but a *vital essence,*—in fact, "the blood is the life," to use an old saying,—and that if you get control of a person's blood you thereby have a certain influence over him; and that is why Mephistopheles insisted on employing Faust's blood. Steiner, in his booklet devoted to this subject, says:

"Occult science says that the etheric body changes the food we eat into vital fluids, and the astral body transforms these vital substances into sentient substance (thinking substance), the raw material of our thoughts, as food is the raw material of our bodies. Blood is therefore an outward symbol or expression of the vitalized etheric body of man,—just as the brain and the spinal cord are the expression of the vitalized astral body. In the same way that the etheric body turns material food into living form, so the astral body, from this vital essence, furnishes a series of inner experiences, which take the form of crude mental pictures of the outer world. When this inner change extends to the etheric body, *blood* is formed. Thus the blood stands midway, as it were, between the inner world of sentience and experience and the outer world of form. It forms the connecting link between the two. The life and memory may be said to be stored within it. It is the physical expression of man's life. Thus, whoever wishes to obtain power and mastery over a man must first obtain power over his blood,—must influence it. Here we have the practical fulfilment of the myths and legends of old times, which always said 'That which has power over the blood hath power over thee!'"

This, of course, is not indorsed by science, but it is the occult tradition; and I give it for what it may be worth, because it is certainly interesting.

Black magic, of course, depended upon the evocation of certain spirits, or demons, and those of you who are interested can find the formulas, the processes, described in various books,—notably in Mr. Waite's work, *The Book of Black Magic, and of Pacts.*

These ''demons'' were summoned by certain magical words, by ceremonies, practices, and by the employment of *sigils* or signatures; by employing these, and pronouncing certain *Words-of-Power,* and going through certain ceremonies,—these demons or evil spirits were summoned and bidden to do the work or will of the magician. The beings who were summoned, in most cases, were sometimes evil spirits, and sometimes ''elementals,''—which must not be confused with ''elementaries.'' Elementals are nature spirits; they are not human beings and never have been,—according to occult teaching; but elementaries are the cast-off astral shells of those who were once human beings, now ''galvanized'' into life. The doctrine is that after a man dies he sloughs off his physical body and assumes the etheric; and after a while this etheric body is in turn sloughed off, and he withdraws to the astral, and for a time this etheric body kicks around the etheric world as a sort of inanimate shell,—before it finally disintegrates, in the same way that the physical body disintegrates; and that during this process of etheric disintegration, this body can be seized upon and manipulated by other intelligences which dwell in it, for the time being, and use it for their purposes. This body is that which appears very often,—it is claimed,—at séances, impersonating other spirits; and it is the basis of many of the legends and traditions of the mediaeval ages, of the *in-*

cubi and *succubi* and "demon lovers," and other semi-material spirits, which came back to torment beings in this world and to "obsess" them.[1] All this is very closely connected with the doctrine of the *vampire*. In the Balkan states, particularly, you will find to this day a belief in the "vampire,"—which is a being said to come back after death and live on the blood of living beings. It is said that when their graves are exhumed these vampires are found to be full of fresh blood, and in no way decomposed! The only way to kill them is to drive a stake through the heart, cut off the head, and then burn the body!

The process of evocation of the dead is really necromancy, sorcery; and this is quite distinct from psychic experimentation, on the one hand, or pure magic, on the other,—in the same way that witchcraft practices are distinct from the higher magical and occult and psychic practices of our own day. It is a perversion of a truth, of a science,—and all magic and occult doctrine should not be condemned because of the practices of the few.

Another belief which is interesting, in connection with occult teaching, is the doctrine of FAIRIES. This is a very wide term. There are, for instance, the "nature spirits,"—the gnomes, who live in the earth; the salamanders, who live in the fire; the Undines, who live in the water; and the sylphs, who live in the air. There are also many other types of fairies. To us, of course, "fairy stories" represent pure childhood imaginings,—superstition; but in this connection it is interesting to know that Mr. Wentz has published a book entitled

[1] See *Heavenly Bridegrooms* by Theodore Schroeder,—being "An Erotogenetic Interpretation of Religion."

Fairy Faith in Celtic Lands, in which he collected over a hundred first-hand cases of people who asserted they had seen fairies, in Ireland and Scotland and North France. These first-hand cases, whatever their scientific value may be, are certainly very curious and very interesting. Apart from them, there is a certain scientific basis for many fairy stories,—as there is for all psychic and occult tradition.

If you study fairy stories, and analyse them, you will find that there are certain factors which are perfectly intelligible to us, in the light of present-day science. For instance, cases of castles or palaces which spring up overnight and again disappear,—as you frequently find in the *Arabian Nights.* Doubtless this was a species of positive or negative hallucination. We can cause a person to see something which is *not* there, or we can cause him *not* to see something which *is* there. Hypnotize a subject, and say to him, "You cannot see that book on the table. You can see everything else, but not that book!" If he is in the proper hypnotic state, he can see everything else but will fail to see the book; and, on the contrary, he will see things which are not there! So that the "fairy," on this theory, would be enabled to cast a sort of spell or "glamour" over the senses of certain people, and cause them to see things which were not there; and this she could do, by waving the magic wand and by other ceremonies,—in other words, hypnotizing the subject.

Also, we hear a great deal of giants and dwarfs,— huge beings and tiny beings; but present-day science, which depoetizes everything, explains these very large or very small people by saying they suffer from certain defects of nutrition,—the functions of certain glands in the body are disturbed, and we have "gigantism," so called,—and "dwarfs."

The case of the "sleeping beauty" is simply one of a long trance. Certain poisons are found to have been utilized in many of the fairy stories. Cases in which objects are moved, without apparent cause,—for instance, where the objects on a table move themselves, or are moved, from one place to another,—are very strikingly confirmed by certain mediumistic séances,—for example, those of Palladino.

Sir Oliver Lodge has given a case in which two glass decanters on the table rose up, knocked against one another, and without any visible hand touching them, poured out a glass of water, into an empty glass, which rose into the air, and finally lifted this glass of water to his lips for him to drink! That, of course, is very similar to many of the fairy stories. In fairy stories, we also have cases in which people become visible and invisible at will,—put on the "cap of invisibility," and this again is very similar to the hallucinations which we have spoken about,—*negative* hallucinations. There are certain occult teachings, in connection with this, which show that invisibility is produced by the controlling of the ether surrounding the body. We have learned before that we only *see* any object because it reflects certain light-waves; and if those light-waves are interfered with,—destroyed,—that object becomes invisible; and the magician, or the person who becomes invisible, at these times, is supposed to possess the occult power of destroying these ether-vibrations, and hence becoming invisible at will.

In Occultism, there are detailed practical directions,— which have been given,—for the production of insurance of invisibility.   Here are the essential requirements, and an outline of the formulae employed.

The requirements are:

A. The shroud of Concealment.
B. The Magician.
C. The guards of concealment.
D. The astral light to be moulded into the shroud.
E. The equation of the symbols in the sphere of sensation.
F. The Invocation of the Higher; the placing of a barrier without the astral form: the clothing of the same with obscurity through the proper invocation.
G. Formulating clearly the idea of becoming invisible; the formulation of the exact distance at which the shroud should surround the physical body; the consecration with water and fire, so that their vapour may begin to form a basis for the shroud.
H.   The beginning to formulate mentally a shroud of concealment about the operator.   The affirmation aloud of the reason and object of the working.

These preliminaries having been settled, the actual process, the magical operation, begins.   I cannot here enter into the details of the process,— which it would be inadvisable to give, in a general book of this character, to those unprepared to conduct or carry-out the required operation skilfully and successfully.   It need only be said that certain conjurations and ceremonies are undertaken, certain mystical and Holy names pronounced, an intense effort of Will is made,—and, as the result of this, the operator is said actually to become invisible,—by reason of the shroud of darkness which he has gathered about himself, and which effectually conceals him from the ordinary sight of those about him. In a very similar manner, certain magical "transformations" are effected—this again reminding us of the earlier witchcraft practices, and also of "fairy tales,"—in which the witch, or the subject of the fairy-spell, was frequently transformed into some animal (so it was said), by the occult power of the enchanter or enchantress.

Magic depends, for the production of its phenomena, upon two factors,—the occult use of the will and the projection of the astral body; that is, the utilization of what is called the "astral light." This astral light is not a "light" at all. It is a misleading term. It really means a fluidic, plastic substance, capable of receiving and storing and retaining impressions,—so that every action we perform, every thought we think, is recorded on this plastic "astral light"; and that, under certain conditions, it is possible to reread the marks or pictures left in this astral light by the actions, the thoughts, the deeds and the words of those who have lived here. Hence we have what is called the "cosmic picture gallery,"—that is, a series of pictures or impressions left in this astral light, by those who have lived in this world.

"*Astral Light* is the important factor in these investigations. It is closely related to the 'radiant matter' of modern chemists, and the 'ether' of physicists. According to a prominent Hermetic philosopher, 'astral light is the universal plastic mediator, the common receptacle of vibrations of motion and of the phantoms of form.' It is likewise the OD of the Hebrews and the learned Baron von Reichenbach; the great Thelesma of Hermes Trismegistus. The control of this force constitutes the great Arcana of practical magic. When the universal light magnetizes the Universe, it is called astral light; when it forms metals, it is denominated Azoth, or the mercury of the sages; when it gives light to animals, it is termed animal magnetism. The astral undulations determine the position of atoms or neutralize them. Herein lies the secret of transmutation, and it becomes the privilege of the Hermetist to acquire the power of controlling this agent.'' (*The House of the Sphinx,* by Henry Ridgely Evans, p. 66.)

We have dwelt long enough on black magic; but this is the side of magic which is usually known. We might say a few words now in connection with WHITE MAGIC, —which is pure magic, or the endeavour to utilize the forces of nature for good purposes.

White Magic consists in using the highest forces, in conjunction with helpful, outside intelligences. Throughout magic there is a certain symbolism, the same as there is in alchemy. In magic, certain paraphernalia are employed,—the circle, the lamp, the sword, the oil, the book, and so forth. I will give you a list of these essentials, also what they signify,—when you will see that the magical paraphernalia all represent inner mental or spiritual phenomena, in the same way as they did in alchemy.

The *temple* is the external universe. The *circle,* drawn on the floor for magical ceremonies, represents the nature of the great work.   The *altar* symbolizes the solid basis of the work,—or the fixed-will of the magician.   The *scourge,* the *dagger* and the *chain* symbolize the sulphur, mercury and salt of the alchemist,—and these again, certain spiritual qualities.   The holy *oil* is the aspiration of the magician.   The *wand* signifies the magical will,—wisdom.   The *cup* represents understanding,—heavenly food.   The *sword* is the analytical faculty, which penetrates everything.   The *pentacle* is the earthly food.   The *lamp* signifies the light of the pure soul.   The *crown* is the attainment of the magician's work,—his ultimate realization.   The *robe* is that which conceals.   (This robe differs according to the grade of the magician.)   The *book* is a book of conjurations, and is a record of every thought and deed of the magician.   The *bell* is the summons that alarms,—and in this connection you must remember the "astral bell" of the theosophists.   The *breastplate* or *lamen* symbolizes the secret keys of his power; and the magic *fire,* as symbolized by incense, is that into which all things are cast. (In the last chapter we learned something of the magical properties of fire,—its spiritual qualities.)

Magic seeks to *control* phenomena instead of being controlled by them.   Certain preparations are necessary; and the best preparations begin from within.   Experienced magicians will tell you to begin with a course in Yoga,—by which you learn centralization, control of self, steadying of the mind, poise, equilibrium, balance, and so forth; and then, when you have controlled the forces within yourself you are entitled to begin the attempt to control those without.

White magic has been defined as "the highest science"

by Dr. Franz Hartmann.   It deals, as we have said before, only with noumena,—that is, realities, invisible things; and not with phenomena, which are illusions. Orthodox science deals only with phenomena or illusions; hence occult science is the highest science of wisdom.   It deals with the forces of the spirit.

One of the practical objects of attainment is the creation of thought-forms, by the magician; and the analogy that has always been put forward is this: in a magic lantern, you have the light, you have the slide on which the picture is painted, and you have the projected image on the screen, in the outer world.   The human will is the light,—the driving power; the mental picture held in the mind corresponds to the image on the slide; and the thought-form, the created external being, in the outer world, is that which the mind has actually created; it corresponds to the image on the slide, in the magic lantern.   In this way, we can conceive that forms are actually *created*,—brought into being,—by the power of the mind; and here we touch upon the phenomena of thought photography,—in which thoughts have apparently been impressed, directly by the power of will, upon photographic plates.

Just a word in conclusion, regarding thought photographs.   It is, of course, inconceivable to us, at first sight, *how* thought can exist in outer space.   So far as we can see, it is intimately connected with our own brain, our own thinking organization's capacities.   "How is it," as William James expresses it, "that thought can exist as an independent variable in the world?"   Are thoughts *things*,—as the "New Thoughters" have contended?   Well, if a thought be sufficiently objective to be photographed, if it can create a swirl or movement in the ether outside the brain, in space,—and recent researches seem to show that it can (doubtless through the molecular action of the brain), it must be far more objective, far more "real," than we have been in the habit of supposing. Thought-photography has thus gone far towards proving the reality of "thought-forms."

Exactly *how* all this is done we do not know,—except that it is probably through the instrumentality or intermediary of a fluidic, vital emanation, issuing from the body. This vital emanation seems to come directly from the etheric body, and not from the physical body, —because experiments show that it has no definite connection with the nerve plexuses or centres, or the nerve-endings. All of which seems to show us that thought is a very tangible and a very real thing; and brings us, also, to the point where we come in direct contact with our better known, though not better understood, psychic phenomena,—of which we will treat in the next chapter.

CHAPTER XI

The Relation of Yoga to "Psychics"

The last chapter dealt with the relationship of Yoga to Occultism, and I tried to show some of the connecting-links between the Yoga practices and the facts and methods of occult teaching,—Magic being the practical part of occultism; and we took up some of the magical practices and their symbolism, and tried to show the connection between these Yoga methods and the occult doctrines.

We will now consider some of the psychic phenomena of the West, and see if we cannot trace the relationship between Yoga and psychic phenomena in the same way.

The first thing we must remember, and understand, very clearly is that, *the unseen is the real.* Most people feel that if they cannot *see* a thing it does not exist—it is not real in the same sense that visible things are; and, of course, in this sense-world of ours, real things *are* visible,—otherwise they would not be "real" to us; but there is a whole category of realities which are quite invisible, although they are equally real. A very important point, I think, to bear in mind is that a thought is as much a reality as a granite mountain; an emotion or a feeling is as great a reality. It is not a visible, tangible, material thing; but it is a reality.

Now, the materialistic doctrine says that matter and energy are the only things in the world; that the interaction of matter and energy are the fundamentals out of

237

which our universe is built; that there is nothing in the universe which is real except matter and energy, and their interactions.   But Huxley admitted very frankly that there is, as he said, a "third thing" in the universe, which is neither matter nor energy,—and that is *consciousness;* so that the mind of man, for one thing, is a reality which is not visible and yet real.   And when we come to think of it,—all reality, all truth, the "essence" of everything, is invisible; all that we see of any energies are their *effects,*—the energies remain invisible; and we have previously seen that matter is only an expression or bundle of phenomena, representing certain realities behind.   The thing to do is to get at the truth by seeing behind this visible veil, into the realm of realities, which we cannot do through the senses.   We "sense" reality,—not through the senses, but through some higher faculty.   Life is certainly a great reality, and yet it is invisible to us.   And this brings us to the question of *life and death.*

One of the greatest problems in biology is the nature and the essence of life.   No one knows precisely what life *is.*   There is a story told of Thomas Edison.   When he was once talking with a very materialistic German scientist, the latter said: "We have now explained practically everything in the universe"; and Edison moved his finger, and said, "Can you tell me what makes that work?"   And the German scientist had to admit that he could not!

You might explain the whole intricate theory of the movement of the bones by the muscles and tendons, and the nervous impulses which move those muscles; but when you come to the connecting-link between the nervous impulse and the will to move it, there is an "impassable gulf" which we cannot bridge,—the *will* being apparently an intangible thing, and the nerve a tangible, physical thing, what is the bridge or connection between those two?

It is merely one aspect of the old problem of the interrelation of mind and matter, which we discussed before. At death, in any case, this life-principle seems to depart from the body. The materialistic theory is that it is snuffed out, like the flame of a candle. The psychic theory, we might say, is that it is *withdrawn;* and it is a question of fact, which of these two theories be true; whether it is extinguished, or whether it is withdrawn; and it is very important, because one leads to obliteration and the other does not. Are there any facts which tend to support one theory rather than the other?

There are numerous facts tending to point to the conclusion that consciousness is withdrawn and not extinguished. Some of the most interesting of these facts are the following: A number of experiments have shown to us that a dying person can be conscious up to the moment of death; the consciousness, the intellect, is perfectly clear, and the individual seems to be conscious of dying up to the very last second.

Now, if consciousness were being obliterated, it would be inconceivable that consciousness could be capable of perceiving its own extinction; but if, on the contrary, it were being *withdrawn,* we could understand that it might be conscious of its withdrawal. Again, there are cases of so-called "visions of the dying," in which dying people have seen visions of dead relatives and friends, who have apparently come to them,—the dying person, in some instances, not knowing that the people they saw were really dead,—though as a matter of fact they were.

After the moment of death, also, many psychic manifestations take place,—as we all know. There are apparitions of the dying,—apparitions which appear to individuals at great distances; and after death this individual consciousness can apparently come back and communicate with us,—the "living"—through the instrumentality of certain peculiar individuals, known as "psychics" or "mediums."

The question may here be raised; why, if communication of this sort be a fact, cannot this person return to *me?* Why cannot he come back to me, if he can come back through a medium? That might be answered by simply saying, "Why does electricity travel along a copper wire and not a board fence?" Because one is a "conductor," and the other is not. The psychic happens to be a conductor for psychic energy. And that is an answer to another objection that has been raised: why more communications did not come from the soldiers in France?

Thousands of souls were shot into the invisible world; why did not more come back? Well, in the first place, I think that more did come back than we know; and, in my book, *Psychical Phenomena and the War,* I collected a large number of cases of this character,—communications, apparitions, and so forth. A large number of cases of this kind *did* occur. However, assuming that the cases are *relatively* infrequent, the answer is that not every one that wants to communicate *can* communicate. The ability to send messages from the spiritual world may be as rare as the ability to receive them. You may have to have some psychic capacity to send messages. No matter how much you may long to, you cannot communicate in all cases,—in fact, very rarely.

After this conscious entity, this "something" in man which apparently survives death, has passed into the next world, then, the question arises as to what the nature of the next life is,—and that has been the subject of many volumes! One often hears the criticism of spiritualistic literature, "If there are spirits that come back, they should be able to tell us something useful about the next life!" Those who make this objection, as a rule, do not know that there are dozens and dozens of volumes which give precisely, in the most detailed outline, the nature of the spirit-world. Unfortunately, many of these volumes disagree fundamentally; and we can only assume that they represent some sort of reality by thinking that these "communicators" have, in most instances, simply given their own views,—their own prejudices and beliefs.

The next life is certainly a mental world of some sort; and we know that in our dreams we create a mental world in which we live, and we create our own environment very largely. Now, the next world has been called a "rationalized dream world," in which we create our mental environment; we see things as we create them, as we want them, very largely. Consequently we see the things that we believe and create, —until we realize the fact that we *are* creating the world in which we are living.

If that were true, it would explain to us very largely

the nature of the disagreement between these messages. Many spirits come back and say that reincarnation is true. Many come back and say it is not true! And the probable explanation is that those who say it is true believe it, and those who say it is not true believe it; neither has much experience, and consequently we must form our judgment entirely upon other facts.

Of course, the question of whether "spirits" come back or not, is not to be settled by dogma or argument or by prejudice, but by *fact;* and I have often made this point: that Christianity, as a doctrine, is founded upon a *psychical phenomenon,*—the resurrection of Christ;—not upon any hearsay or upon any authority. St. Paul himself said, "If Christ be not risen, then is our teaching vain; then is your faith also vain";—from which you see that Christianity is based on a psychical phenomenon,—the same sort of thing that we see today.

To return, however, to the nature of the next world. The Theosophists have a very clear-cut view. They state that there is an "astral" world, and this astral world is made-up of three classes of beings: *the dead,*—that is, human spirits; *the non-human,*—the astral bodies of animals,—and "elemental essence," and so forth; and the *artificial world,*—elementals formed unconsciously,—human artificials, guardian angels, etc. This astral world presents many other phenomena; in fact, the majority of "psychic phenomena" are put down to the activity of the astral.

Above this world, according to the Theosophical teachings, is the mental or Devachanic plane; and this corresponds more nearly to the traditional conceptions of spiritual life of some sort,—not the orthodox heaven, but to a mental or spiritual state. These Theosophical teachings are quite different, in many respects, from the spiritualistic doctrine,—which says that, after a man dies, he is precisely the same being that he was before, only in a different environment, and with changed powers, to some extent; and that he proceeds to progress from that moment, more or less rapidly, according to his own internal efforts. There is no external justice meted-out to him; that all progress depends entirely on himself; he will gradually progress; there is no reincarnation; and that the whole morality of the next world,—its ethics, is merely cause and effect,—justice, without any partial exterior judgment of any kind.

It is hardly necessary to enumerate the different types of psychic phenomena, most of which are doubtless familiar enough,—telepathy, clairvoyance, clairaudience, apparitions, haunted houses, physical phenomena of all kinds, mediumistic phenomena, and so forth. How are we going to connect these odd phenomena with the Yoga teachings,—with their doctrine? Is it that they have a fundamental basis unknown to the Westerners,—to those who practise and obtain psychic phenomena? If you question any ordinary medium, he will probably say, ''I don't know *how* these phenomena are produced. I know that I enter a certain state; certain results happen. *How* they are produced, I do not know.''

The occultist claims that he *has* a very good knowledge of the underlying causes; and the student of Yoga will say the same thing. Is it that, in all these cases, the pineal gland and the pituitary body have been unconsciously stimulated? Or that the kundalini has been partially awakened, unknown to the psychic? That is

precisely what Swami Vivekananda says *is* the cause.
He writes:

"Wherever there is any manifestation of what is ordinarily termed supernatural power or wisdom, there must
have been a *little* current of kundalini which found its
way into the sushumna."

It is doubtless owing to this fact (that the *Kundalini* is sometimes spontaneously aroused without the
knowledge of the subject) that many curious and troublesome cases of psychic phenomena are due. A beautiful example of this is to be found in the *Proceedings*
of the American S. P. R., Volume 13, Part 2,—where
a case is published under the title of "A Case of Incipient Obsession." Writing of his own experiences and
sensations, the "subject" says:

" 'I know just exactly what the trouble is. It is a
fluid—proper place in the lower centre of body—it leaves
its home very easily—it is a strain on me to hold it
here by *breathing* in a certain way. When the "fluid"
gets out and gets in my head, it is enough to set me
crazy. My nervous strength soon gives out. . . .' "

Doctor Hyslop, summarizing the explanations given
by this subject of his own inner experiences, in a series
of letters, says:

"In the first place, he (the subject) referred to a
sort of 'fluid' which seemed to disturb him about the
'solar plexus,'—though he did not use that term. He

merely pressed his hands upon his bowels, or the lower portion of his stomach, and indicated that at times he could feel this 'fluid,' as it were, roll and dash about, and it seemed to be a signal of his going into or coming out of the body, as he described it. He frequently mentioned his getting outside of the body, on the left hand side, and this feeling was accompanied by the sensations described. He also remarked that he frequently felt sensations 'up and down the spine,' and that there were something like strings, wires, or cords, pulling at the top of his head, a little to the left side.''

It is interesting to note, in this connection, also, that at a certain period, this subject heard a variety of "noises" or "sounds" within himself—resembling, of course, to a certain extent, the Voice of the Nada, mentioned above.

This means that these psychic phenomena depend upon the same fundamental psychic energy,—which has found its way into the body, started these psychic currents going around the body, and initiated all these phenomena. There are certain "currents" of energy in the body which, theoretically,—according to occult teaching, —revolve or circulate in different ways. In the mystic, they are said to revolve in a counter-clockwise fashion, in an hourglass form,—through the head, down through the heart and solar plexus, and up on the right side, and cross at the neck; whereas, in the occultist, they revolve in a clockwise fashion; and, within these swirls of energy, there are also minor circles or swirls, in the head and in the heart, which revolve counter-clockwise or clockwise, as the case may be.

In the Adept, however,—one who has passed through both these stages,—there is only the one current of energy, which revolves through the head and the heart and the solar plexus, in the hourglass fashion, and there are no inner swirls of energy at all; they are all absorbed into the main stream. This psychic energy, circulating in the body, arousing certain astral centres into action and stimulating them into activity, is, then, the fundamental cause of many of these psychic powers.

We must not forget that many of our psychic phenomena depend upon the activity of the astral body. Clairvoyance is said to depend on the activity of the astral eyes; clairaudience upon the astral ears, and so forth. And physical phenomena depend upon the activity of the astral body, and the projection into space, of this energy.

The French experimenters, who,—as I have remarked before,—are ahead of all the world, in many lines of psychical research, have conducted many useful experiments on what they call *exteriorization of sensibility,* and *motivity,*—that is, the sensory power and the motor power. If I place my hand over a match box in order to move it, I have to touch it. If, however, I am a medium, and I place my hand at the distance of half an inch from the match box, and then *will* that the box shall be moved, it really *is* moved,—the theory being that, in this case, I can project from my fingers an energy which bridges the gap between the fingers and the box,—and so really moves it. That is the projection of motive force.

On the other hand, if I prick my finger, I feel it only if my finger be touched; but when the sensibility is projected beyond the body,—as it is in some cases of deep hypnosis, and trance;—then you can prick a space half an inch *from* the finger, and you will feel it; and that has gone so far, in the experiments of Col. de Rochas, and others, that they have taken out the astral body altogether, from the physical, and set it to one side,—the feeling body, the body of emotion;—and, by pricking this body,—which was distant in space perhaps five feet from the original, physical body,—every prick on the astral body "repercussed," as we say, or was felt in the original, physical body, wherever the prick was made in the astral body. All this, of course, bears a very striking resemblance to the "witchcraft" phenomena,—in which the witch was supposed to turn into a dog or a cat; and if that dog or cat were shot, or had an eye put out, the next day the witch was found with an eye out,—"repercussion"! It is a striking similarity, —curious and interesting.

Now, when we come to the *mechanism* of many of these psychic states,—the laws under which they operate, we know in many cases very little of the actual facts. Take, for instance, clairvoyance. Mr. Leadbeater, in his work on *Clairvoyance,* outlines five chief methods by which clairvoyance is facilitated or rendered possible. The *first,* according to him, is by the assistance of a nature-spirit. This is done either by evocation or invocation; the spirit sees the distant scene and reports to the operator what happens. A *second* theory is "by means of an astral current." In connection with this he says:

"What is really done by the student who adopts this method is not so much the setting in motion of a current in astral matter, as the erection of a kind of temporary telephone through it. It is impossible here to give an exhaustive disquisition on astral physics. All I need say is that it is possible to make, in astral matter, a definite connecting line, which shall act as a telephone wire, to convey vibrations, by means of which all that is going on at the other end of it may be seen. This is accomplished,'' he says, ''by an effort of will, and through it all the atoms of the ether are affected, and are held for the time with their axes rigidly parallel to one another, so that they form a kind of temporary tube along which the clairvoyant may look.''

In this particular kind of clairvoyance, the picture is seen as very small and highly coloured, it is said,—as though one were looking through the wrong end of a telescope; then, by an effort of will, it is made larger and ''brought up,'' so that it can be inspected.

The *third* form of clairvoyance is by the projection of a thought-form,—this projected being travelling to a distant place, seeing what is happening, and returning to its projector. It is very similar to the *fourth* method, which is, by travelling in the astral body. The *fifth* method is by travelling in the mental body.

All these relate to clairvoyance *in space;* but there are various kinds of clairvoyance,—clairvoyance of great distances; magnifying clairvoyance,—bringing up minute objects; X-ray clairvoyance,—in which you look through a solid object, apparently; and so forth.[1]

[1] See *Your Psychic Powers: and How to Develop Them* for details and discussion of the various forms of clairvoyance, and how the power is usually developed.

Now we also have clairvoyance *in time,* when you apparently travel back the stream of time for indefinite periods, and can project yourself forward into time and see what is going to happen,—which is premonition or precognition, or prevision. How are we to conceive that the future is in any way known to us? It is inconceivable, apparently, that what is to happen tomorrow, or next year, could possibly be seen. The only way in which actual prevision of the future could be explained is to assume,—as some philosophers do,—that the future already exists, in one sense, and that can be made clear by this analogy: Suppose that you are standing on the rear platform of a train which is travelling through the country. You look about you, and as the train travels, new scenes are constantly brought into being on either side of you; you perceive them as you come up to these scenes. As these scenes are unfolded, you do not actually *create* them,—you merely perceive them at the time you come to them. *For you,* they are "created," for the time being, but they already existed.

In the same way, it is held that we only perceive the future *as present* when we come to it, when we experience it; but it already exists in some form, in some world, and it is only real to us when we experience it,—when we come to that point. Practically, of course, from the point-of-view of common-sense, the principle does not hold at all; but it is a philosophical doctrine, and all philosophers love hair-splitting, and so it has been advanced as a conceivable hypothesis.

Certainly if the future is ever seen in detail, *some* theory must be advanced; and apart from such a view there are only one or two others which in any way "hold water.'' One is that there may be a higher sphere of mental or spiritual activity, from which the tendencies or currents of our daily life can be foreseen. If, for instance, you see a man walking down the street, and you know that there is a strong wind blowing down the street at right angles to it, you can prophesy or ''predict'' that when he gets to the corner his hat may be blown off. The reason is that you know facts which he does not know. You have, as it were, a higher mental point-of-view on life. You see more about his environment than he does; and it is conceivable that a ''spirit,'' or a being occupying this higher mental point-of-view,—seeing your life, its trends and tendencies,— might be enabled to convey to you, or prophesy directly or indirectly, what is going to happen in the near future, if certain lines are followed; and that would enable us to say why it is that, out of the large number of prophecies, only a certain number become true,—even with the best psychics,—because they can only see *tendencies;* they can only see possibilities; and they cannot see the idiosyncrasies of human nature.

In this connection, you may perhaps remember Bergson's remark, that ''You can predict an eclipse a thousand and two years from now, but you cannot tell what a pugdog will do if you tweak its tail,''—because immediately you introduce *life* into the problem, you have a complicated factor, and you cannot tell how it will react.

To return, however, to the relationship of Yoga to psychic phenomena. This energy, which is liberated in the system, and which is capable of being projected, at times,—is the basis, theoretically, of many psychic phenomena; and, as you see, we have here,—in this mystical, inner energy,—a connecting-link between many of the Yoga practices and many of our Western, psychic phenomena. For instance, it is this energy which produces many "physical" manifestations,—as we have said,—and which radiates from the body in the form of an *aura*. There are said to be various auras,—physical, mental,—a health aura, an emotional aura, a mental aura, and so forth; and all these auras are tinged and influenced by the state of health, the condition of the body, mind, emotions, and so on; and much work has been done on studying these auras,—though not nearly as much work as *should* have been done.

This "aura" is coloured, and there is a whole symbolism of colours which has been worked-out,—the mystical interpretation of colours, which we cannot go into now in detail; but for the moment this doctrine of *energy,* resident in the body, and forming a substratum or basis for psychic manifestations, enables us to explain many otherwise puzzling phenomena,—such as *psychometry,* in which an object handed to a medium seems to stimulate the psychic productiveness of that medium,—and you get "phenomena," you get facts, which you do not get otherwise.

Dr. Hodgson, in working with Mrs. Piper, found that objects which belonged to "dead" persons, if handed to the medium, had the effect of stimulating the production of phenomena very much; and he recommended that objects, which were preserved with that in mind, should be wrapped in oiled-silk and handled by nobody until they were presented to the medium,—to preserve this influence. Whether that influence be resident in the object, or whether it be a purely psychic, or whatever it may be, it seems certainly to stimulate very remarkably the production of phenomena; and that was proved by actual experiments with Mrs. Piper,—because immediately the object was handled by her, a flood of communication was opened, which seemed to have been dammed or shut-up before.

Of course it is inconceivable, in a sense, that an object should be like a sponge, and soak-up a sort of energy from a certain being, a human being, and that it should be tinged with that human being's personality to the extent that it would supply anything more than the feeling of a presence. How it stimulates facts, *knowledge,* is very difficult to account for,—except you suppose that the mere sensing of that person's aura, or personality, through the aura, puts you in touch with the mind of that person who is resident in some other sphere. In other words, it forms a sort of bridge between the material and the spiritual worlds,—a sort of psychic link, through this resident energy; and here again we get back to the theory of the mystical energies of the body, which are connected with Yoga,—kundalini, and so forth.[1]

Mr. Prescott Hall has published two very illuminating and valuable articles in the November and December, 1916, issues of the *Journal* of the American Psychical Research Society, and a few extracts from these articles will, I think, prove interesting. We dealt before, if you remember, with vibrations,—I showed the value of rhythmic vibrations, and the fact that, while there is no

[1] See my book *The Coming Science* for a lengthy discussion of this question.

sound, in one sense of the word, at all, yet this harmonic series of vibrations which music represents, does symbolize a perfectly definite conception; and this view is held by occultists to this extent:

"It is alleged by certain occultists that 'spirits' communicate in three ways. The lowest grade of spirits use ordinary words; the intermediate grades impress ideas upon the brain of the sitter; such ideas are vague and general and would be subject to confusion. The higher grades of spirits use *music* as the universal language, which is the same at all times and in all spirit worlds. This language is made up of tones and chords, and these are similar to Chinese ideographs. In the case of the latter, for example, a simple mark means *liquid;* when another mark is hitched on to the first one the meaning becomes *water.* When a second mark is hitched on to it, the meaning becomes *red water,*—that is, wine; and so forth. In the same way, in this musical language, a simple tone stands for a general idea, and this is rendered concrete, precise and definite by the addition of overtones and harmonics. Owing to the fact that an almost infinite number of tones exist, of which our ordinary scale uses only a few, there are plenty of signs for that language. It is further stated that many musical composers get their themes and motives through hearing astral music,—that Wagner in particular received, by the intuitive method spoken of above, an understanding of what some of what he heard meant; therefore by comparing the text of some of his operas, especially *Parsifal,* with the music, it is said that one can begin to learn the language. Whatever may be thought of this doctrine, it is perfectly consistent with other spirit teachings.''

Colours appear to affect ''spirits'' entering the earth-plane. Bad spirits are said to dislike blue; therefore blue clothing is good for a person who is developing to wear. On the other hand, good spirits like blue clothing, but dislike black.

There is also a great deal said in occult lore about the connection of music and colours. We spoke before about the sensation of colour, which people experience on hearing certain musical sounds; and many people have a colour-sensation when a note is struck on the piano. The colour red, for instance, is said to correspond to the note C, orange to D, yellow to E, green to F, blue to G, violet to A, grey to B.

The fundamental tone in nature is said to be the sub-octave of F, corresponding to a soft green. Mr. Lead-beater, in his book on the ''Devachanic Plane,'' has gone quite thoroughly into what he calls the *music of the spheres,*—that enormous vibratory activity which is said to pervade the higher mental worlds, and which has been interpreted, in this mystical way, as *music.*

Levi, in his little book on *Self Culture,* says regarding colour:

''Light analysis reveals the fact that there are seven distinct tones, and seven colours, and we are informed by the great esoteric masters that each of the creative spirits appropriated one musical tone and one colour, as follows: Michael, the colour red, and the tone C; Raphael the colour orange, and the tone D; Gabriel the colour yellow, and the tone E; Samael the colour green, and the tone F; Uriel the colour blue, and the tone G; Zadkiel the colour Indigo, and the tone A; Cassiel the colour violet, and the tone B. . . . Red also corresponds symbolically to ice, and to Kama-rupa or animal life; orange to air and to Prana, the life principle; yellow to water, and to Buddhi, the spiritual soul; green to air and to the lower manas or animal soul; blue to steam, and to the auric envelope; and Indigo to air and to the Spiritual Intelligence. . . . The human trinity and its correspondences may be thus stated; the physical body is the red of colour, and the C of music; the soul is the yellow of colour and the E of music; the spirit is the blue of colour and the G of music. As in music, C is the keynote and G is the dominant note, so in the human scale, the physical body is the keynote, because it manifests the rest of the scale, and the spirit is the dominant note."

Speaking of the methods of developing,—the first step is abstinence from stimulating foods and drinks. The pituitary body and the pineal gland are said to be stimulated excessively by these things,—which affect the blood-stream in the brain. The second step in development, is to withdraw the imagination from the physical body, so that it may be centred upon the astral body. It must be borne in mind that what we ordinarily call "imagination" is really exercising the astral senses. Whereas in this world, if we imagine ourselves as going to a certain city, our thought is the only result,—in the astral world we actually *go* there,—at least, if we wish; so, if we imagine our astral body as climbing out of the physical, or swinging from side by side, which is one of the exercises given,—we have nothing as a result except the fact of our imagining; but in the astral world our thought has actually set the astral body in motion,—though we cannot, while in the body, see that this *is* so. In other words, thought is creative in the astral world, and whatever we *will* tends to be brought about.

So, as we said before, thought tends to create our environment in the next sphere of activity.

"As a person begins to develop, his radiations become more luminous. This fact attracts the attention of spirits both good and bad. The former try to assist, but the latter to hinder him in his efforts."

A propos the question of *light,* it is interesting to know that spirits usually speak of mediums as "lights." "I am going to visit another light," they will say. And Andrew Jackson Davis, in his clairvoyant descriptions and diagnoses, would say that he always saw the nervous system in the interior of the body as though full of light; and you must remember an interesting remark in this connection: "If thine eye be single, thy whole body shall be full of *light,*"—which means, "if the third eye,"—the eye of Shiva,—"be developed, you become clairvoyant,"—in other words, you become psychic; consequently your whole body is full of "light." This psychic energy is connected with light in various ways, —symbolically and actually,—in all these psychic experiences; and it is rather significant that the activities of the nervous system are very much bound-up with phosphorus,—which, of course, is a light-producing substance; and that seems to connect us, even in the chemical and physiological worlds, with a certain light-energy.

It is doubtless true that many psychic phenomena originate in darkness. Life originated on our globe in dense darkness; and it certainly originates now in darkness; conception takes place in darkness; and life, even if originated at the bottom of the sea, was in darkness,— since the sun's rays only penetrate a few fathoms below the surface; and beneath that is darkness for ever; so that all creative energy seems to originate in darkness; and we know that light is a very destructive and a very disruptive agent.

The ultra-violet rays of sunlight, for instance, sterilize and kill germs in solutions and in objects; and for this reason it is quite conceivable that any subtle forces and energies, which are liberated,—as they might be during a séance,—would be absolutely destroyed by a gross physical energy, such as light.

Water, it is said, has the power of warding off evil spirits. A dish of water near one sitting tends to keep away elementals and other objectionable personalities; and so does the vapour of water, or putting one's hands in water. A dish of water loses its protective power unless it is fresh, and so must be frequently changed. The image of water in various forms is much used in development; thus drawing water from a well, considering the physical body as a pool of water, or dwelling in the image of a pool of water, are all splendid exercises.

A propos all this, it is rather interesting to remember that in India meditation is nearly always done by running water or brooks. We can imagine that there is some subtle connection in this action.

Regarding breathing exercises, it may be held,—and of course has been pointed out,—that by these long breaths which are taken in *pranayama*,—a certain quantity of carbonic acid gas, carbon dioxide, accumulates in the system, and poisons the nerve-cells and induces these visions; and Dr. Jacolliot in his book, *Occult Science in India,* pointed out that the huts of the Hindus seemed to be so constructed that they would retain a large percentage of this carbon dioxide. But, even granting that to be true, the late tendency in medicine is to regard carbon dioxide as very valuable under certain conditions; and physicians are now administering it for cases of shock on the battlefields,—with apparently good results; in fact a work has lately been published, *Carbonic Acid Gas in Medicine,* which deals entirely with this subject. The reason is that *"an increase of carbon dioxide in the inspired air calls forth deep, rapid respirations."* (See "Shock at the Front" by W. T. Porter, p. 100.)

It seems curious, at first, that a number of short, shallow breaths should not supply the body with as much oxygen, or as much "prana," as one long breath; but the theory is that, the rhythm of the body being established, it is capable of absorbing more prana, and the internal adjustments of the body are so arranged that they absorb more prana, from one long breath than they can from a number of small ones; and that seems to be borne out by the fact that you *do not* get the same results from a number of short breaths as you do from one long one. In the same way, a number of small taps do not give the same result as one steady push. That is the analogy,—one long breath has a certain effect in the body which a number of short ones do not.

In development work, the mental image of a *mirror*

is used for much the same purpose as water. The manipulation of one's own image in a mirror is useful. A mirror being a device for picturing three dimensions in two, it has uses in suggesting that three-dimensional pictures are the image of fourth dimensional objects,—getting out into the astral apparently involving four dimensions.

If you think of it, a mirror, being a flat surface, is two-dimensional, and yet it apparently gives a picture of a three-dimensional world, and seems to give not only height and breadth, but depth as well;—in other words, it throws out, into the mirror-world, the same distance that it receives light rays from in front of the mirror,—as we said in discussing the fourth dimension. So that, in the mirror, you apparently have a three-dimensional world on a two-dimensional plane.

The effect of certain electrical and other waves upon psychic development is a subject for further investigation. Mr. Prescott Hall attempted, at one time, to investigate the assertion made by some electrical experts, —that ultra-violet light of the 51st octave had pronounced effects in developing psychic power. The results, however, were not conclusive. Miss Marie Corelli has made a literary use of the idea that "psychics" are attractive to lightning in her *Romance of Two Worlds*.[1]

To return, however, to our question of the relationship between Yoga teachings and psychical phenomena.

---

[1] Mr. Oliver Bland, in his *Adventures of a Modern Occultist*, states that the radiations of radium are destructive to astral or spirit bodies—though it is not yet known whether the a, β or γ rays are the disruptive agents. Here is a whole field suitable for strictly scientific investigation in a "psychical laboratory."

We have seen that many psychical phenomena,—especially the ''physical,''—are dependent upon certain *energies* which are generated within the body; and these same energies are doubtless a factor in mental manifestations also,—though the connection here has not been so adequately proved. As Swami Vivekananda, in his *Raja Yoga,* says:

''In this country, there are Mind-healers, Faith-healers, Spiritualists, Christian Scientists, Hypnotists, etc., and if we analyse these different groups, we shall find that the background of each is this control of the *Prana,* whether they know it or not. If you boil all their theories down, the residuum will be the same. It is the one and same force they are manipulating, only unknowingly. They have stumbled on the discovery of a force, and do not know its nature, but they are unconsciously using the same powers which the Yogi uses, and which come from *Prana.*''

What is the attitude of the Hindu student of Yoga towards Spiritualism? How does he regard the phenomena, and what does he think of the teaching?

Swami Abhedananda, in his little booklet *Does the Soul Exist After Death?* says:

''As regards the retaining of the individuality, Vedanta says that each soul after death takes with it all the experiences, impressions and ideas which it gained on earth; it takes its mind, its intelligence, its intellect and powers of the senses,—and enjoys, or reaps, the fruits of its own thoughts and deeds.''

It does not seem, however, that the individual *preserves* all these attributes in the next state; and Swami Vivekananda, in his *Raja Yoga,* practically says that he does *not* do so; but that, on the contrary, he is *"absorbed,"* as we have been accustomed to think.

Again, P. S. Acharya, in an article on "Spiritualism: From the Viewpoint of Hindu Philosophy," in the May, 1918, number of *Kalpaka* says:

To a Hindu, Spiritualism is a philosophy, a religion, a science and an art. To him it implies, not a mere gospel of spiritism, but the supreme religious or philosophical science and Art of evolving a spiritual consciousness. Thus, properly speaking, genuine Hindu Spiritualism is included in Yoga Sastra or Mantra Sastra.

The Hindu calls Spiritualism by the name of *Para Vidya* (supreme science), *Brahma Vidya* (the Eternal Art or Divine science), etc. He traces the origins of this great science of Spiritualism to God, the Supreme Spirit of Purity, Beauty and Love Who is immanent, immutable and transcendental. According to the Hindu, spiritual things are discerned spiritually, *i.e.,* by the third eye or the spiritual eye of the sadhaka (aspirant) as well as by other spiritual senses. Briefly, Spiritualism is, from the Hindu view-point, nothing more, nothing less, than, the Realization (sakshatkara) of the spiritual Life by virtue of one's own spiritual evolution (Yoga).

The root and fruit of the spiritual life, say the Aryan Rishis and our Dravidian Alwars and Nayanmars, is *Ananda*—Divine Love, the vital principle of Bliss supreme; pure and unalloyed Love and Bliss deep-rooted in *santi* or the peace of *manas* that passeth knowledge. This sweet mellowing fruit of spiritual Love gives birth, in its turn, to the undying seed of selfless service— service that is joy, rendered with absolute faith (*sraddha*) in the Name of the Supreme Spirit of *Paramatma*.

According to Sri Ramanuja, *Bhakti* is the force through which each *jivatma* (spirit) evolves *Jnana* (Wisdom) in all the changing worlds of men and gods. The spirit starves without *Bhakti* or the bread of life, even as the body which is the physical sheath of man (Annamayakosa) starves without *annam* or food. The physical man gains by getting or grasping. He hoards and hoards, early and late and he is awfully afraid, like Mahamad the Idol-breaker, of the day when he has to bid his cold adieux to the world. But the spiritual man or Bhakta gains by giving; he grows richer and richer by constantly and cheerfully giving himself in whole-hearted service to the children of God. He knows that the more of this joyous service (kainkaryam) he renders, the more expansive his Bhakti becomes. Such a Bhakta, living and moving in an uninterrupted "God-consciousness" or spiritual or cosmic consciousness, is counted truly among the Elect who can possess and exercise at will and, as it were, by Right Divine, God-given gifts of the spiritual life whereby the humble servants of God alone know how to "minister to the mind diseased" of an "Orphan Humanity."

While entering the enchanted Realm of psycho-spiritual Research, the sadhaka should have and use a clear head, clean hands, a pure love-inspired heart, a serene joyous mind, an easy conscience and an enlightened faith. For he has to deal in this new realm with forces much finer and far more etherial than those he has hitherto been accustomed to deal with.

Thus we see that according to the Hindu Shastras, the sadhaka or seeker after psycho-spiritual truths should prepare himself before he can have communion with pure and highly-evolved spirits. He should strive to evoke his spiritual faculties more by the purification of the heart by love and service than by any other sadhana which ignores or tends to ignore the path of duty wedded to Bhakti. It is when pure, spiritual love rules the heart, when marvellous spiritual peace rules the *Manas,* when joyous spiritual service rules the hands— it is then and then only—that the true beauty and grandeur of the spirit life can reveal itself to the astonished gaze of the aspirant. Then the sadhaka hears celestial voices and songs. Then he beholds the beautiful etherialized forms of spirit friends. Then indeed he realizes the unseen realms of life and love and can, at will, walk and talk with the *Devas* and *Pitris.* For verily Bhakti or pure love that is modest and wise can see much farther and deeper, than the purblind knowledge which is "proud that it has learnt so much."

"Let go thoughts and emotions that tax and stir you;
Repose on the Bosom of Peace;
Close thy physical window of the soul and open the spiritual;
Shut the five doors that make manifest the boundless Nature;
Meditate with thy utmost spiritual love on Him who is the Pure
    Essence of Beauty and Love;
Thus, through the Gate of Dhyana that opens but to the magic
    Key of Love Divine let the sadhaka vision the more real and
    sublime worlds of life bright with shining ones."

More specifically, Swami Abhedananda, in his *Spiritualism and Vedanta,* says:

"In India, from very ancient times, the belief in departed spirits has played an important part in shaping the religious ideas of the Hindus. This belief found expression in the oldest scriptural writings of the Vedic period. As early as the time of the *'Rig Veda,'* which goes back at least five thousand years before the birth of Christ, this idea was very common, and there we read many hymns with invocations addressed to the *'Pitris,'* or departed Fathers. (We hear of the *'Pitris'* and their power to produce phenomena, in Jacolliot's book, *Occult Science in India.*) They are invoked, praised, and invited to accept the offerings made to them at the time of the *Shraddha.* . . . The realm of the Fathers, or ancestors, corresponds to the heaven of the modern spiritualists. . . . Spiritualism, whether ancient or modern, cannot describe any stage *beyond* the realm of the Fathers. . . . Spiritualism leads human minds only a step beyond the grave, in the world of phenomena, and opens the way to the belief in this realm of departed spirits. . . . This realm is phenomenal, and subject to the laws which govern the phenomenal universe. . . ."

The point raised here is important, and but rarely understood by investigators; namely, that psychic phenomena represent, or bring us in touch with, the *psychic* realm only, and not the *spiritual* world direct; the borderline between the spiritual and material worlds constitutes the "psychic realm"; when the two meet and generate "sparks," as it were; these "sparks" are "psychic phenomena,"—which we study. We do not study the spiritual world *direct*—by this means.

Those "spirits" who can communicate with us, the Hindus believe, are only "earth-bound spirits,"—as many of *our* spiritualists believe.   While admitting there is a certain truth in spiritualism, therefore, the disciple of Yoga does not attach as much weight to the phenomena as we in the West are inclined to do.   Swami Abhedananda concludes by saying:

"So long as you do not recognize the true nature of your Self, so long as you do not feel that reunion of the individual soul with the Universal Spirit, you shall not attain to spiritual freedom and perfection. . . ."

From every point-of-view, therefore, we should study Yoga, and practise it; and, just as Occultists recognize the value of this initial training of Self,—before attempting practical experiments in Magic,—so our psychics and mediums should be made to undergo a prolonged course of instruction in Yoga,—before they become "mediums,"— in order to attain that self-mastery which is so essential.   Did they but do this, they would obtain not only more striking phenomena, but they would obtain them without that danger to themselves—from "obsession" and other causes—which is so evident among our mediums of the present day.

CHAPTER XII

The Projection of the Astral Body

In the last two chapters I endeavoured to show the connection between the Yoga Philosophy and occult science on the one hand, and psychic phenomena on the other.

We found that there was a certain inter-relationship between all these schools of thought,—more intimate between Yoga and occultism than between Yoga and "psychics,"—because Yoga and the occult sciences both deal with the positive attitude,—that is, the process of controlling phenomena, by cultivation of the inner powers, rather than by passive methods,—such as in psychic and mediumistic development,—in which these phenomena are merely awaited, and, as it were, allowed to come by themselves spontaneously. Therefore, there is a more clearly distinguishable connection between occultism and Yoga doctrines than there is between Yoga and psychic phenomena.

In fact, in spiritualistic and psychic manifestations, as such, you might say there is no clearly distinguishable connection,—because the psychic manifestations,—the ordinary spiritualistic manifestations,—are mere "phenomena" which *occur;* they result as the product of certain inner, psychic experimentation, and they are observed at the time they occur, by the sensitive,—the medium,—without his knowing anything, in the majority of cases, as to *how* these things are produced.

266

As I have said before, most mediums, if questioned, would simply say: "I don't know the laws and causes underlying these phenomena,—their mechanism; I merely sit in the dark,—or in the light, as the case may be,—and these phenomena develop; but as to *how* they develop I don't know!"

Now, occultism claims that it has a more or less consistent explanation for these phenomena; it understands the hidden causes and laws at work; and Yoga Philosophy claims still further, that it has a complete system of interpretation,—by which these manifold phenomena *can* be interpreted.

You will see that, in all these psychic and occult manifestations, there are certain energies employed, which originate within the system, and are projected or "exteriorized" beyond the body,—in the production of physical manifestations,—and perhaps in what we call purely mental or psychic phenomena,—such as telepathy, and phenomena of that character. In fact, as I think I mentioned before, Mr. Frederic Myers coined the word "telergy" to designate the hypothetical energy which accompanies telepathic action and mental action at a distance, outside the body.

If you try to make a graduated scale of phenomena, from the normal to the supernormal, you will find that you have to begin with highly sensitized and acute sense-perceptions, which lead us into what we call "hyperesthesia,"—that is, excessive sensitiveness; and from that, we are led into "psychometry,"—or the ability to sense impressions about objects, apparently in a supernormal way; and from that, to the further extension of psychometry,—which is the sensations we derive from other people, or from objects, and by which we "sense" *presences,*—perhaps apparitions in haunted houses,—or derive or obtain telepathic impressions, or intuitive impressions, from those people or some place or influence.

This "exteriorization of sensitivity," as it is called, has been studied by the French; and its complement, its opposite, is the "exteriorization" of the motive force or "motivity,"—where the nervous energy of the body is projected beyond the surface of the body, into space, and there moves material objects, or has some effect upon the material world.

Of course, it is inconceivable to us that either sensory or motor energy should exist without nerves! The physiologist would say to you: "It is absurd to suppose that the nervous current can exist beyond the body, where there are no nerves on which it can travel." And from the purely materialistic point-of-view, of course, it is inconceivable and impossible. But these psychic phenomena seem to show that it is a *fact;* that nervous energy *can* exist apart from the body;—in these experiments a few inches only, but in those cases in which the astral body is projected to some distance from the physical body, by experimental means, we have cases in which the neuric energy, the nervous forces of the body, are externalized beyond the surface of the physical body for a considerable distance.

This "astral body," which is the feeling body, the emotional body, has been experimentally detached from the physical, by means of deep magnetic passes; and when the subject is in a mesmeric trance or "magnetic" trance, as distinct from the hypnotic. Mesmeric and magnetic phenomena are *not* the same as hypnotic. Hypnotism deals entirely with the mind, and is due to "suggestion,"—mental influences; but magnetism and mesmerism depend upon a certain physical effluence or influence, which passes from the operator to the subject, —that sometimes forms a sort of vital connecting-link, establishing a *rapport* between subject and operator, in the same way that the vital energy is enabled to move a material, physical object, when that object is charged with it.

One step beyond this experimental detachment of the "astral body" is *voluntary* projection,—where the astral body is, by an intense effort of will,—accompanied by other inner practices,—detached and projected from the physical body *during life*,—when the physical body is entranced or asleep,—and sent to some considerable distance. Cases of "experimental apparitions" seem to prove that this has been done more or less spontaneously, and unknown to the operator; the astral body has been seen at some distance from the sleeping person,—or the entranced person,—when an attempt has been made to project this body during sleep or in trance.

Let us come, however, to the more directly experimentally controlled phenomena. In this connection I shall first of all quote a few extracts from the chapter on the "Projection of the Astral Body" published in my *Modern Psychical Phenomena*. A great deal of work has been done in this connection by Col. de Rochas, of Paris, by M. Hector Durville; by Dr. Baraduc, and others; but most of the scientific experiments, in this connection, have been conducted by M. Charles Lancelin of Paris.

"According to M. Lancelin, there is a real 'science and art' in this astral duplication, which consists, essentially, in the ability to externalize the neuric (nervous) force, composing the astral body, and the 'sensibility.' The right or suitable temperament must be chosen for the experiment; and if this is not found, the experiment is liable to fail, or only to succeed partially. 'Temperament' must not be confused with 'character,' or mental make-up. Temperament is a physiological state produced by the predominance of an element, organ or system in the human body. There are four chief types of temperament—nervous, bilious, lymphatic and sanguine. Of these, the nervous temperament is the best for psychic experiments of all kinds; the bilious is the most receptive; the sanguine is liable to hallucinations, both subjective and objective; while the lymphatic is the least suitable of all, from every point-of-view. Of course, one's temperament is usually a compound of all of these, which are rarely found in their ideal state; but the predominantly nervous temperament is the one best suited for this test—as for all other psychic experiments.

"Now, there is at all times a certain outflowing of nervous force,—or 'externalization of neuricity,' as it is called,—in all individuals; but this becomes very pronounced in certain types of individuals known as 'mediums' or 'psychics.' In them, this force, which is thus radiated, can be measured by means of specially constructed instruments, known as Biometers, Sthenometers, etc. Several instruments of this kind have been devised by French experimenters. They show that there is a repulsive force generated from one side of the human body, and an attractive force from the other side.

In normal human beings, these forces should be equal. When they are not, odd things are likely to happen in their immediate environment. Their relative power can be tested by means of instruments.

"These energies depend upon the state of the health, the emotions, the mind, and also upon the *will*. For the experiment to succeed, as we shall see, the subject must be in good health; the emotions calm; the mind placid; and the will exceedingly strong. However, it is not the *conscious* will which performs the miracle; but the *subconscious will*—the will which is active in sleep. It is this which is difficult to train, and can only be reached by psychic and occult methods. Once reached and strengthened, however, it is capable of performing all sorts of marvels, while the subject is asleep or entranced.

"This subconscious will has its own psychology; it is said to consist of four essential elements—possession, deliberation, determination and action. The last three of these are the so-called 'solid' states of will. (The medium Eusapia Palladino was wont to say she could succeed in moving objects at a distance if her will were sufficiently 'solid.') Within this mystic citadel, a double action takes place—(1) the will acts within itself, and (2) it controls its environment. Upon the degree of power which this subconscious will possesses depends the success of the experiments.

"The first thing to do, then, to ensure the success of our 'astral projection,' is to *dynamize the will*—to hyperdynamize it, in fact, so that it is over-charged, and capable of bursting out, like champagne when the cork is removed! There are various methods of doing this.

One of the simplest is to repeat to oneself many times, just before dropping off to sleep, 'I have will,—I have energy!' This must be kept up until sleep actually supervenes and memory is lost. Then one may think of the next day's work clearly, in detail, and make up one's mind not to deviate therefrom, even under great pressure and temptation. This will give the subconscious will a force that nothing else can equal.

"The subconscious will thus strengthened, the next step is to create a 'division of self,'—so as to loosen the astral body from the physical body. The subject, to do this, should go over his entire body in thought—while lying in bed—covering every inch of its surface, and *willing* that the astral body shall be detached from the physical body at that point. Try to feel this body loose inside you. Then focus all your mental energy upon the 'solar plexus,'—at the spot where the ribs divide,—or, preferably, at a point low down on the forehead, between the eyes,—and, while breathing quietly and deeply, *will* that you go out from your physical body at that point. Project yourself outwards into space. Imagine yourself going out; try to transfer your consciousness to the body without you. Try to look out of its eyes, hear with its ears, feel with its body. You will suddenly find yourself enabled to do so; then your first great step will have been taken."

A good exercise for this purpose is to close the eyes, then roll up the eye-balls until they are fixed at a point on the forehead, between the eyes—in much the same way as the Yogis do—and make a concentrated effort to gather together your psychic energies *at* that point.

Will, with the whole force of your being, that you are *there;* and when you have concentrated your full Self at that spot, then *will* that you shall be projected outwards, in space, from that point of departure. This method is a strain upon the eyes, but is one which has been found very effective,—as the result of numerous experiments and experiences.

A propos all this, I might say one can do that sitting in a chair. *Will* that a duplicate or replica of yourself shall stand before you in space, and when this phantom or double self has been created, so that it becomes visible, then transfer, by an effort of will, the consciousness, to the phantom,—so that, as it were, you can see out of its eyes. When that transference has taken place, you have progressed far in your development.

"When you have progressed thus far, you must try to look around you, in your newly-acquired 'astral body,' and notice the furniture in the room; notice everything in detail. Then try to go out through the door of the room, go down stairs, and out of the front door into the street. (It does not matter whether the doors are closed or not; in your astral body you can go through them easily.) Then walk along the street—into the door of your friend's house, to whom you wish to appear—and go upstairs into his or her room. Notice everything as you go. When there, try to make your presence felt or seen. This is the hardest step,—and the one we know the least about as yet, in its technical details.

"The person to whom you are to appear must be more or less 'clairvoyant' or 'psychic.' He must be quiet and receptive, in darkness or semi-darkness; and should, if possible, aid you by *drawing* you by an effort of will —so that his duty is not altogether passive, but active also. One of the best states for the perception of the astral body of another person is the hypnotic trance. The French experiments were nearly all made in this condition—though it is not necessary.

"Once by the side of the 'seer,' the astral phantom should endeavour in every way possible to make its presence felt. It may do this by becoming visible, by speaking (becoming audible), or by touching the 'seer.' The phantom may also be able to rap. If not, it has been found by experience that the astral form may be enabled to prove its presence by impressing photographic plates (by placing its hands upon them), by touching sulphide of calcium screens, or by operating some delicate instrument,—such as a Biometer. Its objectivity is thus established."

I might say that we made use of these experiments in our psychical photoplay serial, *The Mysteries of Myra;* we placed the sulphide of calcium screen by the side of Myra's bed, so that, when the astral body of the Grand Master visited her and tried to strangle her, the screen *glowed;* and this was connected by a delicate mechanism, with Dr. Alden's room,—the psychic detective,—and rang a bell in his room, so that he was immediately awakened. He hurried over to her house, and arrived just in time to thwart the intentions of the villainous astral body! To resume, however:

"As to the 'trip' between one point and the other, the necessary things for the phantasmal form to develop are—(1) self-conscious will, and (2) sense of direction.

"Various factors have been found to influence the results advantageously, or the reverse. We may thus summarize the most important of these:

"*Sex.* This should preferably be male for the projector, female for the recipient or seer of the phantom.

"*Humidity.* The air should be dry and clear, barometer high.

"*Atmospheric electricity.* If high, this is prejudicial to the experiment.

"*Temperature.* This is best if slightly above the normal heat of the room when the experiment is taking place.

"*Clothing.* No restrictions of any kind can be allowed.

"*Light.* Complete darkness is by far the best; a dim twilight in any case is all that may be allowed.

"*Sitters.* If possible, projector and seer should be alone; if any others are present, they must understand what is happening, and be in sympathy with the experiment.[1]

"*Silence* must be preserved throughout,—no noise must disturb the sitter at either end of the 'line.'

"*Time.* The best time is between 11 P. M. and 3 A. M. —that is, when natural sleep is most likely to supervene.

"*Position.* The most comfortable—in an arm chair, on a couch, or in bed. If lying down, it should be on

[1] The *Tantras* warn the Yogi against undertaking any psychic experiments in the presence of an "unbeliever." (v. *Tantrik Texts*, vol. viii, p. 21.)

the *right* side.   You must *not* lie upon the front of the body.

"The *Mind* must be calm; and the *emotions* placid.

"It is well to *eat* very little on the day of the experiment.

"There are certain *dangers* attendant upon this experiment—especially if undertaken rashly, and by one unaccustomed to such trials.   (1) There are *material* dangers—such as would accompany any dissociation experiments.   These should be known.   (2) *Intellectual and Moral Dangers.*   Those having weak characters, weak wills, or uncontrolled lives are liable to be influenced by outside, evil intelligences, and 'open the door' to possible 'obsession.'   Sound advice by a master or adept is advisable here.   (3) *Psycho-physical dangers.* These are dangers which happen in the astral world, and react upon the mind and body of the subject.   (4) *Hyper-physical dangers,* which leave the door open to dangerous principles.

"To avoid these, one should have technical instruction in this matter of self or astral-projection; and, in any case, care, *sang froid,* fearlessness, moral force and a strong will are essential.   If these are lacking, the subject had best leave the experiment alone.   But if he has them, or can develop them, a road is opened to him which is one of the most fascinating in the occult world; he will be enabled to leave his physical body at will, and soar upon the wings of the wind in the astral and ethereal worlds; and he will see things there beyond words to describe; he will behold visions and hear that which 'it is not lawful to utter'—for they pass the ordinary comprehension of man."

To facilitate the projection of the astral body, certain devices have been employed, and certain experiments must be performed,—physical and mental. For instance, anesthetics are said to "blow" the astral body out of the physical body. When one faints, the astral body leaves the physical; when one becomes unconscious, from any source, the astral leaves the physical body. That is what unconsciousness *is;* it is the withdrawal of the consciousness from the body.

After sufficient development, one is said to see and hear with any part of the astral body, without using special sense-organs. When the astral body is out of the physical body, it has an atmosphere of its own, called its "aura," which can be seen by the person developing, at a certain stage of his work. The "aura" appears to consist of coloured vibrations, which act as clothing for the body. The astral body, when "out," is connected with the physical body by an elastic cord, which has sufficient connection to enable the vital processes of the physical body to continue; and when a person is sufficiently developed the physical body can be directed from the outside. The aura is the only atmosphere it has.

This astral cord,—the "silver cord" of *Ecclesiastes,*— is that which connects the astral to the physical body, and is said to be elastic, so that it can stretch almost indefinitely; and along this cord, vital currents travel to and fro, between the astral and the physical. If that cord should be snipped or cut or broken in any way, then the astral is permanently *out,*—in other words, "death" has taken place; and that is apparently what *has* taken place, in certain séances, when the "body" has been seized,—which, in such cases, proved to be the astral body of the medium. It was prevented, as it were, from returning to the physical body. In some cases,—which are on record, I believe,—the medium has died in the cabinet. Says Mr. Prescott Hall:

"The astral body is said to grow in size, as the person develops, and can be seen by him to the same extent as the physical, even before it is fully formed. It cannot travel in space until its aura is fully formed; but when it does move, it leaves a trail of light, and can go in any direction. It can see the vibration of physical objects. In leaving the physical, it usually goes out in a zigzag or spiral movement, but afterwards travels in a straight line to the point desired."

In an endeavour to ascertain the composition or structure of this astral body, a number of interesting experiments were undertaken by two Dutch physicists,—Drs. Matla and Zaalberg van Zelst, of the Hague. They constructed an instrument, extremely complicated in character, which they called the "dynamistograph"; and by means of this instrument, they claim, they have been able to obtain "direct" communication with the spirit-world, without any medium at all! In other words, they put this instrument in a room by itself, observed its actions through a small glass window, which had been cut in the wall, and the instrument was thereupon manipulated by apparently spiritual intelligences, and long "communications" spelled out, by means of a lettered dial, which was at the top of the dynamistograph.

There is a book, in French, entitled *The Mystery of Death,* which gives a long account of these experiments. I have summarized it in *Modern Psychical Phenomena,* in the chapter entitled "Instrumental Communication with the Spirit World." From this article I abstract a paragraph which deals with the astral body,—the existence of the astral body having been established by their experiments.

They, being physicists, said to themselves, "Let us investigate and determine the exact physical and chemical structure and composition of this body,—its molecular arrangements and activity,—and discover, if possible, its exact composition, as we would any other body." Their conclusions,—arrived at as a result of a long series of experiments, which we cannot now go into,—were these:

"The body is capable of contraction and expansion, under the action of the will of the energy resident in the body,—that is, the will of the astral body,—the expansion being about 1.26 mm., or about 1/40,000,000 of its own volume; its contraction being much greater,—namely, about 8 mm., or 1/6,250,000 of its volume. Its specific weight is about 12.24 mgs. lighter than hydrogen, and 176.5 times lighter than air. The will acts upon this body mechanically, causing it to expand (rise) or contract (descend) as the action takes place. It is thus subject to the law of gravitation. There is an 'X' force (unknown force) which holds the molecules of this body together,—as yet unknown. The atoms composing this body are extremely small, widely separated and heavy. The internal density of the body is about the same as that of the external air.   If the pressure of the air outside the body be increased, that inside the body will increase in exact proportion.   If, however, the body rises too high it tends to disintegrate.   The weight of this body was also calculated, and found by them to be about 69.5 gr.,—approximately $2\frac{1}{4}$ oz.''

These results, I may say, agree more or less with certain experiments conducted by Dr. Duncan McDougall, —of Haverhill, Mass.,—some years ago, in which he weighed a number of patients dying from consumption, at the moment they died.   He placed the cot, containing the patient, on a delicately balanced scale,—so that the patient, bed and all, was weighed; and at the moment of death the beam of the balance went up and struck the upper arm instantly.   The weight was calculated, and was found, in four out of six cases, to be between 2 and $2\frac{1}{2}$ oz.[1]   This seems to be a rather interesting confirmation of these Dutch experiments.   It also seems to show us that the astral body is, in a sense, a material thing,—very tenuous, probably, but still material in *one* sense.

It does not prove to us that consciousness is diffused throughout this astral body, any more than it is diffused through the physical body.   The consciousness might be, as it were, a point-of-force within the astral body,—in the same way that it might be within the physical body now.   We do not know about that.

The chief connections between the physical and astral

[1] These experiments may be found described at length in my book, *The Coming Science,* also in *Death: Its Causes and Phenomena.*

body are said to be the throat and the base of the brain, but more particularly the solar plexus. The first motions of the astral body are said to be felt usually just above the nose. (The Ajna chakra.)   Says Mr. Hall:

"During sleep the vibrations holding it down are relaxed. The same is true during severe illness, when it often tries to escape. During development, the astral seems to get a will of its own, and may try to go ahead too fast, even without the person knowing it. It does not always completely resemble the physical body. Before separation, part of the soul is in the astral and part in the physical. At death, the soul and the astral together leave the physical. The astral cannot be killed, and it is impossible for a spirit to commit suicide, nor can it be injured."

An ingenious theory has been put forward by the author of *The Maniac*,—viz., that her insanity was caused, not so much by purely mental defects or physical troubles, in the brain, as by the disturbance of the etheric or vital *intermediary,* between the physical and the astral bodies. Her theory is that her insanity was caused by the disturbance of this etheric *link* or *connection;* and she proposed the rather ingenious method of devising some instrument,—possibly an electric couch, —on which the subject might be placed, which would have an attractive force for the astral body,—in the same way that anesthetics drive it out. The subject, that is, would be placed within the area of force generated by an electric current, from a wire circulating about him; and in that way, the astral body would be attracted and held to the physical, more firmly than it ordinarily would be.

It is estimated that about 15,000 persons now living "see" more or less on the astral plane; and that about fifty persons can consciously go out into that plane at will.   Says Mr. Prescott F. Hall:

"As soon as the astral body is untwined from the physical body, and separated from it, and the space between them is filled with aura, to prevent the bodies coming together again, the astral can go out into space and travel many miles and see at great distances.   Thus, it can see other souls miles away, which may appear at first but small blue lights.   On first coming out of the body, the astral world appears hazy, or the person may be blinded by the brilliance of the light; but he can look back and see the physical body clearly, and at first must keep it in sight, in order not to lose his way back.   Circulation also has to be established between the two bodies, so that the vital processes may go on as usual.   Balance is necessary for rising, as, after "getting out," it is necessary to learn to stay still in one place.   This is because the person tends to continue in motion, and therefore sees other things in motion which are really at rest.   Hence he cannot see spirits in their true dimensions, or the true relations between objects until he himself is stationary.   In sitting for development, a person often feels cold.   This is because the physical body lowers its vibrations as the astral body takes form, and the process may go so far as to produce local anesthesia (loss of sensibility), or even rigidity and catalepsy,—owing to the interruption of nerve currents.

Such a condition is only temporary, and a person should rest after sitting, so that normal feelings should be restored.''

In this connection, it is interesting to note that many materializing mediums, when the materialized form begins to develop, feel cold,—particularly about the feet and lower limbs; and in fact many psychic phenomena induce the sensation of clamminess and coldness. Blasts and currents of ''cold air'' are very frequent manifestations present at all psychic circles, and accompany the presence of a ''ghost'' and other psychic phenomena.

''After the astral body has detached itself from the physical, seeing and hearing on the astral plane begin at once; but getting adjusted to the space-relations takes a little time, and the person may need some assistance. In going out, one should have an open mind as to what the experience will be like, as he will see, otherwise, that his prepossessions will tend to objectify themselves in thought forms, and he will be unable to discriminate between them and the real objects of the astral world.''

(This I think I made clear in the last chapter, in connection with spiritual communications. It enables us to understand the difference or disagreement between so many communications from the other side. They create their own environment or world about them.)

There are several interesting mental pictures or objects which can be held in mind, which facilitate astral projection. One of them is to see a mental image in a mirror,—your own picture. Construct, as it were, or imagine, a mirror about twenty feet behind you in space, and picture yourself walking backwards into that mirror.[1]

Another exercise is to endeavour to lift yourself out of your body to a point about eighteen inches above your own head,—like Baron Muenchhausen lifting himself by his own bootstraps!

A third very good image to hold is that of exuding or steaming out of the body,—coming out of all the pores, as it were; and analogous to this is the image of a damp cloth from which steam issues. This must be held in mind, and you must fancy yourself rising from the physical body in the same way that the steam issues from the moist, hot cloth.

Another very good exercise is climbing a ladder,—which I think we tried before, in connection with concentration exercises.

Another very good exercise is climbing a rope. These exercises give movement to the astral body, and facilitate its detachment from the physical.

Another good exercise is to imagine a tank gradually filling with water,—on the top of which one floats as a point of light. The object is to find a small hole in one side of the tank through which one passes out.

Another good exercise is to imagine oneself as whirling. Whirling objects are much used in development work, and you will remember, in this connection, that the dervishes and the other Orientals resort to whirling exercises,—which doubtless have this fundamental object of loosening the astral body from the physical, and inducing ecstatic states of consciousness as a result.

[1] I am indebted to Mr. Prescott Hall's excellent work for a number of exercises which follow.

The image of a revolving star is used to stimulate the activity of the astral body. Concentration upon the image of a whirlpool, or going up and down through a whirlpool; the sense of expanding and contracting the body is also very useful, as is that of being carried along on the surface of a wave. The image of drawing water from a well is said to strengthen the muscles of the astral body.

One very useful exercise is the image of a cone. The image of a cone in one form or another is quite common in development work, because it involves the idea of contracting to a point or expanding from a point; thus passing through a waterspout or an hourglass shaped space is an image used. Constructing a cone of circles becoming smaller or larger, and turning such a cone inside out, or making a revolving disc assume the form of a cone or flatten out again to a disc, is another. Holding the image in mind of a flame of fire, and endeavouring to identify yourself with the flame, is another very useful mental image, to stimulate the activity of the astral body.

As you develop this astral projection, you will probably first of all go through certain preliminary experiences of sight and hearing. You will see lights, images, figures,—hear sounds of various kinds,—all the way from inarticulate noises to beautiful strains of music.

Mr. Prescott Hall, in his work on "Astral Projection," summarized his own experiences in this connection as follows:

"The most definite objects seen were a Greek profile and the head and shoulders of a Hindu in a turban.

These were perfectly distinct. A brilliant red object. Third, large, round, blue lights. Fourth, a small blue and yellow light. Fifth, landscapes, sometimes of two tones and sometimes of natural colours. Sixth, luminous spaces or patches of mist or colour; frequently outlines of persons, but showing no definite details. Seventh, irregularly shaped figures of all kinds, white in colour and usually seen in a patch of blue sky, . . . or tissue-paper figures. These were perhaps the rarest sights, and required the most effort to produce.

"The principal sounds heard were the following: a hissing or whistling, as of escaping steam; single musical notes; musical phrases, generally new to the hearer. Hymn tunes and other tunes, which were known. Harmonics,—often very beautiful. Two or more notes, alternating in regular sequence. The sound of a bell or bells, sometimes in harmony. Metallic noises like the striking of an anvil."

As you will remember, these noises and sounds and musical harmonies of all kinds are typical of Yoga development,—as we said when we discussed the "Voice of the Nada,"—the inner "soundless sound," which is heard in various stages of development.

This question of the projection of the astral body is a very important one, because, in the first place, it is one of the most interesting of all psychic experiments; and, as you will see, it is, in one sense, the object of attainment of all three schools,—the Yoga, the Occult and the Psychic. They all endeavour to arrive at very much the same result, by different means; and they attain it in different degrees of self-mastery and self-consciousness. When the Yogi has obtained the degree of perfection in which he can project this astral body at will, he can travel to great distances and see and hear distant events,—which accounts for the Hindus' extraordinary power of knowing things which are happening at a distance; and also renders possible voluntary interment for long periods of time,—burial, and so forth, —the astral body being removed from the physical. The body of sensation being entirely gone, the physical body merely keeps up its vegetative functions, for the time being, sufficiently to allow life, in some sense, to remain in it. But you will see that the physical body is supported, on this theory, by a continuous life-current, which travels to it from the astral body, through this "astral cord" or connection, connecting it with the astral; and after he is revived and has been restored from the trance state, the Yogi claims that he remembers the experiences which he has passed through, during this period of interment,—when he was apparently "dead" to the outer world.

This astral body is, of course, supposed to function in the astral or fourth dimensional plane,—and during ordinary sleep, constitutes one of the "Invisible Helpers," which we mentioned before,—a Being which is enabled to help other people who are asleep but unconscious; those who have newly died, and so forth.

The astral or spirit world, over a battlefield in Europe, for instance, was said to have been a very busy place. The spirits of those who had died were constantly endeavouring to assist those more newly arrived, —to help them out of their physical bodies, and assist them in locating or finding themselves;—to get them in touch with each other, and later on, with their own relatives and friends;—and perhaps later to communicate with us, through mediums and other psychics.

The astral body is, of course, very closely connected with the *dream body,*—with which it is more or less identical.   Dr. Van Eeden, of Holland, conducted some extremely interesting experiments upon himself, in his dream body.   He endeavoured to transfer his consciousness to this body, so that he remembered everything that transpired during sleep; and to control that body so that, through it, he would be enabled to manipulate physical objects in this material world.   He did not succeed fully in doing so, but came very near it,—and succeeded to the extent that he induced a complete dual consciousness.   He remembered clearly that he was asleep in bed, with his arms folded across his breast; and *at the same time* he remembered clearly that he was looking out of the window, and saw a dog run up and look at him through the glass, and run away again,—and details of that character.

He then remembered gliding towards the couch on which his physical body was lying, lying down beside it,—and a moment later he woke up and was again, of course, in the physical body.   But he had that extreme sense of duality of consciousness of two bodies.

Now, this brings us to a psychical experiment, which I think you will be interested in trying,—and that is: *dreaming true.*   You may perhaps have heard a great deal about this subject.   There is a practical experiment which can be conducted, by which ''true dreams'' can be induced.

It is very important to observe yourself in the process

of falling asleep; to observe the consciousness while it is in the process of passing into the dream state. If you conduct experiments of this character, on yourself, you will be enabled gradually to keep conscious control of yourself up to the moment you fall asleep; and this self-observation,—the consciousness of going to sleep,—is extremely interesting. When you have learned to do that, then construct before yourself, mentally, a definite scene, which you must hold firmly in mind. Then, as you are falling to sleep, holding this scene before you, at the very last moment,—before you fall to sleep,—consciously transfer yourself *into* the scene,—in other words, *step into that picture;* and, if you have developed yourself to the requisite point, you will be enabled to carry-over an unbroken consciousness into the dream picture; and in that way you have a perfect continuity of thought; there is no break in consciousness; you step into the dream picture and go on dreaming consciously. That is the process of dreaming true, and after this dream is fully enacted, then you should remember perfectly all that has transpired during the sleep period.

. . . .

We have now travelled, I think, the road which we set out to travel; we have given a résumé of the main Yoga teachings,—shown their relationship to Occultism and Psychic Phenomena,—and have concluded by explaining this practical, experimental method of projecting the astral body.

I can only hope, in conclusion, that this work has given a clear idea of the Yoga teachings, and that it will prove useful—not only in aiding your thought, but in practical, daily life.

GLOSSARY

YOGA. A System of Graduated Ascetic Practices.

YOGI. One who practises Yoga.

YAMA. Restraint; purification.

NIYAMA. Self-surrender; mortification, etc.

ASANA. Bodily Posture.

PRANA. A Psychic Energy, indrawn in breathing, etc.

PRANAYAMA. The scientific direction of *Prana*. (Breathing Exercises.)

MANTRA. A rhythmic verse or prayer, often repeated.

MANTRAYOGA. That section of Yoga devoted to Mantras.

PRATYAHARA. Introspection; meditation.

DHARANA. Concentration.

DHYANA. Unification; the Outpouring of the Mind.

SAMADHI. Cosmic Consciousness; Unification with the Absolute.

KUNDALINI. The Secret, Sacred Energy, upon which phenomena depend.

KUNDALI YOGA. That form of Yoga which deals with the Kundalini.

CHAKRA. A Psychic Center in the Body, aroused by *Kundalini*.

KARMA. Action and reaction; Cause and Effect; Consequence.

TATTVA. Ether: According to the Hindus, there are several Tattvas.

SHAKTI. Creative or Generative Power.

SHAKTA. A worshipper of the Shaktis.

BRAHMAN. The absolute.

(Other Sanskrit or Unusual Words and Terms are explained in the Text.)

INDEX

INDEX

INDEX

Lao-Tze, 16.
Layayoga, 4; 170.
Leadbeater, C. W., 140; 141; 150; 247-48.
LeBon, G., 92.
Levi, E., 60; 78; 254-55.
Levitation, 57.
Life, Nature of, 36-37.
Life and Death, 238-40.
Light, 116-17; 197; 256-57.
Lodge, Sir Oliver, 134; 230.
Lombroso, 52; 76; 147.

MacDougall, Dr. D., 280.
Manas Chakra, 150.
Manipura Chakra, 147-48.
Manning, Prof., 160.
Mantras v. Mantrayoga.
Mantrayoga, 62-75 *passim.*
Marquis, Don, 61.
Matla, Dr., 278.
Maudsley, Dr., 67.
Maya, 5; 9.
Metabolism, 156-57.
Mind and Brain, 87-90.
Mirror, Use of, 258-59.
Mirror-Writing, 165.
Morselli, H., 208.
Mozumda, A. K., 193.
Mudras, 153-54; 176-77.
Muladhara Chakra, 146-47.
Music, Occult, 252-55.
Myers, F. W. H., 267.
Mysteries of Myra, 274.
Mysticism, 200.

Nada, Voice of the, 138; 169-72.
Nadis, 46; 138-39.
Niyama, 16-17.
Nyaya, 3.

Occultism, 212-14.

Ojas, 152.
OM v. AUM.

Palladino, E., 58-59; 230; 271.
Papus, Dr , 212-13.
Patanjali, 2-3; 6; 41; 183-84.
Pearl of Great Price, 171.
Perfumes, 75-79.
Persian Yoga, 194-97.
Petals, 140-41.
Pineal Gland, 200-204.
Pingala, 142.
Piper, Mrs. L. E., 251-52.
Pituitary Body, 200-204.
Plato, 91; 189.
Poltergeist Cases, 145-46.
Porter, W. T., 258.
Powder of Sympathy, 220-21.
Prana v. Pranayama.
Pranayama, 19-20; 42-61 *passim;* 137; 258.
Pratyahara, 21; 79-83 *passim.*
Prayoga, 153.
Prince, Dr. Morton, 205.
Psychic Powers, 155; 168.
Psycho-Dynamic Theory, 208.
Purva Mimansa, 13.

Questions and Answers, 126-28.

Ramacharaka, Yogi, 3; 4; 55-56.
Redgrove, H. S., 217.
Reincarnation, 185-86.
Relaxation, 38-39.
Repercussion, 247.
Relativity, 135-36.
DeRochas, A., 269.
Royce, J., 111-12.
Russell, Bertrand, 94.

Sahasrara Chakra, 146; 149.
Samadhi, 22; 103-125 *passim.*

INDEX